Affect, Embodiment, and Place in Critical Literacy

This book engages the entanglement of sensation, affect, ethics, and place in literacy learning from early childhood through to adult education. Chapters bridge the divide between theory and practice to consider how contemporary teaching and learning can promote posthuman values and perspectives.

By offering a posthuman approach to literacy research and pedagogy, *Affect, Embodiment, and Place in Critical Literacy* re-works the theory-practice divide in literacy education to emphasize the ways in which learning is an affective and embodied process merging in a particular environment. Written by literacy educators and international literacy researchers, this volume is divided into four sections focusing on Moving with Sensation and Affect, Becoming Worldmakers with Ethics and Difference, and Relationships That Matter in Curriculum and Place. The book ends with a final invitation for readers to work with assembling theory and practice in posthuman literacy learning.

Affect, Embodiment, and Place in Critical Literacy is the perfect resource for researchers, academics, and postgraduate students in the fields of literacy education and philosophy of education, as well as those seeking to explore the benefits of a posthuman approach when conceptualizing theory and practice in literacy education.

Kim Lenters is Associate Dean, Faculty of Graduate Studies and Associate Professor of Language and Literacy at the University of Calgary, Canada.

Mairi McDermott is an Assistant Professor and Chair in Curriculum and Learning at the Werklund School of Education, University of Calgary, Canada.

Routledge Research in Education

This series aims to present the latest research from right across the field of education. It is not confined to any particular area or school of thought and seeks to provide coverage of a broad range of topics, theories and issues from around the world.

Recent titles in the series include:

Affect, Embodiment, and Place in Critical Literacy
Assembling Theory and Practice
Edited by Kimberly Lenters and Mairi McDermott

The Complex Web of Inequality in North American Schools
Investigating Educational Policies for Social Justice
Edited by Gilberto Q. Conchas, Briana M. Hinga, Miguel N. Abad, and Kris D. Gutiérrez

Fear and Schooling
Understanding the Troubled History of Progressive Education
Ronald W. Evans

Applying Cultural Historical Activity Theory in Educational Settings
May Britt Postholm and Kirsten Foshaug Vennebo

Sonic Studies in Educational Foundations
Echoes, Reverberations, Silences, Noise
Edited by Walter S. Gershon and Peter Appelbaum

Designing for Situated Knowledge Transformation
Edited by Nina Bonderup Dohn, Stig Børsen Hansen and Jens Jørgen Hansen

For a complete list of titles in this series, please visit www.routledge.com/Routledge-Research-in-Education/book-series/SE0393

Affect, Embodiment, and Place in Critical Literacy
Assembling Theory and Practice

Edited by Kim Lenters
and Mairi McDermott

NEW YORK AND LONDON

First published 2020
by Routledge
52 Vanderbilt Avenue, New York, NY 10017

and by Routledge
2 Park Square, Milton Park, Abingdon, Oxon, OX14 4RN

Routledge is an imprint of the Taylor & Francis Group, an informa business

© 2020 Taylor & Francis

The right of Kim Lenters and Mairi McDermott to be identified as the authors of the editorial material, and of the authors for their individual chapters, has been asserted in accordance with sections 77 and 78 of the Copyright, Designs and Patents Act 1988.

All rights reserved. No part of this book may be reprinted or reproduced or utilised in any form or by any electronic, mechanical, or other means, now known or hereafter invented, including photocopying and recording, or in any information storage or retrieval system, without permission in writing from the publishers.

Trademark notice: Product or corporate names may be trademarks or registered trademarks, and are used only for identification and explanation without intent to infringe.

Library of Congress Cataloging-in-Publication Data
A catalog record for this book has been requested

ISBN: 978-0-367-13662-8 (hbk)
ISBN: 978-0-429-02784-0 (ebk)

Typeset in Sabon
by Apex CoVantage, LLC

Contents

Foreword—The Gradual Instant   viii
DENNIS SUMARA

Preface   xiii
MAIRI McDERMOTT AND KIM LENTERS

Introducing Affect, Embodiment, and Place in Critical Literacy   1
KIM LENTERS AND MAIRI McDERMOTT

ORIENTING MAP I
Mapping Posthuman Concepts   19
KIM LENTERS AND MAIRI McDERMOTT

PLATEAU I
Moving With Sensation and Affect   29
KIM LENTERS AND MAIRI McDERMOTT

1. Listening to Junk: Sensorial Assemblages and Community Engagement   33
STEPHANIE BARTLETT AND ROBERT LEBLANC

2. How Minor Gestures Generate Relational Transformations in the Act of Literacy Teaching and Learning   43
CHRISTIAN EHRET AND RACHEL MACDONALD

3. Experimentations in Affective Reading for Adult Language Classrooms   51
MONICA WATERHOUSE AND ANITA CHAUDHURI

4. Planning-as-Burden, Planning-as-Gift: Shifting to Gift-Economy Approaches in Teaching and Learning   62
JENNIFER MACDONALD AND KEVIN M. LEANDER

ORIENTING MAP II
Opening Minds, Eyes, Ears, and Doors: Emergent Learning Opportunities for Literacy Educators Weaving Theory in Everyday Classrooms   73
BARBARA COMBER

PLATEAU II
Becoming Worldmakers With Ethics and Difference   85
MAIRI McDERMOTT AND KIM LENTERS

5 What Nose Hill Taught Us About Boundary-Making, Boundary-Knowing, and Boundary-Becoming   91
JAYE JOHNSON THIEL AND MELODY PELLING

6 The Literacy is in the Listening: Honouring Multiplicity and Interrelatedness as Early Grade Teachers   103
MAREN AUKERMAN AND KRISTA JENSEN

7 On Being Thrown Together: Living and Learning in Diversity   115
GUY MERCHANT AND DIVYA DEVENDER-KRAFT

8 Classroom Cosmopolitics: Worldbuilding for Mutual Flourishing   126
T. PHILLIP NICHOLS AND BRIANNE O'SULLIVAN

9 Ways of Being and Becoming in the Adolescent Classroom: An Invitation to Consider the Possibilities of Throwntogetherness   135
ERIN SPRING AND AMANDA HUDDLESTON

ORIENTING MAP III
Knowing/Be(com)ing/Doing Literacies: (Re)Thinking Theory-Practice With a Personal Narrative Game Board   147
CANDACE R. KUBY

PLATEAU III
Relationships That Matter in Curriculum and Place   161
MAIRI McDERMOTT AND KIM LENTERS

10 Walking Together In and Through Stories   165
PAM WHITTY AND HEATHER McKAY

11 Wibbly-Wobbly-Timey-Wimey: Place-Based Pedagogy Across Time and Space 176
MEGAN HIRST AND CATHY BURNETT

12 Red Dresses and Sequined Bras: Encountering Materiality, Place, and Affect in Pop-Up Installation Pedagogy 189
MICHELLE A. HONEYFORD AND PATTI TRUSSLER

13 Relationship Matters in Adult Education: The Practice of Literacies In-Between 203
MIA PERRY AND KEITH SEEL

PLATEAU IV
(In)Conclusions 213
MAIRI McDERMOTT AND KIM LENTERS

Traveller Review I: Space Matters: How a Change in Space Can Influence Learning 215
MIRIAM RAMZY

Traveller Review II: Used Once and Disposed: Collaborating With Youth Environmental Activists in Posthuman Times 218
GINA KO

ORIENTING MAP IV
Why Theory? Thinking, Being, Doing Literacy With Posthumanism 221
KIM LENTERS AND MAIRI McDERMOTT

Index 226

Foreword—The Gradual Instant

Dennis Sumara

It is October 2017, and I am in a classroom at the University of Calgary with a group of university- and classroom-based researchers and teachers. I am here to offer some introductory comments and listen to the opening of a 3-day workshop. People who have never met one another prior to this week are paired and given the challenge to find some shared work about which they will eventually write and publish. There are some constraints in the form of rituals, relationship building, and routines of presenting and discussing. But not much more. The constraints are minimal—creating the degrees of freedom that lead to ambiguity, uncertainty, and some obvious anxiety associated with not having an explicit thesis statement.

There are several presentations made by university-based participants that make use vocabulary not well known by some participants—*posthumanism, assemblage, affect, embodied knowing, cosmopolitanism*. At one point, it feels like the tentative new threads of interpersonal connection will break. There are murmurs of discontent as perceptions and professional knowledge are challenged. I leave at the end of the first day curious about what might happen to this disruption of the entrenched habits of sustaining unproductive gaps between university- and school-based work—gaps the workshop organizers, Kim and Mairi, were hoping to bridge.

I arrive the next day to join a talking circle. Participants situate themselves personally in this very public work. I hear some of the new vocabulary tentatively used to describe the juxtaposition of cross-cultural, interpersonal, interprofessional, interdisciplinary ideas and stories. The mood has shifted. The tone is more animated and, at the same time, more intimate. A creative and productive place of learning has emerged, one in which the usual binaries between what I call the us/not us, me/not me no longer exist.

According to Merleau-Ponty (1962), our sense of self co-emerges with interactions with others and the tools and practices that animate those experiences. While is it the case that the authors of each chapter in this volume worked mostly at a distance from one another using now ubiquitous forms of technology enabled communication, it is important to remember that the genesis of writing occurred in a shared interpersonal, physically embodied space where the air in the room was shared. There was eye contact. There were hugs. There were food and perhaps even some wine. Along with the embodied, situated materiality of the week-long encounter with new people, new ideas, and new vocabulary, there also were what I describe as literacy events of reading and writing as a focal practice—an interpretive event that occurs when readers and writers become committed to making something that provokes new perception and attention to detail; requires development of new interpretation and production skills; and sustains attention, energy, and interest (Sumara, 1996). Most importantly, focal practices are inherently creative practices out of which both new ideas, new forms, and new identities co-emerge.

Guided by theory identified with words such as *affect, materialism, assemblage, posthumanism, cosmopolitanism, and embodiment*, the authors of the chapters in this book provoked for themselves an encounter with what Gadamer (1990) explains as the inextricable relationship between what is considered to be *true* and the methods used to perceive and interpret those truths. The challenge to erase boundaries of identity positionality, genre conventions, and perceptual habituation eventually required creative uses of language by these authors (e.g., *gifting, aliveness, throwntogetherness, allatonceness*). Rorty (1999) argues that changes in perception require some "creative misuses of language—familiar words that initially sound crazy" (p. 204).

Each of the chapters represent in different ways the complexity of the authors' shared engagement those theories, ideas, vocabularies, and emergent practices. As I read and reflected upon each chapter and, importantly, the volume as a whole, I was moved intellectually and emotionally by how the authors have not only presented what has emerged from their shared work but also the ways they also have provided a record of their processes and unfolding perceptions (including instances when they have allowed vulnerability to become a vital part of their work).

I understand the importance of that responsibility. An ethic of attention and care is particularly important when writing is understood as a process of learning to create insight into personal, interpersonal, private, and public aspects of experience. This understanding of writing eschews beliefs that writing is a simple act of recording or transcribing thoughts, facts, or ideas. Instead, the act of writing is a complex one of finding words to substitute for the confluence of remembered and imagined experiences that fold over one another in something we experience as the present moment.

Of course, this process leads to new ideas and thoughts—ones that sometimes emerge unexpectedly and, when they do, cannot be ignored. As Winterson (1995) explains, "The act of writing, itself, is an evolution;

from the Latin *volvere, volvi, volutum*, to roll. The unrolling of the secret scroll, the thing suspected but not realised until present" (p. 160). As Ann Michaels (1996) shows through her characters in the novel *Fugitive Pieces*, what is influential to daily perception is often not available to consciousness without a deliberate practice of remembering, recording, and interpreting. The sometimes dramatic moments of understanding seem sudden and often are associated with surprising and unexpected emotion are similar to the way the earth prepares for thousands of years for events leading to earthquakes and volcanos. In *Fugitive Pieces*, the archeologist Athos Roussos calls the moment of geographical cataclysm "the gradual instant".

Conceptualizing writing as a process of ongoing emergence challenges commonly believed ideas about curriculum. Even though instrumental approaches to curriculum development and use have been soundly critiqued by Dewey in the early 1900s and many contemporary curriculum theorists since the mid 1970s (Britzman, 1991; Pinar, 1975), it is still commonly held that curriculum is the program of study that teachers teach and students learn.

Over the past several decades, I have argued for a more complex understanding of curriculum process (Sumara, 1996, 2002)—one that focuses not so much on the artifacts or actors of schooling but instead on the complex relations between and among them. When one understands curriculum as a constantly emerging relational process, the unproductive private/public, body/mind, self/other binaries are understood instead as complex, inextricably intertwined, and co-emergent phenomena. As I compose new text, new text composes me. Of course, this is not an easy experience. And, as such, as educators, we are challenged to follow some advice from Anne Berthoff (1990), who in her discussion of writing process explains:

> We need to teach ourselves and our students to manage the complexity of *allatoncessness*, to learn to tolerate uncertainty and ambiguity, to recognize the value of *not* knowing what your thesis statement is and thus discovering the uses of chaos.
>
> (p. 86)

Not surprisingly, it was Louise Rosenblatt who in her 1938 book *Literature as Exploration* argued that it was the relationship between reader and text that produced the reading—not the reader, not the text. Positing the relationship between reader and text as an exploration of possible worlds, Rosenblatt was prophetic in shifting authority from the author and/or the text and moving it into the interaction between reader and text. For Rosenblatt, reading is theorized as a productive activity in which readers can learn to better understand an ever-evolving world.

Rosenblatt's theorizing literary engagement as convergence of reader and text was so antithetical to the New Criticism of the day that it remained largely ignored until its reprinting in 1968. It is not merely coincidental that this reprinting followed closely on the heels of the Anglo-American seminar on the teaching of English Language Arts held in Dartmouth, New Hampshire in 1966 and the subsequent publication of John Dixon's (1967) report of this conference where a "growth" model versus "skills" or "cultural transmission" model of English teaching was endorsed. In effect, the conference and report authorized an approach to literature reading and teaching that was aligned with the reader-text-context reader response model theorized and described by Rosenblatt.

Again, these ideas were not new. Rosenblatt and those who followed her lead were profoundly influenced by Dewey's (1916/1966) *Democracy and Education* in which he argued that schooling must not be understood as a preparation for life but must be understood for what it is—life itself. The problem Dewey identified is (and continues to be) the unfortunate gap between schooling and education—or what I have argued (Sumara, 1996, 2002) as the separation of the private and the public.

It is precisely the separation of private and public, between schooling and education that is being strongly addressed in all of this volume. Not only are the theories, concepts, and insights presented as important, but they are also a vivid call to action for educators to use new vocabularies describing ways of being, knowing, and doing in a world where *wallmaking* is being prioritized over *worldmaking*, where *thrownapartness* is taking the place of *throwntogetherness*, where *taking* is replacing *gifting*.

One pragmatic and productive response to these amplifying problems is offered in this volume in the form of writings emerging from situated, embodied assemblages of people, theories, stories, objects, and focal practices. It always has been the case that experience will exceed the forms we use to describe it. However, we have forms that come close. Rorty (1989b) argues that written genres such as ethnographies and novels have been and continue to be able to demonstrate the associations between theory and social hope owing largely to their ability to show how experiences arises from complex relations among history, memory, and identity.

The chapters in this volume—and, I argue, the *collection as a whole*—are vivid demonstrations of this complexity. Not only do they depict what can happen when there are deliberate disruptions to perception and expression, but they also perform an important form of resistance to wallmaking and thrownapartness. As such, they inspire and provoke educators to actively engage with theories, concepts, and practices that function to reproduce the unproductive gap between education and schooling.

References

Berthoff, A. (1990). *The sense of learning*. Portsmouth, NH: Heinemann.
Britzman, D. (1991). *Practice makes practice: A critical study of learning to teach*. New York, NY: State University of New York Press.

Dewey, J. (1916/1966). *Democracy and education*. New York, NY: The Free Press.
Dixon, J. (1967). *Growth through English*. Oxford: Oxford University Press.
Gadamer, H.-G. (1990). *Truth and method*. New York, NY: Crossroad.
Merleau-Ponty, M. (1962). *Phenomenology of perception*. London: Routledge and Kegan Paul.
Michaels, A. (1996). *Fugitive pieces*. Toronto, ON: McClelland-Stewar.
Pinar, W. (Ed.). (1975). *Curriculum theorizing: The reconceptualists*. Berkeley: McCutchan.
Rorty, R. (1989a). *Contingency, irony, solidarity*. Cambridge, UK: Cambridge University Press.
Rorty, R. (1989b). *Philosophy and social hope*. Toronto, ON: Penguin Books.
Rorty, R. (1999). *Truth and progress: Philosophical papers* (Vol. 3). Cambridge, UK: Cambridge University Press.
Rosenblatt, L. (1938). *Literature as exploration*. New York, NY: Appleton Century.
Sumara, D. (1996). *Private readings in public: Schooling the literary imagination*. New York, NY: Peter Lang.
Sumara, D. (2002). *Why reading literature in school still matters: Imagination, interpretation, insight*. London: Lawrence Erlbaum.
Winterson, J. (1995). *Art objects: Essays on ecstasy and effrontery*. Toronto, ON: Afred A. Knopff.

Preface

Recently, a pre-service teacher in our Bachelor of Education program courageously commented to a class of her peers that she is scared about becoming a teacher. She did not mean that she didn't think she was up to it; we were in the midst of a course considering social justice education, and she recognized that what she was about to step into professionally *matters*. She opened the space for the class to reflect on their "why's" for pursuing teaching as a career. Many in the room, like many of those out in the classrooms who take up the enormous work of teaching, care about being "good teachers"; they care for and about their (future) students, and they want to be able to do right by them. There are many layered and drifting components that teachers are asked to tend to, and when you add the global emphasis on the importance of literacy to the mix, literacy educators can feel both inundated with "best practices" through disconnected professional learning while at the same time feeling inadequately supported in meeting the ever-increasing and shifting demands for literacy education in their classrooms.

So, it is here where we begin; we believe that classrooms have always been contingent spaces, politically charged and rife with uncertainty while grounded in the crucial nature of the work (of both teaching and learning). We also believe that this contingency, the potential for messiness and chaos, can be repositioned as generative rather than issues to be quelled, ignored, or managed. This is why we have written this book. Our hope is to encourage and support literacy teachers and researchers in actively seeking and cultivating the potentialities hidden in mess and chaos through a particular shift that is (re)orienting academic literacy research: posthumanism.

Why Theory? Where Does Theory Reside? Who Theorizes?

Some readers might feel that this is the same old game whereby university research and theory are imposed on teacher practices, where theory is made distinct and separate from practice. We, too, struggle with this, for we believe in what posthumanism offers to literacy teaching and learning, and yet, by starting with theory, are we simply fueling the dichotomous (and some might say contentious) relationship between theory and practice? Indeed, posthumanism helps us (re)think this dichotomy, conceptualizing a different relationship between theory and practice. That is, that theory emerges in practice and, importantly, ought to be a *useful* tool for pedagogically (re)imagining literacy.

Theory as Invitation

As we animate across the assembled chapters in the book, we work theory as a practice: theory can help explain what is happening in a situation or a classroom/school as a whole; theory can provide a language to name and discuss what we are sensing or what we would like to see (more/less of); theory can help us in thinking and becoming differently as we (re)organize ourselves for instruction. Literacy educators and researchers, perhaps most of all, recognize the power of language in shaping our worlds, ourselves, and our place(s) within complex socio-material relations.

One of our main purposes in writing this book is to invite teachers into a theory—posthumanism—as a language, that they might find helpful in their ongoing mappings of the contours of literacy teaching and learning. Furthermore, our hope is that literacy researchers who are interested in posthumanism can think with the chapters in the book to better understand the lived tensions, implications, and possibilities of posthumanism in shifting the terrain of literacy education.

Throughout the process, and as you will read in the following chapters, there is a politics of naming; even if we sense we are doing similar *things* in our literacy teaching and research, having a language to name and mark what we are doing and to (re)orient ourselves to our practices enhances our noticings and ability to reflect on and take up moments of openings and possibilities. When working closely with the literacy educators who participated in the work, we were reminded that this is, indeed, the case. We were also encouraged by the stories of how coming into the language through participation in the project helped these educators sustain broader changes in their classroom and curricular work. Theory, as such, is only one entity that, when separated from entanglements in literacy teaching and learning, can only do so much. That said, in believing in the possibilities of posthuman literacy, one of our core commitments was with amplifying educators' voices.

Amplifying Educator Voice

We began this project believing that educators *are* doing many things in schools and classrooms that are creative and critical approaches to literacy, approaches that both dovetail with *and* expand posthuman approaches. The sense that we could and should learn from the everyday practice-theory literacy educators enact remained central throughout the project. We attempted to hold the space open[1] for educators' voices and experiences to be positioned on a level plateau with university research as we collectively reimagined pedagogical possibilities of posthumanism for literacy.

Part of our commitment towards amplifying educator voice was enacted through our organization of writing partnerships. Each chapter in the text was co-written by a literacy educator affiliated with a local school board in Alberta, Canada, and an international literacy researcher whose university-affiliated work explicitly takes up posthuman possibilities for and with literacy. In line with our interpretations of posthumanism and a politics of difference, we are cautious about re-inscribing hierarchies between the university researcher and the practitioner. However, it is precisely the different perspectives, experiences, and orientations to the work each individual brought that opened the space for critical and sustained dialogue. With this in mind, we name the contributors through the language of "educator" and "scholar" as a way to animate and honour the various orientations with theory-practice their work offers to literacy education. Through this move, our desire is to work with these different voices as generative and necessary for broader sense-making to encourage the flourishing of posthuman literacy approaches in teaching and research.

On Positionings and Response-Abilities: Inviting a Call to Action

Each of us has a role and response-ability in the gravitas of literacy teaching, learning, and research animated in the opening story of the preservice teacher, and we dream of a time when we are taking this work up in a more sustained collaborative fashion that unfurls our different positionings and materializes the potentials flowing through these collaborations. As such, we invite you—teachers, researchers, administrators, policy and curriculum writers—to bear witness to our processes, thinkings, beings, and doings with posthuman approaches in (re)imagining literacies' possibilities. We invite you to read between the lines, to bring your stories, experiences, and practices to bear on the writings presented here. We humbly offer you our narratives as you take them into your worldmaking—past and present—recognizing your abilities to respond (response-ability) to literacy teaching, learning, and research.

Note

1. At all moments in the work, we had to resist the inclination towards sustaining the divisive and hierarchical relationship of university-theory-knowledge production/practitioner-practice-knowledge implementation.

Introducing Affect, Embodiment, and Place in Critical Literacy

Kim Lenters and Mairi McDermott

> *August 31, 2017: Local literacy educators from early years through adult learning—13 in total—trickle in, perhaps a little uncertain about what is to unfold. This is the first official reading group in preparation for a 3-day workshop the educators were invited to at the university. While the first meeting outlined our goals for the reading groups and provided a framework for reading and familiarizing themselves with the texts, we (Kim and Mairi) wonder what is going on in their minds and bodies, how they are feeling about the work ahead, and what really brought them to this place at a particularly busy time of the year* (school start-up is just around the corner).

To begin this volume, we invite you in to the unfolding of a collaborative project, organized by Kim Lenters and Mairi McDermott, in which we assembled 13 local literacy educators and 13 international literacy scholars. The events in the vignette arose in a preparatory reading group with the local literacy educators prior to a 3-day workshop in which our goals were twofold: 1. to create curricular materials to support educators in rethinking possibilities for literacy teaching and learning for the 21st century classroom and 2. to push literacy scholars into thinking about the implications of their research for classroom practices. As the title of the volume suggests, we are particularly interested in the ways in which learning is an affective and embodied process emerging in a particular place. Thus, before introducing the rest of the chapter, we return to some of the sentiments among the local educators, as they were introduced to the ideas we flesh out later in the chapter.

> *Cautiously, the educators begin to give voice to the feelings they experienced while reading BarbaraComber's (2016) book,* Literacy, place, and pedagogies of possibility. *They wonder aloud about the teaching context of the educators Comber introduces in her text. They hesitantly share their sentiments, connected to a wider public discourse on educators' work, a discourse in which they are positioned as not*

doing enough—one that implies they are not creative enough, not critical enough.

Together, we (the educators as well as Lenters and McDermott) lament the ways in which educators often become scapegoats for a "failing educational system." With these circulating discourses swirling through the room, space opens for discussions around their embodied responses to reading Comber's work. In this space, the educators express feelings of being implicated in narratives that misrepresent them and the desire to be heard and acknowledged in the work they are *doing*.

Passion for and commitment to expanding literacy practices beyond test score foci begins to seep through the conversations, wafting through the air, claiming space in the here and now. As we talk together and acknowledge the affect we feel within the narratives we encounter, we sense a common passion that we explore with each other as we continue to dialogue. While each of us experiences and embodies this passion in a different way, we share a commitment to expanding literacy practices beyond a test score emphasis, beyond a focus on individual literate kids learning fixed skills to do fixed things with fixed texts. We are united by the commitment, which already threads throughout our teaching practice. But we also recognize that literacy teaching, as we know it, can and should continue to expand and that we can be a part of that expansion.

Ah, so this is why we're here; something deep inside of us knows that we need to and can do more. But, how? *A slow wave of affirmation swells, and we begin to position ourselves collectively—together, we become willing participants in expanding literacy; together, our next question is how we might convince policy makers.*

Over the course of three reading group meetings, ideas churn, conversations flourish, no longer hindered by disembodied theoretical abstractions. Thinking-with-theory, the educators weave in examples of expanded literacy from our shared readings [see Figure 5] and their own classroom projects—past and present. We allow ourselves to be caught up in the imaginative possibilities, *taken away on the swelling prospects and then bringing ourselves back to cautionary tales of how easily great ideas can fall flat and become stagnant.*

It is with this vignette that we open the introduction to the volume to invite you into the worldmakings flowing from a series of collaborative encounters among educators. In the rest of the chapter, we briefly map the historical trajectories of

> While we are working specifically with post-human approaches to literacy in this volume, please see other closely aligned orientations named in the Mapping Posthuman Concepts portion of the book.

literacy as they relate to the contemporary needs of a global 21st century classroom. Throughout the volume, then, we want to underscore the importance of various literacy instructional approaches accumulated through the time and commitment of dedicated educators and scholars. From there, we offer and animate another layer of possibility: a posthuman approach to literacy pedagogy.

> **Posthumanism:** An orientation that considers the ways in which humans, non-humans, and more-than-humans are entangled in ongoing and ever-shifting relations. It critically questions the historical location of agency as human-only and, rather, expands agency to incorporate objects, materials, texts, feelings, and so on.
>
> Examples of the ways posthumanism shifts our focus to entangled webs of relations that constitute sensemaking in literacy classrooms may be found in:
>
> - Young children's enchantment with Pokémon or superheroes and the ways these characters and storylines seep into their playground play and classroom writing
> - The infectiousness of internet memes, which circulate through YouTube and social media and show up in classroom discussions and artwork
> - The graphic novel a student risks reading in class when they are supposed to be researching or writing
> - The power of a film based on a Shakespearean play to motivate students to read the actual play despite its difficult language

Finally, after briefly framing the context of emergence for our collaborative experimentations, we provide an invitation for you to navigate the text and terrain of posthumanism and literacy via the routes that provoke and move you.

Literacy in the Global—Political 21st Century Classroom

What does literacy mean in contemporary times? Concerns around effectively preparing children, youth, and recently arrived peoples for an interconnected knowledge economy, with increasing semiotic resources, technological advances, and subsequent literacies necessary, are of utmost importance for multiple stakeholders. As a society, we are confronted with digital and networked cultures that have precipitated an unprecedented state of ongoing social change; boundaries (be they nation-state or between the material and virtual) are being reconfigured through the rapid change brought on by technological advances and information that is readily available through the immediacy of digital platforms (Jenkins,

Clinton, Purushotma, Robison, & Weigel, 2009). To begin our exploration of these matters, we share an emerging conceptualization of literacy that frames the work we do in this volume.

> **Literacy**: Communicative practices for forming and making sense of the world through intentional and sustained encounters with human and more-than-human entities and for opening spaces for new becomings.

Considering the above, literacy scholars have recently begun to engage a particular approach through posthuman theory, which enables us to imagine possibilities for expanding literacy and literacy education through thinking of the **classroom as an assemblage** of people, objects, materials, ideas, policies, practices, texts, events, and places, each with its own histories and trajectories.

> **Classrooms as assemblages:** In schools, deliberate choices may be made by educators and administration to configure the assemblage, for example, which students are placed with a particular teacher or how learning groups are formed or which novels will be read in class contribute to the forming of a classroom assemblage. However, because people, things, practices, and events are always emerging or becoming something new, we cannot know how the various participants in a classroom assemblage will engage with each other. And so the classroom, like every other assembled space, has a quality of unpredictability, contingency, or indeterminacy.

While posthumanism inflects and informs the way many involved in educational research think about the work they do or understand what they are seeing in classrooms and schools, it has not yet seeped into the terrain of the educational system. With a few notable exceptions (e.g., Comber, 2016; Davies, 2014; Kuby & Gutshall Rucker, 2016; Kuby, Spector, & Thiel, 2018; Leander & Ehret, 2019; Lenters, 2019; Lenz Taguchi, 2010), discussions on the gritty materialities of what posthumanism does for classroom literacy instruction beyond preschool are minimal. What we have found interesting in the examples we see of posthumanism in the classroom is how readily it is taken up in preschools and even into the early years (e.g., Hackett & Somerville, 2017; Thiel, 2015). This body of work has set the authors in this volume on a trajectory that considers the possibilities of posthumanism across a wider range of educational settings, from the early years into adult learning educational spaces.

This book, which brings together school-based educators and literacy scholars who engage with posthumanism, enters into this space. Our aim is to animate the potential for posthumanism in the classroom and, in particular, to consider how a tripartite focus on affect, embodiment, and place may help us do, be, and know literacy pedagogy more generatively. As we noted earlier, while we are interested in mapping posthumanism in literacy education, we want to do so while also recognizing the historical journey through different approaches to literacy. In the next section, we do just that.

Mapping the Turn to Posthumanism in Literacy Education

Where Have We Come From, and Where Are We Going?

Understandings of literacy as a concept are continually shifting, which speaks to the dynamic role literacy plays in school and society. Over the past few decades, educators have progressed from thinking of literacy as referencing only the mechanical skills of reading and writing, to considering the social, cultural, and linguistic practices that are part of the meaning-making associated with encoding and decoding texts. Literacy was once considered solely a linguistic endeavour, and it is now thought of as multimodal—that is, meaning-making associated with visual, auditory, spatial, and gestural modes of communication, as well as the linguistic. While the practice of one-correct-response comprehension assessment continues in some educational circles, there are educators worldwide who recognize the limitations of this practice. Flowing from this recognition, critical literacy—that is, asking who or what is "behind" a text and the consequences of circulating that text—is now a regular feature in literacy instruction starting in the early years and continuing throughout high school and into adult learning.

All of these movements—the sociocultural, sociolinguistic, multimodal, and critical turns, to name a few—have added tremendously to our understanding of what literacy is and have shaped the ways literacy is pedagogically approached in schools. However, while engaging the sociality of literacy, each of these turns positions literacy as beginning in the brain—an individual cognitive process that becomes social through practice with less articulated focus on the role of the body as part of the work of literacy. When understood to originate and flow solely from the brain, literacy becomes a disembodied process of decoding symbols or a process whose end goal is a representative product that symbolically encodes meaning or thought. This line of thinking draws from a Cartesian dualism that separates the mind and the body, a duality that posthumanism repositions. We explore this further in the next section.

> See Plateau I for a more in-depth discussion of affect and embodiment in literacy.

As we move through this introduction to the volume, we explore what gets overlooked and forgotten with a cognitive focus on literacy and how a posthuman approach to literacy and literacy learning can help address these lapses. In the next two sections, we consider where we might go with literacy and posthumanism, considering what posthumanism contributes to critical literacy as we conceptualize a post-critical literacy pedagogy. We introduce a number of concepts that are key to thinking with posthumanism in literacy learning. As we name them, we italicize and bold the term. In some cases, we embed a definition, and in others we invite you to refer to other sections of the book. And finally, all of the concepts we work with can be found in the next chapter (titled Mapping Posthuman Concepts), which is dedicated to explicating the posthuman concepts at work in this volume. Additionally, we provide a list of articles that explore literacy and posthumanism, to further any exploration you may desire (see Figure 5 located at the end of this chapter).

A Posthuman Understanding of Critical Literacy

Three overarching concepts ground, launch, and animate the conversation between posthumanism and literacy that we engage in this volume: *affect* , *embodiment*, and *place*. With its attention to these material aspects of life and living, posthumanism requires us to rethink separation of mind and body (Cartesian dualism) and the representational understandings of literacy associated with it. Posthumanism views the body and the mind, working in tandem as an important site of learning; in other words, the body and mind are seen as inextricably linked and always working together—the ***bodymind*** (Semetsky, 2013).

> For those interested in taking a deeper look at representationalism and education, we provide a list of resources in Orienting Map IV.

Affect refers to the preconscious, visceral responses of the bodymind during any type of encounter. In literacy encounters, these unarticulated, felt responses initiate the process of understanding and responding to literacy encounters. Encounters with literacy are also inseparably entangled with place. Our tendency may be to think of place as something rooted or fixed and therefore static and immutable. Posthumanism emphasizes affective relations, emergence, and fluidity and, as such, understands place as formed through ongoing relationships among things, people, and events, materializing in space and time. Schools and classrooms,

> See Plateau III for further discussion of place and literacy learning.

as places, provide excellent examples of entangled relationships between literacy and place. When literacy is anchored in specific places, its connection to *ethics* comes into view.

A conventional understanding of critical literacy refers to what people do with literacy—of the political and social practices associated with literacy. Many educators have taken up the four-part framework conceptualized by Lewison, Flint, and Van Sluys (2002) as they engage critical literacy in their classrooms. The framework, which draws on the work of multiple critical theorists, involves students and educators in four practices: disrupting the commonplace, interrogating multiple viewpoints, focusing on sociopolitical issues, and taking a stand and promoting social justice.

Post-Critical Literacy

Engaging with posthumanism in relation to critical literacy affirms the value of these four critical literacy practices, particularly the idea of acting as part of the work of literacy. However, as posthumanism moves us toward understanding learning as more than cognitively framed ways of knowing, that is, toward an understanding of learning as being/doing/knowing, the way we approach critical literacy must shift.

Posthumanism disrupts the notion that in the engagement of critical literacy, the reader/writer, viewer/composer must step back from the topic, creating critical distance in order to approach the topic. Rather, a posthuman understanding of critical literacy—post-critical literacy—acknowledges that we are always already entwined, to various degrees, with the topic through our ***intra-action*** (Barad, 2007) with it. Affect matters in post-critical literacy. And so posthuman critical literacy engages the student and educator in attuning to their own affective responses to texts and authors, as well as the events and practices referenced and animated in those texts.

A posthuman understanding of critical literacy also indexes the relationship between ethics and empathy, foregrounding the importance of ethics and ethical response. Karen Barad (2007) and Rosi Braidotti (2013), two scholars in the areas of feminist new materialisms and posthumanism, help us think about this relationship between ethics and critical literacy. Thinking with Barad's work, we engage with critical literacy as a matter of ethics and ethical response, a critical consciousness that opens up "suggestive, creative and visionary" possibilities (Barad, in Dolphijn & van der Tuin, 2012, p. 50). Engaged in respectful and detailed ways, these "inventive provocations" propel us toward intra-actions that matter in the world (p. 50).

As Rosi Braidotti (2013) puts it, by enlarging our sense of interconnection between self and others, including "non-human or 'earth' others" (p. 49), posthumanism focuses on affirmative bonds between entities in our ongoing relationships. This focus, when brought into conversation with critical literacy "combines critique with creativity in the pursuit of alternative visions and projects" (p. 54) and provides "new starting points that bring into play untapped possibilities for bonding, community building and empowerment" (p. 54). Taken up in these ways, an ethical post-critical literacy becomes:

> **Post-critical literacy:** A generative worldmaking practice, one that goes beyond critique as an endpoint and looks towards ongoing commitment and action

As educators involve themselves in post-critical literacy, they can gauge the efficacy of their pedagogy through asking: How have students been changed by their engagement with the text/author and the practice of critical literacy? In Figure 1 we provide further questions educators might ask in moving towards a post-critical literacy.

Post-Critical Literacy Pedagogy

Posthumanism understands living and learning as ways of being and doing (*ontologies*) *and* ways of knowing (*epistemologies*) with(in) the world. Ways of being/doing and ways of knowing are understood to operate in tandem and not separately or in binary opposition to each other. Rather than thinking of being/doing as occurring in the body and knowing in the mind, **onto-epistemology** considers being/doing/knowing as fully embodied and entwined, that is, engaged in by the bodymind. It also signals the ways that being/doing/knowing are inseparably connected, not only to each other but also to ethics—for being/doing/knowing always take place in relationship with others. Furthermore, ways of being/doing/knowing

> *How have my students and I been changed by our engagement with the text/author and the practices of critical literacy?*
>
> - In what ways have my students reflected on the words and background knowledge or cultural narratives that inform their understandings of the text?
> - When, where, and how are my students and I open to allowing new ideas to interfere with our preconceived notions or belief systems?
> - How might we engage with texts and practices that foster new ways of being with the world?
> - What worlds have opened up for my students and me as we critically engage with text(s)?
> - How has engaging with texts set us on a trajectories of re-imagining and re-making our own worlds?

Figure 1 Questions for be(com)ing post-critical literacy educators

are considered to be multiple within an individual or an *assemblage*. This posthuman notion of the entanglement of being/doing/knowing moves us away from thinking in *either-or* (binary) terms and encourages us to think "*and-and*" (non-binary) in relation to all we are, do, and know.

Post-Pedagogy

As suggested earlier, a posthuman approach to literacy pedagogy moves us to think of instruction as relational. Rather than training students in ways of doing literacy (a hierarchical relationship between educator and student), post-pedagogy unsettles this rank ordering, urging us to think of attuning with students to myriad practices of literacy and how they might intra-act with these practices, texts, and events. In the sections that follow we elaborate on these ideas by focusing on two ideas: the importance of process in post-pedagogy and the idea of "and-and."

Process and Product

In addition to bringing our attention to the affective aspects of literacy, posthumanism also leads us to reconsider that which is produced during encounters with literacy—both for the humans involved and the more-than-human. Moment to moment affective responses are understood to "count" as products of an encounter. Posthumanism views that which is produced—for example, affective responses, drawings, stories, essays, videos, reports—as never fully completed but rather as snapshots of the *emergence* of what a student is doing with literacy and what they are *becoming* at a particular moment in time. Thinking with emergence, becoming, and processes of literacy encounters, educators also consider how the products themselves are becoming and might further become as they intra-act with students. Process thus becomes a key consideration, and unfinished drawings, stories, and essays are considered valuable and important players in the performance of literate becoming. Next we offer an example of intra-action between process and product.

> We might ask how a student's reading of a well-worn textbook comes to be guided by the extra wear on a portion of the page where a clammy finger went over the text multiple times—text changed in the intense work of a previous body's sense-making. This subtly altered text, then, is acknowledged as having agency in leading to another student's noticing/attention about plastic waste in the oceans and setting them off on a line of flight, provoking them to become activist letter-writers or prompting them to become involved in a student-led social media campaign that moves beyond the bounded classroom timespace.

Furthermore, in keeping with the concept of the bodymind, the kinds of (un)finished literacy products that symbolically encode meaning (the stories, essays, videos, and so on) are not viewed as higher forms of learning but of equal value to responses of affect such as desire, curiosity, excitement, frustration, or ennui.

And-And Literacy Pedagogy

As we think with this non-binary, posthuman approach to life and learning in the literacy classroom, new possibilities open up. In putting forward an *and-and* approach to literacy instruction, we are not proposing replacement of the "tried and true". Literature circles, novel studies, guided reading, close reading, readers theatre, grammar mini-lessons, mentor texts, word walls, drop-everything-and-read, to name a few, are longstanding literacy teaching strategies and practices that have proven to be highly effective over the years. But their effectiveness is not universal.

When thought of as one-size-fits-all strategies that an educator may plug into a literacy program, in any context, at any time, even the tried and true can backfire. When they have been part of a classroom or school repertoire for a long period of time, they can become common-place or worn out. The point is that literacy instruction, like all instruction, must be responsive to its space and place; it must move with the participants in its setting. When we think of the classroom as an assemblage of people, objects, practices, policies, events, and places, each with its own histories and trajectories, we begin to glimpse the uniqueness of every classroom. When we add to that considerations of the ever-changing relationships amongst these participants in the classroom assemblage, we can begin to appreciate the complexities of literacy teaching and learning and the difficulty of one-size-fits-all literacy programming.

Educators who work *with* emergence, those who move with the emergent identity and moment-by-moment compositions of their classroom's assemblage, are well-positioned to provide effective literacy instruction. But such an approach most definitely complicates teaching and disrupts the status quo. Unit and lesson plans cannot simply be recycled from year to year. What currently works for the educator down the hall may not work in your classroom. What worked well with your class last month may not work this month. One year students may have already grasped certain spelling patterns or the three-paragraph essay when they come into your classroom, making teaching and assessing these explicitly redundant and unnecessary. And the next year, a significant number of students in the class may not have these under control, requiring you to make instructional time for ensuring students know how to use these tools of writing.

And-and pedagogy provides a way forward for engaging literacy learning that meets students at their present state of literacy development. Rather than thinking in binary terms, such as literacy programming that explicitly teaches grammar *or* literacy programming that immerses students in literature, and-and literacy pedagogy asks, "What do *these* students need at this time?" It then develops literacy encounters that respond to these particular needs and interests. And-and pedagogy would have these hypothetical students experience immersion in literature *and* instruction in specific elements of grammar that can move them forward in their capacities to engage with and respond to that literature.

And-and pedagogy brings to the classroom assemblage that which is needed, from a curricular perspective *and* from an affective perspective. It encourages educators to ask, how do I cover that which is laid out in the state or provincial curriculum *and* what do I need to bring together to make this happen? (See Figure 2 for other questions for educators prompted by and-and pedagogy.)

What we have put forth so far in this introduction consists of some of the many directions we believe a posthuman approach to literacy offers. The subsequent chapters work with and through some of these propositions to further consider possibilities for expanding literacy landscapes. In the next, and final, section of our introduction, we provide a brief overview of the assemblages that the composing partners worked within through a description of the 3-day workshop that brought us (13 literacy educators, 17 literacy scholars, including McDermott and Lenters as well as the two keynotes and critical friends, Comber and Kuby, and 3 graduate assistant researchers) all together in shared physical space. Following that, we provide a possible itinerary for you to consider how you would like to move through the terrain of posthumanism and literacy!

- How do I cover that which is laid out in the state or provincial curriculum *and* what do I need to bring together to make this happen?
- How do I take into consideration the affect that is produced as I bring these literacy learning strategies together with students and materials?
- What ways can this learning become inviting and provocative for students?
- What would happen if I worked *with* my students to bring them into the selection of materials and planning of experiences?
- As I consider the materials and experiences my students and I will engage with, how do we assemble people, objects, and practices in ways that will matter to/for my students?
- How can I work with each student, my class as a whole, our texts and our practices in ***differenciated*** ways to encourage literate becomings that open up new possibilities and capacities?

Figure 2 Questions for be(com)ing affective literacy educators

A Closer Look at the Terrain: A Three-Day Encounter

As noted in the preface, the and-and attention in the overall project had much to do with the bringing together of literacy educators *and* literacy scholars on a lateral plane wherein both voices were necessary for the sense making (see comments in the preface regarding our intentions with naming the groups as seemingly distinct). Admittedly, while we (Kim and Mairi—as the organizers of the workshop) had ongoing and extensive discussions about how we would assemble the event, we, too, had to be open to emergence, and emerge we all did! In this section, we try to capture bits and pieces of the 3 days that surge through the writings assembled in this book.

Prior to the workshop, we paired each educator with a scholar based on the age group with whom they work most closely. We soon came to see the audacity of this proposition. Not only did we want folks to think with posthuman approaches to literacy but to do so in completely unfamiliar collaborative composing partnerships—and produce a draft or outline of the chapters herein in three days! As you will read in the chapters that were crafted, this notion of ***throwntogetherness*** is woven throughout. Different composing partners navigated the terrain of voice, experience (in the classroom; in research; in writing "academically") in various ways, and some explicitly tend to these tensions (as generative) in their chapters.

So, we began; a beautiful October Calgary morning, no signs—only stories—of the early snowfall the week before! (Un)Settling into the room where we would spend our collective time together, fresh baked goodies (homemade by our graduate assistants) and coffee (also made by our wonderful graduate assistants) in hand, the literacy scholars—who mostly know each other from working together and going to similar conferences—and the local educators—who now knew each other from the preparatory reading group in the weeks leading up the workshop—chat in separate groups. Quickly, though, the day began with a dean's (Dr. Dennis Sumara) welcome and brief introduction to the purpose of workshop.

Our Dual Goals

- Create curricular material that literacy educators interested in expanding literacies' possibilities in 21st century classrooms can engage, something they can take a hold of in understanding what posthumanism offers literacy learning.
- For literacy scholars to be challenged in how their thinking with this theory could be materialized in the literacy classroom

To prepare for the work ahead, we (Kim and Mairi) convened a reading group with the literacy educators to begin collectively navigating the language and ideas of posthumanism, as well as surfacing their wealth of experience regarding the emergent spaces of literacy learning in our local schools. We opened this chapter with a snapshot of the discussions in the reading group that played a crucial role in our last-minute tending to details for the 3-day workshop. In the following box, we outline the texts we read as part of the reading group and in the last section of this chapter we come full circle to map where each writing pair went in their thinking/being/doing together.

An Invitation to Map Your Journey Through the Plateaus

At some point, many who take up posthuman approaches to literacy wind up encountering the French scholars Gilles Deleuze and Felix Guattari, whose individual and collective oeuvres substantively contribute to the overall posthuman orientation. One piece of their writing, in particular, that we are working with in our articulation of posthuman literacy is titled *A Thousand Plateaus: Capitalism and Schizophrenia* (Deleuze & Guattari, 1987/2004). Deleuze and Guattari invite us to reorient ourselves to conventional approaches to reading texts sequentially through their use of the plateau. When standing on one plateau, you are able

---

Reading group meeting 1:
Comber, B. (2016). *Literacy, place, and pedagogies of possibility.* New York, NY: Routledge.

Reading group meeting 2:
Nichols, P., & Campano, G. (2017). Post-humanism and literacy studies. *Language Arts, 94*(4), 245–251.

Reading group meeting 3:
Zapata, A., & Van Horn, S. (2017). "Because I'm smooth": Material intra-actions and text productions among young Latino picture book makers. *Research in the Teaching of English, 5*(3), 290–316.

Ehret, C., & Hollett, T. (2014). Embodied composition in real virtualities: Adolescents' literacy practices and felt experiences moving with digital, mobile devices in school. *Research in the Teaching of English 48*(4), 428–454.

Waterhouse, M. (2012). "We don't believe media anymore": Mapping critical literacies in an adult immigrant language classroom. *Discourse: Studies in the Cultural Politics of Education, 33*(1), 129–146.

Figure 3 Reading group texts

14 *Kim Lenters and Mairi McDermott*

to look across the landscape to other plateaus, each created through its own histories and relations while also being interconnected. Extending the possibilities of this idea, we have named the sections of this volume as "Plateaus" and "Orienting Maps" and invite you to move between them in any order you desire. In Figure 5, we expand upon what work is being done in the differently named "sections."

Plateaus: In what might otherwise be named a "section," the three plateaus are organized as assemblages of chapters that take up common themes and concepts in posthuman literacy:

- Moving with Sensation and Affect
- Becoming Worldmakers with Ethics and Difference
- Relationships That Matter in Curriculum and Place

Within each plateau, you will find chapters written by the composing partners. As noted previously, these partners (a literacy educator and a literacy scholar) were tasked with focusing their experiments around a particular age group. We have organized the chapters within each plateau sequentially, moving through the ages from early years to adult learning. Additionally, to open each plateau, Kim Lenters and Mairi McDermott provide a brief introduction to the core concepts being animated in the subsequent chapters as well as signalling what each chapter does with those concepts. These can be read as a tool to help decide which chapters to read, or simply as an overview of the ideas in the plateau.

Orienting Maps: Otherwise thought of as "interludes," the orienting maps are placed amongst the plateaus to help guide the reading and understanding of posthuman literacy approaches. These maps take different forms to provide a variety of entry points into the terrain:

- *Orienting Map I*: This map focuses on briefly introducing the lay of the land. In the first part, we locate posthuman approaches to literacy within a rich history of literacy practices. In the second part, we provide another entry point into the language and concepts taken up throughout the volume.

  - Introducing Affect, Embodiment, and Place in Critical Literacy (Kim Lenters and Mairi McDermott)
  - Mapping Posthuman Concepts (Kim Lenters and Mairi McDermott)

- *Orienting Map II*: In this map, Comber addresses the ways in which educators (can) use theory as generative for their literacy teaching. Starting with the educator, rather than theory, Comber notes how theory helps us to understand our pedagogical decisions and what we notice (e.g., assessment) of students' work in different ways, thus opening up possibilities for continual growth.

  - Opening Minds, Eyes, Ears, and Doors (Barbara Comber)

Introducing Affect, Embodiment, and Place 15

- *Orienting Map III*: Kuby takes us on a journey through posthuman theory, locating it more prominently within her discussion than Comber. Through her theory-practice orientation, Kuby asks "what counts as literacy"?
  - Knowing/Be(com)ing/Doing Literacies: (Re)Thinking Theory-Practice with a Personal Narrative Gameboard (Candace Kuby)
- *Orienting Map IV*: Again thinking-with-theory, the purpose of this map is to animate, from our perspectives, why we believe in (posthuman) theory and how drawing out our theoretical assumptions helps us to better understand the implications of our practices.
  - Why Theory? Thinking/Being/Doing Literacy with Posthuman Theory (Kim Lenters and Mairi McDermott)

Travelers' Reviews: Staying with our theme of moving through the terrain of posthumanism and literacy teaching and research, we include one final type of chapter in the book. In these travelers' reviews, we learn about two of our Graduate Assistant Researchers on the project whose doctoral research did not directly take up posthumanism or literacy. As they came into the project, they participated in the reading group with the local literacy educators, and were asked to take notes on our conversations throughout the workshop. Afterwards, they had many reflections about what they now thought the theory might do for their own sense-making and literacy more broadly. The travelers' reviews, then, provide another entry into the ideas from the perspectives of two emerging scholars just being introduced to the orientation.

- Traveler Review I: Space matters: How a change in space can influence learning (Miriam Ramzy)
- Traveler Review II: Used once and disposed: Collaborating with youth activists in posthuman times (Gina Ko)

Figure 4 Naming the organization of the book

So, we close this introductory chapter, as part of Orienting Map I, with a final invitation to you, the reader, to join us on this emergent terrain of possibility. Of course, we have put much thought and consideration into how to organize the book yet in doing so hope that you find it open enough to put together your own itinerary for our various experimentations with posthuman approaches to literacy. Wherever you begin and whatever path you map out for yourself ahead of time, we hope that you keep yourself open to being surprised and going off the trail; stay for a while, dwell, or return periodically when a reprieve is needed. We

Posthumanism and Literacy Learning

Aukerman, M. (2015). How should readers develop across time? Mapping change without a deficit perspective. *Language Arts, 93*(1), 55–62.

Boldt, G., and Leander, K. (2017). Becoming through 'the break': A posthuman account of a child's play. *Journal of Early Childhood Literacy*, 17(3), 410–425.

Burnett, C., & Merchant, G. (2016). Boxes of poison: Baroque technique as antidote to simple views of literacy, *Journal of Literacy Research*, 48(3), 258–279.

Ehret, C., Hollett, T., & Jocius, R. (2016). The matter of new media making: An intra-action analysis of adolescents making a digital book trailer. *Journal of Literacy Research, 48*(3), 346–377.

Hewes, J., Whitty, P., Aamot, B., Schaly, E., Sibbad, J. & Ursuliak, K. (2016). Unfreezing Disney's Frozen through playful and intentional co-authoring/co playing, *Canadian Journal of Education, 39*(3), 1–25.

Honeyford, M. (2015). Thresholds of possibility—mindful walking, traditional oral storytelling, and the birch bark canoe: Theorizing intra-activity in an afterschool arts space. *Literacy Research: Theory, Method, and Practice, 64*, 210–226.

Leander, K., & Ehret, C. (Eds.) (2019). *Affect in Literacy Learning and Teaching: Pedagogies, Politics, and Coming to Know*. New York: Routledge.

Kuby, C. R. & Gutshall Rucker, T. (2015). Everyone has a Neil: Possibilities of literacy desiring in Writers' Studio. *Language Arts, 92*(5), 314–327.

Kuby, C.R., Spector, K., & Thiel, J.J. (Eds.) (2018). *Posthumanism and literacy education*. New York: Routledge.

LeBlanc, R.J. (2017). Time, labour, texts: New English Language Arts teachers' selective use of instructional documents. *International Journal of Critical Pedagogy*, 8(1), 105–128.

Lenters, K. (2016). Riding the lines and overwriting in the margins: Affect and multimodal literacy practices. *Journal of Literacy Research, 48*(2), 280–316.

Lenters, K. (2019). Nerdisms, Almina, and the petsitter: Becoming social commentary composer. *Research in the Teaching of English, 53*(4).

McDermott, M. (2014). Mo(ve)ments of affect: Towards an embodied pedagogy for anti–racism education. In G. J. S. Dei & M. McDermott (Eds.). *Politics of anti–racism education: In search of strategies for transformative education*, (pp. 211–226). New York, NY: Springer.

Nichols, P., & Campano, G. (2017). Post-humanism and literacy studies. *Language Arts, 94*(4), 245–251.

Perry, M., Wessels, A., & Wager, A. C. (2013) From playbuilding to devising in literacy education: Aesthetic and pedagogical approaches. *Journal of Adolescent and Adult Literacy, (56)*8, 649–658.

Spector, K., & Jones, S. (2007). Constructing Anne Frank: Critical literacy and the Holocaust in eighth-grade English. *Journal of Adolescent and Adult Literacy, 51*(1), 38–48.

Spector, K. (2010) Classroom Provocateurs and Ethical Classroom Practice, *Changing English, 17*(4), 363–373.

> Spring, E. (2016) Where are you from?: Locating the young adult self within and beyond the text. *Children's Geographies, 14*(3), 356–371.
> Thiel, J.J. (2015). "Bumblebee's in trouble!": Embodied literacies during imaginative superhero play. *Language Arts, 93*(1), 38–49.
> Waterhouse, M. (2012). "We don't believe media anymore": Mapping critical literacies in an adult immigrant language classroom. *Discourse: Studies in the Cultural Politics of Education, 33*(1), 129–146.

Figure 5 Posthuman Literacy Resources

have provided signposts to help guide and position you, but ultimately, we hope you playfully create your own journey through the terrain of posthumanisms and literacy—enjoy the trip!

References

Barad, K. (2007). *Meeting the universe halfway: Quantum physics and the entanglement of matter and meaning*. Durham, NC: Duke University Press.

Braidotti, R. (2013). *The posthuman*. Malden, MA: Polity Press.

Comber, B. (2016). *Literacy, place, and pedagogies of possibility*. New York, NY: Routledge.

Davies, B. (2014). *Listening to children: Being and becoming*. New York, NY: Routledge.

Deleuze, G., & Guattari, F. (1987/2004). *A thousand plateaus: Capitalism and schizophrenia* (B. Massumi, Trans.). Minneapolis, MN: University of Minnesota Press (originally published as *Mille Plateaux*, volume 2 of *Capitalisme et schizophrenie*. Paris, France: Minuit, 1987).

Dolphijn, R., & van der Tuin, I. (2012). *New materialism: Interviews & cartographies*. University of Michigan and Open Humanities Press. Retrieved from https://quod.lib.umich.edu/o/ohp/11515701.0001.001/1:4.3/-new-materialism-interviews-cartographies?rgn=div2;view=fulltext

Hackett, A., & Somerville, M. (2017). Posthuman literacies: Young children moving in time, place and more-than-human worlds. *Journal of Early Childhood Literacy, 17*(3), 374–391.

Jenkins, H., Clinton, K., Purushotma, R., Robison, A. J., & Weigel, M. (2009). *Confronting the challenges of participatory culture: Media education for the 21st century*. MacArthur Foundation. Retrieved from https://www.macfound.org/media/article_pdfs/JENKINS_WHITE_PAPER.PDF.

Kuby, C. R., & Gutshall Rucker, T. (2016). *Go be a writer! Expanding the curricular boundaries of literacy learning with children*. New York, NY: Teachers College Press.

Kuby, C. R., Spector, K., & Thiel, J. J. (Eds.). (2018). *Posthumanism and literacy education*. New York, NY: Routledge.

Leander, K., & Ehret, C. (Eds.). (2019). *Affect in literacy learning and teaching: Pedagogies, politics, and coming to know*. New York, NY: Routledge.

Lenters, K. (2019). Nerdisms, Almina, and the petsitter: Becoming social commentary composer. *Research in the Teaching of English, 53*(4).

Lenz Taguchi, H. (2010). *Going beyond the theory/practice divide in early childhood education: Introducing an intra-active pedagogy*. New York, NY: Routledge.

Lewison, M., Flint, A. S., & Van Sluys, K. (2002). Taking on critical literacy: The journey of newcomers and novices. *Language Arts, 79*, 382–392.

Semetsky, I. (2013). Learning with bodymind: Constructing the cartographies of the unthought. In D. Masny (Ed.), *Cartographies of becoming in education: A Deleuze-Guattari perspective* (pp. 77–91). Rotterdam, The Netherlands: Sense Publishers.

Thiel, J. J. (2015). Vibrant matter: The intra-active role of objects in the construction of young children's literacies. *Literacy Research: Theory, Method, and Practice, 64*, 112–131.

Orienting Map I

Mapping Posthuman Concepts

Kim Lenters and Mairi McDermott

In this chapter of Orienting Map I, we provide an explication of the concepts referenced in this volume. It is our intention that this section might further assist you in attuning to the language of posthumanism as it relates to the literacy classroom. As a result, we have written it as a chapter and placed it early in the text (as opposed to a glossary located at the end of the volume). If we could, we would have provided the chapter on perforated pages, intended for you to pull out and put to work as you read the various sections of this book. Perhaps instead you will wish to dog ear this page, tab it, or insert a bookmark!

In the previous chapter, we identified posthumanism as an orientation that considers the ways in which humans, non-humans, and more-than-humans are entangled in ongoing and ever-shifting relations. Furthermore, posthumanism critically questions the historical location of agency as human only and, rather, expands understandings of agency to incorporate objects, materials, texts, feelings, and so on Flowing from a number of philosophical and theoretical traditions, as Taylor (2016) states, "Posthumanism is perhaps best considered as a constellation of different theories, approaches, concepts and practices" (p. 6). Next we provide a list of some of the various strands that have developed alongside posthumanism and helped shape its trajectory.

Other strands of poststructural and postmodern theory have developed alongside of posthumanism:

- *feminist new materialisms* (e.g., Barad, 2007; Bennett, 2010; Braidotti, 2013);
- *relational materialism* (e.g., Hultman & Lenz Taguchi, 2010);
- *assemblage theory* (e.g., DeLanda, 2006);
- *affect theory* (e.g., Gregg & Seigworth, 2010; Massumi, 2015);
- *actor-network-theory* (e.g., Latour, 2005);
- *science and technology studies* (e.g., Law, 2004; Haraway, 1988; Stengers, 2010); and
- *socio-materiality* (e.g., Fenwick & Edwards, 2012).

> This list is by no means exhaustive but provides a reference for those curious about the close relatives of posthumanism in the world of philosophy. Although variously named, these strands of poststructural theory share many common features that mutually enhance each other when put into conversation. While we use the label "posthumanism" in this volume, the work we have produced draws on a constellation of these various strands of poststructural and postmodern theory.

In this chapter, we are more deliberate than we were in the previous with citing the scholars whose works have provided a conceptual basis for so much of the research into posthumanism and literacy learning. Again, consider it or work with it as a reference chapter. Many of the scholars you see in this chapter have opened pathways the scholars contributing to this volume follow and branch out from, as we each pursue the myriad possibilities for posthumanism in the literacy classroom in our own work. We are greatly indebted to and appreciative of their ground-breaking contributions and pleased to introduce them to you in this orienting map.

In what follows, we provide an alphabetized list of the concepts you will encounter in this volume. You may note the overlaps between many of the concepts as you move through them. This entanglement of ideas is an important part of posthumanism because it endeavors to acknowledge the deep and always shifting interconnections within human and material worlds.

Posthuman Concepts at Work in This Volume

- **Affect:** A form of knowing, it first begins as unconscious and visceral knowing and often informs our immediate, practical actions (Gregg & Seigworth, 2010; Semetsky, 2013). "It precedes the articulations of language and thought. It is felt in the body before it is overladen with meaning" (Gannon, 2009, p. 74). Affect comes before emotion—it is a visceral, pre-conscious response of the body (individual and collective). Brian Massumi (2015) reminds us that the term *affect* is double—it refers to the "ability to affect and to our ability to be affected" (p. 48). To affect and to be affected are two simultaneous aspects of the same event. Affect is what drives students to become those who love to intra-act with texts and literacy practices and, conversely, it is also that which can present a barrier to such engagement.
- **Agency:** As taken up in this volume, agency reconceptualized to expand notions of who or what is considered agentic and how agency is produced. Rather than agency being an individual (human) possession or quality, "agency is an enactment" (Barad, 2007, p. 112). That is, agency is enacted relationally as entities in assemblage come

into association with each other, as they intra-act. Importantly, in this conceptualization, more-than-human entities also have the ability to *move* others with whom they come into contact, and likewise, to be changed in these associations. Therefore, agency is not held or summoned by an individual person; rather, posthumanism views it as a "commotion of co-activity" (Manning & Massumi, 2014, p. 14).

As an enactment, agency offers "possibilities for reconfiguring entanglements" (Barad, 2007, p. 54) among human and more-than-human entities. Understandings of agency connect intimately with the concept of affect through emphasizing the ways in which human and more-than-human entities have the capacity to affect, or move, other entities when in relation. It is, thus, closely related to the ideas of **thing power** and **vibrant matter** (Bennett, 2010).

- **Assemblage:** The concept of assemblage understands entities as moving through the world by producing assemblages. These assemblages are heterogeneous groupings of human and more-than-human, which may be either material or expressive, gathered within a particular context (see DeLanda, 2006). Entities in an assemblage are conceptualized as participants, and relationships between these participants (human and more-than-human participants) are understood to be non-hierarchical. Thus, when an assemblage is mapped, people are significant participants, but the assemblage will also include things such as signs, material objects, events, practices, and utterances. The participation of humans is not automatically foregrounded in the functioning capacities of the assemblage, and as the role of the human in assemblage is de-centred, the role of the material comes more clearly into view (see Latour, 2005).
- **Becoming:** Because assemblages are always in a state of flux, as participants come and go, an assemblage is always changing, and its participants, likewise, are always becoming something new or simply put, *becoming*. As Deleuze and Guattari (1987/2004) state, "we can be thrown into a becoming by anything at all, by the most unexpected, most insignificant of things. You don't deviate from the majority unless there is a little detail that starts to swell and carries you off" (p. 292). In Deleuzo-Guattarian parlance, this becoming, spurred by pre-conscious affect, occurs when participants (human and more-than-human) come into association with each other.
- **Bodymind:** The term bodymind (Semetsky, 2013) signals the indivisibility of the body and the mind. As applied to literacy learning, it reminds us that literacy is an embodied practice—it takes place in the bodymind and therefore is always both cognitive and material. Learning is produced when the bodymind comes into relation with other entities.
- **Collectivity:** Posthumanism seeks to move away from the radical individualism of Western humanism and proposes a society based

on mutual accountability, collectivity, and relationality (Braidotti, 2013). Considerations of collectivity in educational settings focus our attention on the capacities of students working collaboratively—with each other, their teachers, and materials at hand.

- **Difference and differenciation:** The concept of differenciation (Deleuze, 1987/2004 provides an important alternative approach to thinking about learning. For Deleuze, difference is the process of continually becoming different—differenciation—and understanding difference is about inquiring into *how* things become different and how they will *continue* to do so as time and assemblages shift. Classrooms typically take up difference in two ways—with intolerance to deviation from what is considered "the norm" or with pre-planned, teacher-designed differentiated instruction (Davies, 2009). Differenciation allows for an alternate focus in literacy instruction by asking how students (and their skill sets, practices, attitudes, ethics, and so on) are emerging, rather than measuring these against predetermined norms. One of the driving forces of differenciation is affect, so attuning to student affect can assist educators in working with student differenciation.

- **Embodiment:** Liberal humanism positions cognition as having precedence over the body—rational thinking and expression, linearity—which ties it up to epistemological questions. Posthumanism, among other orientations, re-centres, acknowledges, and values the role of the body in sense making. Embodiment is a reminder of the ways in which we come to know our selves, our worlds, and our complex relations therein with, in, and through our bodies. Our bodies are integral in the entangled ways of knowing and being posthumanism amplifies, thus situating the impossibility of separating ideas, materials, bodies, and knowledge.

- **Emergence:** The term *emergence* addresses the idea that bodies (e.g., people, things, places, assemblages) never remain in stasis. That is, they are always in the process of emerging or becoming something new. Emergence in relation to literacy learning reminds us to think of it as an ongoing process of doing, being, and knowing (Lenz Taguchi, 2010) and not something that has fixed endpoints.

- **Ethico-onto-epistemology:** This concept is an important one in posthuman thought because it reminds us that the body and the mind, and therefore, being/doing and thinking cannot be separated, and, furthermore, that ethics are intimately entwined with being/doing/thinking. As Karen Barad states, "questions of ethics and of justice are always already threaded through the very fabric of the world. They are not an *additional* concern that gets added on or placed in our field of vision now and again by particular kinds of concern" (in Dolphijn & van der Tuin, 2012, p. 69, emphasis added). Indeed, she continues, "Being is threaded through with mattering. Epistemology, ontology, and ethics are inseparable. . . . This way of thinking ontology, epistemology, and ethics together makes for a world that is always already an ethical matter" (ibid.)

- **Ethics:** Rather than an ethics informed by an exterior code or set of rules, posthuman ethics flow from relationalilty. Posthuman ethics "evaluate relations as they emerge, rather than judge them a-priori" (Hickey-Moody & Malins, 2007, p. 3). As Brian Massumi (2015) states, inquiring into the ethics of a particular set of actions "means assessing what kind of potential they tap into and express" (p. 11). A posthuman account of ethics has to do with what an entity does and its interdependencies—what it is capable of doing and how its relations with other bodies enhance or constrain those capacities. Because of this relationalilty, ethics are inextricably tied to being, doing, and knowing, and therefore are an integral part of learning.
- **Intra-action:** The term *intra-action*, as we take it up in this volume, indicates this performative entanglement of human and more-than-human relations (Barad, 2007). This strand of posthumanism views reality as a process of becoming through relational encounters, that is, reality is constituted in the moment of encounter between entities. As the concept of intra-action highlights, the inseparability of entities in assemblage as they are doing/being/thinking together, it also highlights the notion that, as entities intra-act, affect is always produced.
- **Lines of flight:** Lines of flight may be thought of as tangents or trajectories on which entities within an assemblage are launched. The term is closely allied with the idea of becoming. A line of flight is generally initiated by affect. As such, lines of flight are very often associated with an unconscious embarking, sparked by something or someone that resonates, carrying the entity off on a trajectory that deviates from their current mode of being/doing/knowing.
- **Non-human and more-than-human:** For simplicity's sake throughout the volume, we use the term *more-than-human* to refer to both the non-human and the more-than-human, recognizing that they are taken up differently by those in the field. Within posthumanism, as noted in our description of agency, we are attuned to the ways in which agency is located in more than just humans but rather speaks to relations among material, expressive, and human entities in an assemblage. Indeed, all entities that come into an assemblage have agency: in their very coming together, they affect one another. In liberal humanist thinking, humans are centred as agentic beings, while the material world, as well as other non-human animate beings are acted upon. The more-than-human, then, serves as a reminder that it is not merely humans who hold agency in our worldmaking.
- **Plateau:** Deleuze and Guattari's *A Thousand Plateaus: Capitalism and Schizophrenia* (1987/2004) maps the main tenets of their philosophy. The volume is written with the intention that its chapters—named as plateaus—may be read in any particular order. Each plateau is

a "stage of a thought-experiment on the creation or renewal of a concept or assemblage of concepts" (Holland, 2013, p. 34). By using a geological term to classify these thought experiments, Deleuze and Guattari remind us of the role of the material world in philosophical spheres whose tendency is to focus solely on a cognitive experience of living. The plateau also reminds us of the role of time in shaping the people, things, events, and practices we are considering in relation to literacy education. Just as a plateau takes millennia to form and is always in the process of becoming something new—contoured and shaped through the forces of human and more-than-human intra-action—so, too, are literate beings, materials, and practices constantly becoming in the classroom.

- **Relational ontology:** In simplest terms, ontology refers an entity's ways of being and doing. As with many of the concepts elaborated in this volume, the work of Gilles Deleuze and Felix Guattari (e.g., 1987/2004) has brought this concept into the mainstream of contemporary philosophical thought. Relational ontology refers to the idea that it is through relations or associations with other entities, that is, through assemblage, that bodies come to be. This ontological becoming is an ongoing process of becoming. Relational ontology moves us away from representational epistemologies (e.g., Cartesian dualism) that locate higher forms of learning in cognitive knowing.

- **Response-ability:** Coined by Karen Barad, the concept of response-ability refers to the capacities made possible through shared response. Response-ability is closely tied to posthuman understandings of agency and ethics. Barad connects the two concepts as follows: "agency is about response-ability, about the possibilities of mutual response, which is not to deny, but to attend to power imbalances. Agency is about possibilities for worldly re-configurings. So, agency is not something possessed by humans, or non-humans for that matter. It is an enactment" (Barad, in Dolphijn & van der Tuin, 2012, p. 55). Patti Lather frames the relationship between agency and response-ability as follows: "Agency is enactment in the possibilities and responsibilities of reconfiguring entanglements. Both determinism and free will are re-thought, and the complexity of a field of forces becomes the focus in assessing response-ability in the face of power imbalances" (Lather, 2016, p. 126).

- **Space and place:** The concept of space, as articulated by Doreen Massey (2005), is dynamic and continually altered or shaped by the contributions and activities of various biological, physical, social, and cultural processes. This understanding of space contrasts markedly from the static view of a space as a container where events take place. Following Massey's (2005) understanding, space is rife with possibility and potentiality. Anderson (2008, p. 228), elaborating on Massey's work, states,

Space is the product of *interrelations*; thus, we must recognize space 'as constituted through interactions, from the immensity of the global to the intimately tiny' (Massey, 2005, p. 9). Space is the sphere of the possibility of the existence of *multiplicity*).... Space is always *under construction*; 'it is always in the process of being made. It is never finished; never closed' (Massey, 2005, p. 9).

While space refers to that which is more ethereal, place denotes materiality—a material place. But even in its physicality, the term, as used in posthuman thought, is recognized as dynamic. As Massey explains, "Place [is] an ever-shifting constellation of trajectories" (Massey, 2005, p. 151). Constituted by multiple entities, who themselves are always becoming, place is not static, nor is it homogeneous.

- **Smooth and striated spaces:** The concepts of smooth and striated spaces build on the idea of space as far more than a static container (Massey, 2005). Elaborating the concepts put forward by Deleuze and Guattari (1987/2004), Hickey-Moody and Malins (2007) conceive striated spaces as follows: "Striated spaces are those which produce particular, limited movements and relations between bodies" (p. 11). Also known as territorialized spaces (Deleuze & Guattari, 1987/2004), striated spaces may also be thought of as rule-governed spaces (DeLanda, 2006). A classroom assemblage is a classic example of a typically striated space. "Smooth spaces, by contrast, are those in which movement is less regulated or controlled, and where bodies can interact—and transform themselves—in endlessly different ways" (Hickey-Moody & Malins, 2007, p. 11).

  While smooth space in the classroom (or any other assemblage) is considered as a generative and open learning space—one that a posthuman informed literacy classroom might strive for—it is important to note that striated space is crucial part of learning. Striations (rules) and striated (rule-governed) spaces hold (or attempt to) an assemblage in a place of predictability and instill a certain kind of calm (DeLanda, 2006). While we wouldn't want classrooms to operate as highly striated assemblages, the constancy of a measured amount of striation is an important aspect of learning and being in these settings. It is the relative stability of a striated space that allows students to find smooth space (spaces of resonance, intensity, excitement, or desire) and embark on personally or collectively meaningful learning trajectories, lines of flight, or flow.

- **Throwntogetherness:** A term popularized by Doreen Massey (2005), the concept of throwntogetherness alerts us to the somewhat random and always changing composition of classroom assemblages. Throwntogetherness acknowledges "the way that very diverse elements that cross categories such as the natural or social come together to foster a particular 'here and now'" (Anderson, 2008, p. 232). As a

concept engaged throughout the volume, it draws us into the situatedness of assemblage entangled in place. In other words, attuning to throwntogetherness animates the contextual and momentary groupings that shape the possibilities and limitations for sensemaking.
- **Vibrant matter:** Closely connected to the idea of "thing power," this concept highlights the observation that things have the capacity to affect other entities (human and more-than-human). Jane Bennett (2010) describes thing power as "the curious ability of inanimate things to animate, to act, to produce effects dramatic and subtle" (p. 6). Things have the ability to move others with whom they come into contact, and likewise, to be changed in these associations—affecting and being affected are not just human capacities. As such, things or matter are understood to have a certain kind of vibrancy or vitalism and play key roles in assemblages.

As you engage with the various plateaus arranged within this volume, this set of concepts will come into play. It is our hope that the present introduction to them will assist your reading and imagining of the possibilities and potentials for posthumanism as you move through the rest of the volume. In the plateaus to come, you will also be introduced to further concepts that elaborate and elucidate posthuman thought in the area of literacy learning. The work you will encounter plays an intra-active role with posthumanism—it is simultaneously shaped by posthuman thought and engaged in the work of contouring posthumanism.

References

Anderson, B. (2008). "For space" (2005): Doreen Massey. In P. Hubbard, R. Kitchin, & G. Valentine (Eds.), *Key texts in human geography* (pp. 227–235). London, UK: Sage Publications.

Barad, K. (2007). *Meeting the universe halfway: Quantum physics and the entanglement of matter and meaning*. Durham, NC: Duke University Press.

Bennett, J. (2010). *Vibrant matter: A political economy of things*. Durham, NC: Duke University Press.

Braidotti, R. (2013). *The posthuman*. Malden, MA: Polity Press.

Davies, B. (2009). Difference and differenciation. In B. Davies & S. Gannon (Eds.), *Pedagogical encounters* (pp. 69–88). New York, NY: Peter Lang.

DeLanda, M. (2006). *A new philosophy of society: Assemblage theory and social complexity*. New York, NY: Continuum.

Deleuze, G., & Guattari, F. (1987/2004). *A thousand plateaus: Capitalism and schizophrenia* (B. Massumi, Trans.). Minneapolis, MN: University of Minnesota Press. (originally publishedas *Mille Plateuaux*, volume 2 of *Capitalisme et schizophrenie*. Paris, France: Minuit, 1987).

Dolphijn, R., & van der Tuin, I. (2012). *New materialism: Interviews & cartographies*. University of Michigan and Open Humanities Press. Retrieved from https://quod.lib.umich.edu/o/ohp/11515701.0001.001/1:4.3/-new-materialism-interviews-cartographies?rgn=div2;view=fulltext

Fenwick, T., & Edwards, R. (2012). *Researching education through actor-network-theory*. Oxford, UK: Wiley-Blackwell.

Gannon, S. (2009). Difference as ethical encounter. In B. Davies & S. Gannon (Eds.), *Pedagogical encounters* (pp. 69–88). New York, NY: Routledge.

Gregg, M., & Seigworth, G. J. (Eds.). (2010). *The affect theory reader*. Durham, NC: Duke University Press.

Haraway, D. (1988). Situated knowledges: The science question in feminism and the privilege of partial perspective. *Feminist Studies, 14*(3), 575–599.

Hickey-Moody, A., & Malins, P. (2007). *Deleuzian encounters: Studies in contemporary social issues*. New York, NY: Palgrave Macmillan.

Holland, E. W. (2013). *Deleuze and Guattari's "A thousand plateaus."* New York, NY: Bloomsbury Academic.

Hultman, K., & Lenz Taguchi, H. (2010). Challenging anthropocentric analysis of visual data: A relational materialist methodological approach to educational research. *International Journal of Qualitative Studies in Education, 23*(5), 525–542.

Lather, P. (2016). Top ten+ list: (Re)thinking ontology in (post)qualitative research. *Cultural Studies ←→ Critical Methodologies, 16*(2), 125–131.

Latour, B. (2005). *Reassembling the social: An introduction to Actor-Network-Theory*. New York, NY: Oxford University Press.

Law, J. (2004). *After method: Mess in social science research*. New York, NY: Routledge.

Lenz Taguchi, H. (2010). *Going beyond the theory/practice divide in early childhood education: Introducing an intra-active pedagogy*. New York, NY: Routledge.

Manning, E., & Massumi, B. (2014). *Thought in the act: Passages in the ecology of experience*. Minneapolis, MN: University of Minnesota Press.

Massey, D. (2005). *For space*. London, UK: Sage Publications.

Massumi, B. (2015). *Politics of affect*. Malden, MA: Polity Press.

Semetsky, I. (2013). Learning with bodymind: Constructing the cartographies of the unthought. In D. Masny (Ed.), *Cartographies of becoming in education: A Deleuze-Guattari perspective* (pp. 77–91). Rotterdam, The Netherlands: Sense Publishers.

Stengers, I. (2010). *Cosmopolitics I* (R. Bononno, Trans.). Minneapolis, MN: Minnesota University Press.

Taylor, C. A. (2016). Edu-crafting a cacophonous ecology: Posthumanist research practices for education. In C. A. Taylor & C. Hughes (Eds.), *Posthuman research practices in education*. New York, NY: Palgrave Macmillan.

Plateau I
Moving With Sensation and Affect

Kim Lenters and Mairi McDermott

Educators working with posthumanism view affective (embodied) responses as key to processes of literate engagement (e.g., Enriquez, Johnson, Kontovourki, & Mallozi, 2016; Leander & Boldt, 2013; Lenters, 2016). The authors in this plateau animate this concept for us as they explore ways that literacy moves with and is moved by sensation and affect. **Affect** refers to the often unconscious, visceral responses of the **bodymind** during any type of encounter (Massumi, 2015; Semetsky, 2013). In literacy encounters, these unarticulated, felt responses activate a process of responding within the *assemblage* of objects, people, practices, and events associated with each other in that moment. That is to say, literate response is felt in the body and not limited to being processed in the mind. With this affective response, the mind may begin to process and respond in discernable ways (e.g., with emotion), or it may not, leaving the encounter as felt but unarticulated.

Viewing the body as an important aspect of intra-action in literacy encounters also takes our understanding of literacy from that which takes place in the individual bodymind, to thinking of it as a collective process, associated with a larger body of people, practices, objects, and events. ***Intra-action*** refers to what happens when participants in an assemblage come into association with each other (Barad, 2007). An example of this kind of intra-action might be the collective affect that is produced when an educator reads aloud from a novel with which the class has been highly engaged or when students and educators watch a humorous YouTube video. Considerations of collectivity in educational settings focus our attention on the capacities of students working collaboratively, with each other, their teachers, and materials at hand. Intra-active collectivity also leads us to consider the ways human, **non-human**, and ***more-than-human*** members of the literacy assemblage work relationally to shape literacy encounters—for individuals and for groups of people—in addition to shaping the objects and practices with which they engage. Waterhouse and Chaudhuri (this volume) do just this as they think with concepts of affect, assemblage, and collectivity. In their example of affective pedagogy for second language and newcomer adult learners, Waterhouse and

30 *Kim Lenters and Mairi McDermott*

Chaudhuri posit the idea that affects are not only the sole property of the individual human body but also live in the assembled body that is the classroom. The selection of text, Shaun Tan's (2006) *The Arrival*, engaged to animate the collectivity of sensed meaning making is particularly relevant for their provocations.

What Can a Body Do?

In the consideration of literacy as embodied, whether within the body of an individual or in the assembled (or collective) body the individual is a part of, posthumanism leads us to consider what that body can do. We can ask, what are its capacities and potentials? What kinds of agency does that body demonstrate? In a posthuman understanding, ***agency*** is not an individual quality, nor something a person has or possesses, but rather that which is produced when participants in an assemblage ***intra-act*** with each other. In this way, agency is closely linked with affect—affect works as a catalyst (Thiel, 2015) or spark to produce agency. In the literacy classroom, educators will want to set their intention to notice that which produces agency and find ways to encourage the production of agency. Ehret and MacDonald (this volume) engage with this intra-action in their exploration of the relationship between affect and agency. As they consider the concept of "minor gestures" (Manning, 2016) in the secondary school English classroom, Ehret and MacDonald make the case that affective moments between teacher and student, often unspoken and fleeting, play transformative roles in the literacy learning assemblage.

Thinking of agency as collectively produced, an educator might ask, "What kinds of agentful responses am I already seeing, as my students engage in classroom literacy encounters?" along with a number of related questions that consider how to nurture those affective responses through configuring the classroom assemblage of people, objects, practices, and events (see Figure 6).

- What kinds of agentful responses are you already seeing as your students engage in classroom literacy encounters? How might you nurture these responses?
- What kinds of materials foster a sense of agency amongst your students?
- How might you work with these materials and students to produce agency that extends to other situations, practices, or events?
- How might we reconfigure classroom assemblages to create new affects in relation to the texts that seem to repel students?
- What new agential possibilities have taken flight as students think with these texts and the worlds they embody?

Figure 6 Questions to consider for promoting agentful classroom intra-actions

Further to the question of what a body can do and the understanding of body as assemblage, posthumanism views things or objects (the non-human and more-than-human) as agentful. That is to say, things play a role in assemblages, just as humans do. Jane Bennett (2010) names this ***thing power/vibrant matter***. Bartlett and LeBlanc (this volume) animate this vibrancy as they examine what is produced when objects, such as "junk," are brought into relationship with student memories and histories in sensorial assemblages. Following a question posed by a student after a field trip to a local recycling facility, Bartlett's elementary students spark a school-wide, arts-focused, interdisciplinary inquiry into junk. Through their narration of this experience, Bartlett and LeBlanc tease out the different ways materials, objects, students, and ideas affect, or change, the composition of individual identities as well as the assemblage as a whole.

As teachers, students, things, and practices intra-act in the classroom assemblage, the assemblage shifts—it becomes something new. Much like Bartlett and LeBlanc's example, educators may be very familiar with the way a topic that arises incidentally during a current events discussion, an event in a student's life, or a class read-aloud seems, out of the blue, to capture the interest and imagination of an individual student or a whole class. In posthumanism, this movement is often referred to as a ***becoming*** or a ***line of flight***.

As we create space in our literacy programming for students, collectively or individually, to pursue lines of flight that spring from their interests and concerns, we not only make room for agency; we also foster curiosity, creativity, and generosity. In the closing piece for this plateau, MacDonald and Leander (this volume) provide us with a provocative example of this as they re-imagine unit planning, a task engaged by all educators, as a mode of gifting. As we think with these ideas, the goal is not to follow every student's whim or fancy or to completely upend teacher planning and meeting of curricular outcomes. However, by attuning to the ***smooth spaces*** that signal potential student lines of flight and making space for some of these trajectories to be pursued or by engaging in activities such as improvisation and body storming (MacDonald & Leander), educators may involve students, in meaningful ways, in the direction(s) of their own learning.

While it may be easy to lament the agency produced when students and particular things intra-act, framing objects, such as smartphones or video games, as harmful distractions may not be productive for students' literacy learning. Ultimately, rather than eschewing them, understanding the agency associated with the things students intra-act with and finding ways to engage those material objects and practices will more effectively move classroom assemblages toward the production of literate dispositions.

An understanding of thing-power also moves us to think about the negative affect students may associate with certain literacy objects—things such as densely written textbooks or plays written in Old English. If these material objects are a necessary part of classroom literacy instruction, how might we reconfigure the assemblage to create new affects in relation to the things that may repel some students?

References

Barad, K. (2007). *Meeting the universe halfway: Quantum physics and the entanglement of matter and meaning.* Durham, NC: Duke University Press.

Bennett, J. (2010). *Vibrant matter: A political economy of things.* Durham, NC: Duke University Press.

Enriquez, G., Johnson, E., Kontovourki, S., & Mallozi, C. (Eds.). (2016). *Literacies, learning and the body: Putting theory and research into pedagogical practice.* New York, NY: Routledge.

Leander, K., & Boldt, G. (2013). Rereading "A pedagogy of multiliteracies": Bodies, texts, and emergence. *Journal of Literacy Research, 45*(1), 22–46.

Lenters, K. (2016). Riding the lines and overwriting in the margins: Affect and multimodal literacy practices. *Journal of Literacy Research, 48*(2), 280–316.

Manning, E. (2016). *The minor gesture.* Durham, NC: Duke University Press.

Massumi, B. (2015). *Politics of affect.* Malden, MA: Polity Press.

Semetsky, I. (2013). Learning with bodymind: Constructing the cartographies of the unthought. In D. Masny (Ed.), *Cartographies of becoming in education: A Deleuze-Guattari perspective* (pp. 77–91). Rotterdam, The Netherlands: Sense Publishers.

Tan, S. (2006). *The arrival.* New York, NY: Arthur A. Levine Books.

Thiel, J. J. (2015). Vibrant matter: The intra-activerole of objects in the construction of young children's literacies. *Literacy Research: Theory, Method, and Practice, 64,* 112–131.

1 Listening to Junk
Sensorial Assemblages and Community Engagement

Stephanie Bartlett and Robert LeBlanc

> *There was a buzz in the school that felt different from a typical day. Spanning the length of two hallways, students worked together in small groups or individually. What was different here? Everyone was enthusiastically involved in the measuring of the holiday lights that students had taped to the floor around the perimeter of our hallways. The conversation was lively as they asked questions, compared notes, and shared materials and techniques. One student came racing up to me in his bike helmet, exclaiming "I love this because it is JUST. SO. GOOD!" He zipped away to continue measuring.*

This short anecdote highlights the activity, excitement, and material of a multi-phased collective art venture, *Project Engage*, that researcher and educator Stephanie Bartlett undertook with her students in Calgary, AB. In this chapter, we detail the work of Stephanie to create and explore with her students the materiality of *junk*—to work with material that was cast off and abandoned—and in doing so to help students rework the experience of *place* at their school. At a moment, when we as teachers are thinking more about our global connections, we ask in this chapter how we might encourage students to see themselves as part of an assemblage (DeLanda, 2016): a collection of different materials, places, objects, and feelings, all of which have different histories and different trajectories and which may have very different futures. In the spirit of place-based researcher Barbara Comber's (2016) call to "position students as active agents in their own learning and the social and political life of their schools and communities" (p. 10), we outline how Stephanie worked with her students to connect themselves to the *stuff* all around them, to see themselves as an active part of the place they find themselves, and to work to actively recreate their own local assemblages for the better. We begin this chapter by outlining the research relationship between Stephanie, a Calgary-based teacher, and Robert, a Lethbridge-based teacher educator. We then turn to talking about our core concept in this project: the *sensorial assemblage* (Hamilakis, 2017), an arrangement of materials, people, and histories that is not just about information but about how we *feel* and *affectively respond* to that arrangement. Finally, we detail how Stephanie worked with her students to create their own sensorial assemblage out of junk, a public art project for their schoolyard that drew on sight, sound, and touch.

Assembling Ourselves

As co-authors, a researcher and an educator, coming together as composing partners added a layer of depth to our writing. Reading a selection of Robert's research, Stephanie understood the threads of anthropology throughout and wondered if Robert's connection to assemblage might offer an alternative line of flight for her work with *Project Engage*. Hearing about Stephanie's work, Robert wondered if *Project Engage* might complicate and nuance notion of the assemblage for an educational setting. Sitting in our composing room, we each assembled our side of the table with computer, books, journal, pen, snacks, and coffee mug then looked at each other and grinned, wondering where we should begin. We started by introducing ourselves by way of who we are, where we come from, and how we came to be in Alberta. Next, we turned to talking about what drives us in our work, scribing each other's thoughts as our partnership began to take shape. The conversation bounced and flowed from rhythm, to time, to possibilities, to "what if" pedagogies, returning often to the themes of rhythm and time (Smith, 2014). Together, we began to draw on the work of the notion of the sensorial assemblage to think through how we might use educational moments to attune our students to their place within it. Educating for this kind of connection requires new tools, new resources, new materialisms, and new networks. In the age of the global connectivity, with its vast architecture of connections, the problem for teachers is how to make these kinds of tools, materialisms, and connections real and tangible, or as Latour (2013) asks, "How do we tell such a story?" (p. 3).

Engaging Project Engage

Central to our discussion was Stephanie's narrative of her student-led collective public art, *Project Engage: Living our Lives for a Sustainable Future*. Both a year-long interdisciplinary school-wide project and a study of school culture, *Project Engage* invited stakeholders to experience learning through the lenses of environmental sustainability, math, and music in a public elementary school in a large urban school district in Calgary. This study engaged teachers, parents, students, and community members to redefine community through the reflection of student voice and ecological stewardship. In doing so, it asked students to create their own assemblages: of memories, of space, of sound, and of junk in service of creating public art. What began as a way to experience a shift in pedagogy from traditional teaching towards experiential learning in the community morphed into a potential for engaging children and their families in their care for their local place. Literacy was embedded throughout as students described their process of assembling junk, reflected upon their work in the community, and created campaigns to promote environmental sustainability. The idea of sensorial assemblages is a powerful and practical way to think through *Project Engage* to wonder how educators might take the interests of children to design an authentic real-world project that matters in their own context.

Assembling the Present and the Future

We like to imagine ourselves as autonomous people, as independent at our very core. But as contemporary scholar Bruno Latour (2013) points out, this would appear to be a contemporary fiction: *We Have Never Been Modern* is Latour's longstanding claim, that is, never been the fully independent rational beings in the model of the Enlightenment. We have always been connected, influenced, embarked by the constituent *outside*, and indeed, Latour's work and others (Bennett, 2009) help us rethink neat boundaries of *inside/outside*. Taking this further, Latour asks how we might reconsider agency in a time of connected globalization, as part of the shifting multi-scaled assemblage of vehicles, suburbanization, geologic time, nitrogen footprints, escalating protein production, extended lifespans, colonial expansion, and the multi-generational decline of democratic institutions. These are educational as much as epistemological questions: how do we educate students to see themselves as active players in the assemblage of our contemporary world?

De-centring the idea that we are autonomous people—and engaging what many call "the posthuman"—is part of an important project to dislodge false and unhelpful notions of rationality from its high perch in politics, education, and other fields (Massumi, 2015). Beyond (and before) argument lays what some posthuman scholars call *affect:* "the potential for bodies—including material things—to move, to compel, before and after direct perception, where direct perception includes 'higher' functions'" (Ehret & Hollett, 2014, p. 432). While we may think of ourselves as "thinking beings" first and foremost, we are profoundly affected by all kinds of *stuff*: the food we eat, the hormones in our bodies, even music (Bennett, 2010). Affect is a kind of intensity, "an intensive *force* that all bodies (whether human or non-human) exert upon one another" (Ott, 2017): one need only turn up a song on the radio to see how we can be affected by things beyond our rational parsing. And where schools are largely considered "thinking" spaces, scholars suggest that we might think about what kinds of embodied affective experiences and virtualities resonate with the affect of our students—movement, remaking, intensity, music, touch—for the purposes of learning.

Sensorial Assemblages

Animating much posthumanist thought is Deleuze's (2002) concept of the assemblage: "a multiplicity which is made up of many heterogeneous terms and which establishes . . . relations between them" (p. 69). Classrooms and communities are assemblages, and assemblage theory helps us unthink objects, spaces, places, institutions, and even individuals as coherent "things" and instead see them as processes which unfold over time. Some of those components are biological, some linguistic, and some geological, meaning an assemblage is a mix of bodies, ideas, words, and things.

Assemblages are more than the coming together of bodies and objects, however. They include the coming together of memory, affect, senses, and time. For example, Stephanie's powerful *Project Engage* brought together stuff but also children's memories, their histories with the playground, and their tactile engagement with the "junk" of the public display. Powerful assemblages like art, the archeologist Hamilakis (2017) suggests, "piece works at different registers: the sensorial and affective, the historical, the political" (p. 169). Commenting on the installation of artist Kara Walker's "A Subtlety or the Marvelous Sugar Baby"—a huge white sugar sculpture of a kneeling black woman, housed in a former Domino's sugar refinery in Brooklyn—Hamilakis notes that its resonance was multiple. The factory smelled strongly of sugar, invoking an olfactory history of industry in New York. The statue itself was slowly melting and left a sticky residue on visitors' hands. Shining in its whiteness, the statue invoked the racialized legacy of colonialism, the brutal slave work of sugar plantations, and the consumption of black labour and women's bodies for European gain. Collective memory and materiality co-mingle as visitors walk through the gallery and around the statue. The participant feels, smells, experiences, and remembers. The multiplicity of the assemblage, shifting with each new participant and stirred memory, evokes an affective response and is affected by the participants. This affective intensity also escapes the logic and intention of production, even the productive intention of the artist, spilling over into novel arrangements, affective responses, and embodied reactions. Affect, then, is a part of any assemblage, and assemblages are recognized, understood, and engaged by way of affect. Like Walker's art, Stephanie's project sought to tap into more than linguistic claims and thinking beings—it brought together sound, memories, senses, feelings, and affective engagements to create a sensorial assemblage for the purposes of education.

Assembling Junk

The following anecdote returns to the holiday light recycling project to highlight that this learning experience was inspired by a student who was not engaged in traditional learning settings, yet he thrived when given an opportunity to think and ask questions:

> "How many strings of lights can go around the school?" "Can we attach them all together and find out?" As I sit writing kindergarten report cards, this boy is the lived curriculum. Traditional methods don't work for him. It is hard to sit, hard to play games, hard to concentrate on a task that he doesn't want to do. And yet . . . he is the first, and often the only, student to come up with an idea during class discussions (in the case of the lights, a huge part of the school took part in his idea). He is a leader in calling out his strategy of how he arrived at a certain point in his thinking. He is my living example to remember to give my students what they need.

Assembling the Scene

Stephanie's work with *Project Engage* offered insight into the possibilities (and limitations) that arise from linking school and community through learning experiences. In composing this project, Stephanie asked: What stories do we want to tell our children about the world today? How can educators help students to engage in their learning differently? What might they be doing? Given our economic and environmental climates and decidedly uncertain future, we wanted to tell the stories of refuge and inspiration, of community, environmental stewardship, of a changing education system, and of how students can be empowered to shift the inert and alter how we live in the world. *These* are the stories that Stephanie wanted to tell. But equally, within and beyond stories, what kinds of affective intensities might these assemblages provoke? To explore these stories, the remainder of this section is written in Stephanie's first-person voice.

The objective of *Project Engage: Living our Lives for a Sustainable Future* was to link school and community together as we cared for our local environment. We collaborated to create meaningful learning opportunities that placed relationships and sustainability at the heart of the students' learning. The foundation of *Project Engage* was inspired 4 years ago by a kindergarten student: this young boy loved metal, and his father owned a scrap metal yard. Assembling from his interests, I brought in various pieces of scrap, and my students began to play with the metal in the classroom, feeling and working with materials artistically. Building on this, we went on a field trip to a scrap metal yard, and this opened up questions about the life cycle of objects and recycling metal—how our system produces waste and where that waste might be repurposed. I began to wonder if we could create a school-wide sustainability project that would teach students to look differently at the world around them. As a school, we wanted to involve students in a meaningful project that incorporated our core values, and we wanted to do it by expressing math and science through art, with literacy embedded throughout as a way of documenting the journey. We did not know at the time precisely what form this project would take. We knew we needed to create a culture of sustainability, so with a partnership with the adjacent high school, we installed a metal recycling bin in our community. This became a common shared experience of living ecologically for our schools. Students and staff began to understand the life cycles of objects and realize that living a sustainable life is more than just recycling your cans and bottles. Their tactile engagements with the stuff of contemporary life, including its under-side of waste, helped to repurpose and re-assemble it together.

The kindergarten student who loved scrap metal became my teacher, as he revealed a wisdom beyond his years through his thoughts and words. As I explain in the anecdote below, Mitchell understood that we are recycling the lights to divert them from the landfill and recover the copper from inside.

> *I paused from our work and stood with 6-year old Mitchell as he surveyed the scene of busy students. He makes me slow down and see the world through his 6-year old wisdom. "Looks like we have a lot of lights here. I think we might need to get a copper shredder in the school." I asked him to estimate how much money we might earn from the lights once we weighed them. Another long pause as he looked around. I rocked figuratively in my chair and looked around, too, nodding my head and listening to the focused chatter nearby.*

Having a conversation with Mitchell conjures the image of two old men contemplating life together as they sit in rocking chairs on a cool porch sheltered from the hot afternoon sun. For me, Stephanie, that conversation was about connections and heart. I seek the time and space to connect with my students to get down on their level and let them know that they matter. This space helps me breathe, connect with those around me, and realize that it is community and generosity of spirit, with learning woven in that is at work here. I like to believe that I helped to show him that he matters as a person in his own right.

Listening to Junk

This needed to be a project that mattered. We needed to make decisions together as a broader school community. A spark was ignited when the adjacent community association invited our students to have input into decisions, through the lens of sustainability, to renovate their building. We began to think about sustainable outdoor shared spaces. An idea emerged to create an interactive musical playground from recycled metal—a sensorial assemblage of memory, objects, space, and time. To create this idea of a musical playground, we knew we needed to foster relationships to help us with the project. We decided to bring in an artist-in-residence and found a luthier, Chris, who built string instruments. The artist had deep musical knowledge but also came with the mindset that the students should be the driving creative force behind the design of the sound sculpture. To reinforce music's connection with math and science and for the purposes of skill development and knowledge building, we engaged the National Music Centre. They also helped us to document our learning. The result of this year-long collaboration was an incredible sound sculpture. Although the product was impressive, the real value of the sculpture was journey students lived through to create it. Every student had a hand in the process. Students worked with Chris to prototype ideas and test them. They played, problem solved, came up with creative ideas, and collaborated together.

We celebrated in the form of a Fine Arts Fair with pop-up performances and an audible exploration of our sound sculpture. It could be heard a block away! If one could measure the success of a year-long sound exploration of sound and music through the joyful noise of participants, this learning experience was a great success. As a researcher, I had been closely observing the reactions of teachers, students, parents, and community experts. This event showed me results that had been building through my data collection: field notes, observations, interviews, and focus groups. Teachers facilitated and guided students through a learning exposition that challenged all involved to use photos, writing, and artifacts to document the process. The street festival–style showcase of learning demonstrated a deep engagement with the learning and strong ties to community.

Each experience in the unfolding of the year-long project added another layer, becoming richer than the last. Once I awakened to this idea of community as an integral part of learning, I was excited by the seemingly endless possibilities that slowly unfolded as time progressed. For each initiative within *Project Engage*, teachers led the task design part of the project, with input from community experts. The work was for the students, who took the knowledge, synthesized it, and gave it back to the community in terms of the environmental message, the different design challenges, and stronger ties to community. Together, we were redefining the values of our community and exploring the value of expert knowledge that the world has to offer our students.

Teaching Take-Aways

- Community art using local resources can help students see themselves as part of a bigger picture.
- Literacy learning can include local experts and local materials to re-create local spaces.

- Even the most "local" activity, object, and resource is connected to a wider network of activities, objects, and resources; invite students to follow these threads.
- Literacy learning can extend from place-based learning as students explore what and who they are in that place and what it means to belong.

Imagining New Assemblages for Schools and Teaching

> *"Will you stay with me tonight?" pleaded my 8-year old daughter. "You can just sit with me; you can read whatever you like. . . ." There was something in her earnest eyes and tone of voice that pulled me from the evening chores. Of late, she has been very worried about our planet. She runs around indignantly turning out lights, even before we are finished in that room. "Just one light at a time" is her mantra. So tonight, I chose a book that might just serve to fuel this fire of mindfulness. I wondered if she would enjoy the words of Thich Nhat Hahn (2016). She lies back, eyes distant while gazing at the ceiling. I read to her of how to love nature and know that we must care for the earth. I read of how it is important to step mindfully thinking and breathing slowly. Deeply. "Yes. Go on." "What do you mean?" "That's beautiful" were some of her comments. And then: "That man? He must really love the earth."*

Imagination is materially embodied in and through *Project Engage*. The sound sculpture of junk, the festival, the scrap metal yard, the holiday light recycling campaign, and the community are all physical manifestations of the children's wonderings, of future assemblages yet to be. It was not enough to think about the work or simply complete a task or project in class. The school and community physically participated in the process and the celebration. The sensorial assemblage of recycled metal, sound, math, and science was brought to life by the relationships among students, teachers, parents, and community, becoming a metaphor for educational change—memory, affect, space, and history overlapping. Being attuned to our local assemblages means asking that we attend to our impact as humans on the planet and to reimagine new ways of living well together in a way that strengthens relationships so that communities can contribute to the well-being of local places and the earth itself on a global scale. It is easy to become paralyzed with climate change and our global crises. Traditional Western models of education and problem solving have not prepared citizens for understanding our impact (Smith, 2014). In creating *Project Engage*, Stephanie sought to untangle traditional classroom assemblages and build towards something that echoed Walker's sensorial assemblage—something which spilled over into novel

Table 1.1 Traditional Classrooms and Project Engage

Traditional Classroom Assemblages	What Unfolded in the Assemblage of Project Engage
Teacher delivers content	Teacher is a guide and facilitator
Student consumes knowledge	Student co-creates knowledge with peers and teachers
Desks	Scrap metal yard
Books	Cross-grade community
Classroom	Attunement to local place + global flows
Teacher-directed art class	Community public art using local resources
Reading and writing programs	Literacy learning can include local experts and materials to recreate spaces in the community
Context of student work comes from a textbook or curricular outcome	Even the most "local" activity, object, and resource is connected to a wider network of activities, objects, and resources; invite students to follow these threads
Student work displayed on a bulletin board	Student work is displayed in the community for a broader audience
Literacy learning follows a specific program, regardless of local context	Literacy learning can extend from place-based learning as students explore what who they are in that place and what it means to belong

arrangements beyond the orderly intention of the teacher, providing affective responses and embodied reactions. Who knows what future assemblages this might provoke? The table below shows a comparison between traditional assemblages and the assemblages in *Project Engage*.

Music and sound became the affective intensities that wove the entanglement together. The need for changes in the education system is a subtext in this narrative, with the stories pointing toward new pathways. *Project Engage* was a living example of humans and non-humans lingering together in a learning experience inherently different than the traditional pedagogy of project-based learning. It became a conversation within a topic rather than between teacher and students with known outcomes. We wondered what it would be like to look at environmental sustainability through the lenses of math, science, music, and junk. Literacy education was woven throughout this work in broader and deeper ways than conventional methods of planning and teaching literacy blocks.

Conclusion

In framing *Project Engage* as a sensorial assemblage, we rethink the well-trodden binary of humans as actors and materials as the things upon which we act. Jane Bennett (2010) asks us to consider *thing power*, "the material agency of natural bodies and technological artifacts" (p. xiii). Things, she argues, have agency in themselves insofar as they produce effects in humans and other bodies—what she calls "the curious ability of inanimate things to animate, to act, to produce effects dramatic and subtle" (p. 6). Here she offers examples like litter and chemical leaches from garbage dumps, worms, electricity, microscopic organisms, bacteria and food in our guts, and stem cells. The story of *Project Engage* is an illustrative example of how large-scale problems with political implications can be re-scaled through the assemblage of things and local action. The purpose of using the sensorial assemblage of community engagement and junk de-centres the traditional role of the teacher and demonstrates how deeply social justice and place-based learning are embedded in the foundational fabric of the project, as well as the diverse entry points for both students and also teachers new to this type of pedagogy. Beyond agency and "attunement"—can educators offer more than just being aware, using critical pedagogies in literacy and posthumanism to create new and different types of learning experiences inviting students to be leaders in global change? Through this work with sensorial assemblages, we hope to have offered a framework to shift practice towards providing opportunities for students to attune themselves to their place and the potential in a rapidly changing world.

References

Bennett, J. (2010). *Vibrant matter: A political ecology of things*. Durham, NC: Duke University Press.

Comber, B. (2016). *Literacy, place, and pedagogies of possibility*. New York, NY: Routledge.

DeLanda, M. (2016). *Assemblage theory*. Edinburgh, UK: Edinburgh University Press.

Deleuze, G. (2002). *Dialogues II*. New York, NY: Continuum.

Ehret, C., & Hollett, T. (2014). Embodied composition in real virtualities: Adolescents' literacy practices and felt experiences moving with digital, mobile devices in school. *Research in the Teaching of English, 48*(4), 428–454.

Hamilakis, Y. (2017). Sensorial assemblages: Affect, memory, and temporarily in assemblage thinking. *Cambridge Archaeological Journal, 27*(1), 169–182.

Latour, B. (2013). *Inquiry into the modes of existence*. Cambridge, MA: Harvard University Press.

Massumi, B. (2015). *The politics of affect*. New York, NY: Polity Press.

Nhat Hahn, T. (2016). *The miracle of mindfulness: An introduction to the practice of meditation* (M. Ho, Trans.). Boston, MA: Beacon Press.

Ott, B. (2017). Affect. In *Oxford research encyclopedia of communication*. New York, NY: Oxford University Press.

Smith, D. G. (2014). *Teaching as the practice of wisdom*. New York, NY: Bloomsbury Academic.

2 How Minor Gestures Generate Relational Transformations in the Act of Literacy Teaching and Learning

Christian Ehret and Rachel MacDonald

Before the Break

> *I had just welcomed the class and gotten the students started. Sam showed up at the door, late. I felt him enter the room; he seemed charged, and out of the corner of my eye I could just sense his shaking.... I can't remember for sure, but it's likely I would have greeted him with a cursory "Hey, kiddo, what's up?" but somehow I knew in that moment that I needed to turn and acknowledge his arrival into the classroom.*

Our classroom was tucked away into a corner of the school, where there were less traffic and less noise. It was not a typical high school English class, where a teacher might lead her students into lengthy discussions about literature, ideas, and philosophical understandings; rather, it was a class where the course material was shared through a digital learning platform and the students worked asynchronously through a prefab curriculum. I, the classroom teacher, worked alongside them, providing instruction and support as needed or as requested. We were housed in a computer lab, where there were no supplies, no colorful pictures on the wall, and really, no free space. Horizontal rows of tables and computers filled the room, leaving only a small space through which I could walk along the row of desks and squeeze myself into the front of the room. The learners sat in front of a large computer screens, squished between learners to the right and to the left. My students crunched over dusty keyboards in the often dark and hot moist air of a computer lab, which for one period in the day became our classroom. This classroom, despite its apparent awkwardness, was a respite for learners who did not thrive in the typical classrooms found throughout the school, preferring instead a classroom where there would be less heavy-handed forms of institutional control and discipline.

Being located in a community that was once its own town, separate from the large, midwestern Canadian city of which it had recently become a part, also made the classroom and larger school culture unique.

Although annexed by the city, the community culture, identity and sense social cohesion persisted. The "original" townspeople, who lived in the former military housing and lower income properties, considered themselves unique from the residents who settled within the community after annexation and bought the expensive and newly built homes along the river. Sam [a pseudonym], like his classmates, had lived this history, feeling the effects of a changing and quickly gentrifying community. He and his friends were feeling more and more socially marginalized from the riverside homeowners and the dominant cultures they brought with them. Like Sam, many students in the class were in their self-professed last attempt at high school, and the class structure provided a space where they did not have to follow a typical high school routine. And so, at the time of this recollected story, I was in the fortunate circumstance of being a teacher in a class full of learners who not only challenged the status quo and rebelled against authority but also who very much represented the history and longstanding community from which the school was built.

On this day, as on any other, this history was present but not necessarily conscious to any of us. In fact, much of what happened that day felt unconscious but intensely felt and present—to myself, to Sam, to the entire class that tensed, breathed, and relaxed together through the moment after Sam entered the room late. There are times in my teaching life when my choices make little sense to the logical eye. Only in retrospect can I recognize the automaticity of the thing, the almost nonchoice aspect of the moment. I have, at least, found this to be true. To be fair, I am acutely aware of the many structures and spaces around me, the things that I believe I am allowed to do or not allowed to do. The protocols that guide my behaviour; responses; and choices in terms of content, instruction, and assessment and in the day-to-day interactions with my students.

In the moment when Sam entered the room, abruptly and late, I could feel these protocols tensing my body and generating intensities between myself and Sam, myself and the rest of the class, and all the bodes in the room, on edge as the moment played out. Thought in the act is potential-full, on the verge of not yet, emergent. And this emerging act—how I would respond to Sam's boisterous late entrance—was full-up with more than potential, as all activity is. Major and minor forces push potential towards a particular action that moved me in the moment (Deleuze & Guattari, 1987; Ehret, 2018a, 2018b). The major: how the protocols that guided my professional life might determine my move to chasten Sam for being rude and late; how the abstract construction of a boisterous male body impinges on singular actions with unfounded fear. The minor: desiring to disrupt these major tendencies of control and fear that do violence in everyday moments and inhibit their potential for change. Breaking moments are full of forces that are not beyond our control but that are pushing us towards their own image of controlling potential. The minor breaks towards disruption of structures and major tendencies that stultify moving human relations toward change.

Before the break, through the events of these ordinary social interactions between teacher and student welling up, the potential to learn and to be together more or less justly, and lovingly, is most at stake. The ordinary event overflows with potential for change, beyond the direct or absolute control of major forces. But how a moment breaks, how we choose to act doesn't always feel like a rational choice. And this is how my choice in this moment unfolded—choicelessly and beyond my own rational determination.

We Have Always Valued the Minor

As former high school English language arts teachers and current teachers and mentors for the same, we never stop searching for how to make a difference. We never stop because our desire for making a difference is constantly changing and taking shape through moments of difference-in-the-making with our students and fellow teachers. No one difference is the same, but we know it when we feel it, and when we feel it, we know why we teach. The teaching material that sustains us exists outside of major theories and texts, like scaffolding, constructivism, curricular books, and our worn, overflowing lesson plan binders and over-the-limit cloud storage. The "teaching material" that keeps us desiring teaching is a feeling that something happened and that in the act of that happening, something transformed in the relationship between us and our students.

We call the feelings "material" because in moments of relational transformation between us and our students, we experience a sense of movement register through our bodies that doesn't always fit into language or emotional categories. These feelings resist registering in major theories and texts both because they resist language and categorization and because each of these moments is singular, connected only in the desiring forward to the next such moment, which we'll know as such as soon as we get there. These moments are the minor and mundane that are everything to our desiring as teachers and nothing to the major but a disruption of its surety and authority. But as teachers, we are surer of nothing more than these feelings, which have an actual existence in our sense of things in the moment as it comes to pass. We therefore *know* relational transformations in moments of teaching and learning through our bodies *in the moment*, the felt-sense of something happening, something moving us urgently into the act of literacy teaching and learning, the sense of becoming a teacher, endlessly, choicelessly.

This chapter is about how minor gestures in the act of literacy teaching and learning generate relational transformations that produce difference (Manning, 2016). It is about how to feel for the potential for such difference in the event of its happening and how to feel forward toward actualizing potential difference. This chapter is also therefore about how teaching and learning in the major key tends towards sameness and towards muffling minoritarian potentials for change (Manning, 2019). Therefore, a central concern for us in this chapter is how to feel the major infringing upon moments with our students and how disrupt the major's tendency with minor gestures. The chapter itself is therefore an effort to disrupt the major's tendency to describe change in familiar ways that actually do not *feel* all that different.

This is because the major values factual accounts of change that can be measured, named, and brought to scale. A structural change in curricular design might "flip the classroom" such that, in place of classroom instruction, high school English language arts students watch a brief video about a critical theory, such as the social construction of gender (see Appleman, 2014), at home. The next day in class, they apply this critical lens, working in groups to analyze gendered images and character actions in new media marketing and television dramas. The flipping continues as the next evening they watch a video on writing arguments about new media and pop culture texts through critical gender theory, and they come to class the next day prepared to write brief arguments and to peer edit. And in our imagined classroom, the fact is: this works! Students' scores increase when their end of unit essays are marked according the standardized state rubric for argumentative writing. And the fact becomes: English language arts teachers statewide ought to flip their classrooms, at least for their instructional units on argumentative writing. The major values factual accounts of change that can be measured, named, and brought to scale.

At the curricular level of transformation, everyday acts of teaching and learning—smiles between teachers and students, students laughing together or arguing over their interpretations of the symbolism of Offred's red cloak—are ancillary concerns. The embodied, mundane joys and tensions of classrooms as living bodies experience them resist quantification or being named by the major. And yet as teachers, we know these joys and tensions amongst the most meaningful moments of change that arise in our practice. We know it when we feel it, and when we feel it, we know why we teach. These feelings force us to consider what qualitative factors of change are left un(der)theorized in the major's wake. And given the major's power, we return to Rachel's story, wondering through it: how does the major tendency to locate educational change in quantifiable transformations affect everyday pedagogical encounters that are the differences that keep us desiring as teachers deeply invested in English education?

A Minor Gesture in the Act of Literacy Teaching and Learning

English language arts is one of those subjects that often, and at instruction's best, creates spaces for learners and teachers to be real, raw, and willing to grapple with their realities of life through discussion, writing, and performance. As an English teacher, I feel especially grateful for the multiple opportunities and freedoms I have throughout the day to connect to learners in a powerful way—human to human connection through writing, talking, and exploring texts together and grappling with the big questions of life, relationships, and the purpose (or lack of) we humans feel in working through all this together. Sam was pushed out of this sort of environment and placed into my class after an incident with another English teacher in the school. He had gotten into an altercation wither her after being late for class. Apparently, the lateness had become a regular occurrence, and his teacher wanted to address it with him in the hall. The result of that conversation? He was removed from the first English class for being "explosive and defiant," according to his referral.

Never "explosive and defiant," Sam seemed to be a good fit in our room. He chose to attend class, mostly. At the beginning, he was neither an obviously central part of the class community, nor was he a disruption to it. He just did not speak up often, and he completed his work slowly. I remember feeling that I needed to tiptoe around his emotions, as I could sense that if I were to upset him, he likely would not return. I also remember trying very hard to make him relax, laugh, and feel comfortable, all in an attempt to get him to complete more of his necessary coursework. About a month into the class, I can say with certainty that I was worried about many students' progress, including Sam's. Would they ever complete their work? How could I be sure that they had shown me enough? Although I had some strengthening student–teacher relationships, I would describe my relationship with Sam as fledgling. He was open to talking to me, but he was also very reserved in his stance towards me.

And then . . . I remember the moment so well.

I remember noticing at once that Sam seemed in a really bad way, almost desperate. His eyes were wide, and his whole body shook. He turned to me and slowly held out his hand, which I could see was bruised and swollen. My action was uninhibited. I grabbed his hand, and I held it gently—something I would not normally do with any student, let alone with one whom my relationship was so new like Sam. As I held his hand, I had him sit down and leaned in. I gently said, "It's going to be okay. You are okay. You are good. I am worried about your hand."

Holding his hand, I moved him farther into the classroom and asked him to share what happened. He told me of a series of verbal altercations he encountered prior to class. He had gotten into it with some students in the hall and with another teacher. In his story, he said, "I snapped." In his frustration, he punched one of the school's brick walls over and over again. Why he turned up in class I will never know for certain. Why didn't he just head home? I remember thinking, "What am I to do?"

It really was a strange non-choice to hold his hand. Normally, if I had been following protocol, I would have first remarked that he was late for class, that he needed to go to the office, or, most likely, that he needed to calm down, relax, chill out. In the moment, I somehow knew that he, that we, as a class, needed something to change, that we needed much more than a teacherly response dictated from a majoritarian image of teacherly and the structures that have been built to support that image. We had to disrupt that image of teaching in order to move forward. This was a moment when I did not necessarily suspended all worries about content, expectations, and my own fears about breaking protocol; rather, it was a moment when the major tendencies of teaching cannot but be broken toward a different form of value—the value of unstructured human relation that exceeds protocol's attempts to confine or even to define it. Relationships transform not through the majoritarian actions of teacher and student but despite them, when teacher and student break from them toward what it is possible for them to do, to learn, and to become.

I admit that I never reported the incident with Sam to anyone else. I became his biggest champion, working alongside him to smooth the fractured relationships he had by with other teachers and administration through sharing stories of his growth within the classroom. He and I shared a moment of connection and from that moment a deep trust persisted, a trust that has never subsided since. Sam turned a corner with me that day because from that moment on, he became more interested in attempting to do the course. He began to ask questions, tentative at first, and then, slowly, surely, he began to chip away at a course that previously he had felt uncompelled and unequipped to complete. He learned how to compose responses to the deeper questions of literature; he worked on his writing, his speaking, and his relationships with others in the room. He ensured that all of the students in that room showed respect both to me and each other.

Sam became a force for change, and he empowered others in the class to begin their work. He continued to work on his course work outside our class. He passed the course with little trouble, and he began to see that he, too, could possibly graduate—that maybe he could set aside some of his frustration with adults and his teachers just enough to work with them to complete his schooling. Something he had given up all hope prior to this moment. He still expressed huge moments of anger and frustration, but he also saw ways out and potential to move out and through those moments to the other side, productive accomplishment. He enrolled for another year of high school, and in the next English class with me—grade 12—and passed it with no problem at all.

Advice for Putting These Ideas Into Practice

- English language arts explores human existence, perspective, and the power in sharing stories. Many of the most relevant stories are sitting in front of you, waiting to find a teacher who will hear their stories and make them relevant and important.

- Personal connection is central to teaching; without safe and caring relationships, students are not reaching their potential. Sometimes these relationships take a long time to develop; don't force them but don't let them disappear from your radar either.
- As a teacher, it is our job to recognize children in distress. Be aware, be present, trust your senses, know when a students' presence has changed. Be ready to shift gears and find a new avenue into the learning.
- Be willing to be vulnerable and be willing to show students safe human connection. These connections are not likely found in the majors; rather, they are in the minors, or "in between the lines."
- Alternative classrooms that combine digital learning platforms with teacher support can create game-changing opportunities for students who have not thrived in typical classes.

Revaluing Educational Change

This is not a teacher's success story or Sam's success story. To call either such would perform at least two fallacies. First, either assertion would assume that an individual made change: Rachel's taking Sam's hand rather than disciplining him or Sam motivating his fellow classmates. Difference making is always already relational, movements between more-than-one that produce something new, such as a shared desire for doing differently. Second, success in this sense is defined through a majoritarian conception of value—success in terms of Sam's finishing the self-directed curriculum or the teacher motivating him to do so. Where in this vision of success and change can we feel the relational transformation that kept Rachel, Sam, and the classroom moving together?

The success of moving more humanely in relation to each other was *the difference that made a difference* (Boldt & Leander, 2017), the break toward a new way of relating rather than towards the same structures, protocols, and ways of being that were keeping Sam's "success" at bay. The quotidian nature of the relations that produced change in this instance, the holding of a hand, is not remarkable for leading to success in major terms but for the majoritarian structures that would keep such humane practices from emerging in the first place. This is not a success story because educational research and practice do not (yet) have words to value minor gestures. The relational transformation between Rachel and Sam exceeds current systems of value both in research and practice that work to count, measure, and re-produce proven change making practice. How does the major tendency to locate educational change in quantifiable, even nameable or categorizable, transformations affect everyday pedagogical encounters? When an event like Rachel's with Sam presents itself, instead of searching through a tool kit of pedagogical moves or for what protocol demands, what if we were ask: what is possible in this moment? What could this moment become? What if these moments determined their own value rather than being valued with existing educational measures and protocols?

And yet, even if we were to follow such pedagogical propositions, we would not know in advance what a moment of change-potential looks or feels like. Rachel could not have predicted that on this day, Sam would enter the room just like that affecting her capacity to disrupt protocol and thereby affecting his relation to her. None of these moments feel the same, and none of them feel like enough. But although they do not feel the same, we feel continuity through these moments across our years of teaching through their production of our desiring teaching. We feel the differences being made through that continuity of desiring because, in the act, something different happened that felt different: a difference that made a difference. None of these moments are enough because they produce desire toward this continuity of change. Relational transformations in literacy teaching and learning that are generated through the minor gesture paradoxically feel like everything and nothing. Nothing, both because they are singular and unique to every situation and feel like "nothing else," and because they make us feel forward to the next moment, they keep us desiring for differences yet to come. None of this can make any sense. Minor gestures move and change because they are choiceless with the systems they disrupt. Teaching and learning that makes a difference is never a choice.

References

Appleman, D. (2014). *Critical encounters in secondary English: Teaching literacy theory to adolescents.* New York, NY: Teachers College Press.

Boldt, G., & Leander, K. (2017). Becoming through the "break": A post-human account of children's play. *Journal of Early Childhood Literacy, 17*(3), 409–425.

Deleuze, G., & Guattari, F. (1987). *A thousand plateaus: Capitalism and schizophrenia.* Minneapolis, MN: University of Minnesota Press.

Ehret, C. (2018a). Propositions from affect theory for feeling literacy through the event. In D. E. Alvermann, N. J. Unrau, & M. Sailors (Eds.), *Theoretical models and processes of literacy* (7th ed., pp. 579–597). New York, NY: Routledge.

Ehret, C. (2018b). Moments of teaching and learning in a children's hospital: Affects, textures, and temporalities. *Anthropology & Education Quarterly, 49*(1), 53–71.

Manning, E. (2016). *The minor gesture.* Durham, NC: Duke University Press.

Manning, E. (2019). Propositions for a radical pedagogy, or how to rethink value. In K. M. Leander & C. Ehret (Eds.), *Affect in literacy teaching and learning: Pedagogies, politics, and coming to know.* New York, NY: Routledge.

3 Experimentations in Affective Reading for Adult Language Classrooms

Monica Waterhouse and Anita Chaudhuri

Mise-en-Scène

What do you do when a book reaches out and grabs you, and you can't resist reading it? If you are a materialist theorist, you study the agentive nature of this book to do something to you. If you are a language and literacy educator, you ask yourself: how could I share this extraordinary book with my students? We happen to be both and so this chapter describes our affective reading experience as teacher-researchers and explores one book's pedagogical potential to be used, and to *act*, in adult language classrooms through a materialist lens.[1]

We frame this collaborative experimentation as a series of interconnected *theory-practice encounters* produced out of our work together: Anita, an English language program specialist at Mount Royal University, and Monica, an assistant professor at Université Laval interested in studying pedagogy in adult immigrant language contexts from an affective, materialist standpoint. Theory-practice encounters signal a dynamic relation in which theory is a toolbox that has to work in practice (Deleuze, 2004). In educational settings, theory-practice means that teacher-researchers are always thinking with theory (even if not consciously aware of it) and that theory underpins how teacher-researchers understand classroom life.

The first theory-practice encounter sets the stage for our pedagogical experimentations by elaborating the valuable insights materialism offers into adult language education generally. We also reflect on our first encounters with one especially potent book, the text-body which ultimately spurred our specific theory-practice project. Encounter two describes the way we shared our reading-thinking-writing around the book, a process we call *affective reading*. This leads into the third encounter in which we present the fruits of our collaboration: potential teaching strategies for a socio-materialist, affective pedagogy appropriate for second language learners, especially newcomers.[2] Moving forward, we challenge other language educators to engage in their own pedagogical experimentations in order to create socio-material, affective teaching practices that counter some of the detrimental effects brought about by neoliberal thinking in education.

Theory-Practice Encounter One: Materialism and Shaun Tan's *The Arrival*

We will discuss *affect* as a materialist concept in detail later, but we begin with materialism more generally to show its usefulness for thinking about specific challenges in adult language education. Charteris, Smardon, and Nelson (2017) explain that:

> materialism recognises the agential nature of matter and questions the anthropocentric narrative that frames the post-enlightenment conception of what it means to be human. The de-centring of human subjects through a materialist ontology facilitates a consideration of the power of objects to affect the spatial politics of learning environments.
>
> (p. 808)

These basic tenets of materialism have several key implications for work in adult language classrooms. First, accepting the power of matter, including non-human objects or *bodies*, to act requires taking seriously the agentive nature of *texts* themselves in language learning contexts and literacy events. Text-bodies, otherwise known as teaching materials, are an important focus in this chapter. In fact, for some time now, we have been struck by how frequently text-bodies (e.g., books, articles, videos, songs), when assembled with reader-bodies (e.g., teachers, students) and a multiplicity of other contingent factors, suddenly become the impetus for unexpected classroom events. Thus, materialism can help to account for the unpredictability of classroom life and "to see the contingencies of teaching and learning not as confounding variables to be overcome, but as a fundamental condition of our work as educators" (Nichols & Campano, 2017, p. 247).

Second, materialism's de-centring of the human subject disrupts the seemingly myopic focus on the human, as human *capital* specifically, in many adult language and literacy programs (Guo, 2015). Job preparation tends to be the raison d'être of these programs, and employment outcomes are important measures of program success. However, a materialist lens brings into focus other stakes in these classrooms (e.g., affective dynamics and emotional forces) that have tended to be downplayed or completely ignored. In addition, socio-material perspectives have the potential to challenge deficit discourses in adult language and literacy education, particularly in programs serving newcomer populations that tend to represent refugee language learners as hapless victims in need of saving rather than as agentive forces in their own right (Anwarrudin, 2017).

The text-body at the centre of our theory-practice experimentations is Shaun Tan's (2006) graphic book *The Arrival*, but it might have been another. In fact, in a materialist way, Tan's text-body was not so much *selected* as it was imposed upon us by its sheer affective power.

Monica's Reflection

When one of my student-teachers at the University of Ottawa introduced me to *The Arrival* a number of years ago, I was immediately hooked. Its narrative, unfolding through evocative sepia-toned artwork, moved me to tears. After the cover and front pages, there were no recognizable words to read, only Tan's own incomprehensible invented language. Yet I *read* this picture-story over and over again in those first days after discovering it, running my hands over the leather-look cover that almost seemed warm to the touch. I shared its reading with apologetic strangers peering over my shoulder on my bus ride home. I experienced it again snuggled on the couch at home with my nieces and nephew, who whined when it was time to go home before the story was finished. This book drew folks in, held them. I couldn't quite put my finger on it, but there was something very special about this book.

Anita's Reflection

My first reaction when Monica shared *The Arrival* with me was "I could read this book for hours." It was a sensory experience, not only visual but seemingly olfactory and tactile, too. Then, as I read the book with my 6-year old daughter, it was fascinating seeing it through her eyes. For me, the cracks at the corners of artwork gave the pages a vintage, old-fashioned photographic quality, but to her, they were "sparkly stars." Before we finished the book, though, she grew tired of our shared reading and fell asleep. I wondered, somewhat ruefully, if my interventions, prompting, and directing her interpretations ultimately curtailed our shared reading experience.

Shaun Tan's pictorial chapter book *The Arrival* is a reading in human aspirations, the definition of success, and the struggles that form the assemblage in a narrative on immigrant experience. In many ways, the text encourages the reader to reel in the intangible aspects of moving away and coming into a setting, the sense of displacement, loss of values or realization of what is valuable. Therefore, the text works the tensions between getting displaced and the act of reconciliation, familiar and alien spaces, and knowing versus literacy skills. These dichotomies are in fact an assortment of dissimilar, albeit familiar experiences. The book displaces the narrative as universal yet unique; everyone can find a part in this storytelling. This variety is the generative power of Tan's art: the visual response effortlessly flows into the act of storytelling. The lack of the written word is a medium via which one can dissociate from narrative practices of telling the reader or, as the author notes, it is a break from "security and authority when it comes to meaning" (Tan, 2010, p. 31). Resisting traditional categorizations such as graphic novel or picture book, *The Arrival* is helpfully described by Arizpe, Colomer, & Martínez-Roldán (2015) as a "wordless narrative," that is, "a text where the visual image carries the weight of the meaning" (p. 34). The images are powerful constructs, the plot, the characters, the disillusionment, the small wins, knowledge generation, and the hopeful future comes together in a way that is open to interpretation. Multiple affective filters play all at once, and that's where lies the text's power of narrative and its value for literary practices in the field of second language learning.

Theory-Practice Encounter Two: Affective Reading and Sticky Note Thinking

Convinced of *The Arrival's* affective force as a text-body and excited about its pedagogical potential, we began our collaborative experiment in affective reading-thinking-writing using sticky notes to make comments of all kinds on our books: some were related to ideas for teaching with the book; others were general impressions and aspects that stood out for us in our own reading experience. Sharing our notes as we re-read *The Arrival* together produced articulations of theory-practice that might work for adult second language educators and their students.

Why Affect?

We have found *affect* a particularly useful materialist concept in our effort to understand language learning and literacy experiences in a more complex way that accounts for the *doing* of text-bodies. Deleuze and Guattari (1980/1987) view affects as powers to affect and be affected, relational capacities to transform (i.e., *becoming*). Affects are not a property of an individual human body but instead create transformative effects out of the relations *between* bodies when they come together to form a particular assemblage. By expanding its viewpoint beyond the affective powers of human bodies, Deleuzian affect theory enables a pedagogical consideration of the affective powers of not only student-bodies and teacher-bodies but also non-human bodies such as text-bodies in language classrooms. Moreover, text-bodies are "entities [that] affect us, prior to and irrespective of our understanding of them" (Charteris et al., 2017, p. 812). In classroom events, assemblages of bodies are continually shifting, reconfiguring, and functioning in unique, and often unanticipated, ways. The affective capacities of a body, including text-bodies, cannot be fully apprehended in advance, so every literacy event becomes, on some level, an experimental (even risky) endeavor with the potential to transform individuals and the relations between them.

In line with this materialist take on reading, Masny (2009) theorizes literacies in terms of affective, transformative processes, rather than predictable, interpretative outcomes. "Literacies constitute ways of becoming with the world" (Masny, 2009, p. 14). The consequence of a materialist formulation of literacy is that sense is no longer about a human subject making-meaning from a text. Instead, sense *happens* as an effect of a reading.

Theory-Practice Encounter Three: Potential Actualizations of Materialist Teaching Practice

In this theory-practice encounter, we summarize some potential pedagogical strategies for working with *The Arrival* in adult language and literacy classrooms that emerged from our collaborations during the workshop. In addition, we draw inspiration from language and literacy scholars in the United States (Benesch, 2012) and Australia (Cole, 2016) who have worked towards imagining what a Deleuzian affective pedagogy might look like in practice with English language learners, as well as specific literacy teaching strategies around *The Arrival* that have been piloted with migrant youth in the United States (Danzak, 2011) and children in the United Kingdom, Spain, Italy, and the United States (Arizpe et al., 2015). We also show that these activities align not only with key linguistic and with literacy objectives driving adult programs but that they also connect with materialist orientations and affective reading practices. In this respect, Nichols and Campano (2017) helpfully remind that a materialist or posthuman theoretical stance "does not require us to abandon our existing practices altogether, but rather provides news dimensions that help better account for the complexities of the classroom" (p. 249).

As an affective teaching and learning tool, *The Arrival*'s compelling images offer semiotic resources accessible to a wide range of learners. Aside from Tan's own invented, fantastical linguistic symbols, the absence of any *existing* language in the book makes the story accessible to learners at all language proficiency levels and any language background. Moreover, it can be used in any language of instruction. This explains, in part, why the book has received international attention from teacher-researchers in Spain and Italy, besides several predominantly English-speaking countries. In our own Canadian context, lessons built around the book could easily be adapted for use in adult language classes for both official languages, French and English. Besides these pragmatic advantages, the lack of any comprehensible printed words strategically facilitates alternative modes of meaning emergence. Moreover, this wordless text-body paradoxically creates the desire to produce language in its readers, both oral and written. This art-story spurs literacy-related classroom

> **Socio-Material, Affective Connections**
>
> How might the introduction of this unconventional teaching *material* create a different assemblage in which "struggling" readers might be repositioned as "engaged intellectual contributors" (Nichols & Campano, 2017, p. 249)? As one teacher who participated in Arizpe et al.'s (2015) study commented, teaching "with wordless texts showed me that the students with whom we worked knew more than their [test] scores said they did" (p. 211). Reading *The Arrival* was a real confidence builder for the migrant children in their study, and we posit that it could have similarly positive effects if adult learners were invited to deploy their array of reading competencies and experiences beyond the purely linguistic.

> **Socio-Material, Affective Connections**
>
> Our suggestion to use sticky notes is not due to any taboo about writing on books. Sticky notes do justice to the way the material relations unfold differently in each affective reading event. They enable

activities that remain open to creative and unexpected responses produced in each unique reading assemblage. Some concrete ideas for working with the text in the classroom might include the following activities.

- Reading *The Arrival* with low literacy learners could contribute to the development of basic literacy skills (e.g., orienting a book right side up, turning pages, tracking left to right) and provides practice following a narrative structure divided into chapters.
- Students, especially beginners or those with emergent literacy, could benefit by responding to the text in non-linguistic modes through drawings or a collage of selected images from the Internet or magazines.
- Students could be asked to write a single word or short phase on a sticky note to be placed at a place in the book they feel is relevant. Then students could share with others and express their reactions orally.
- Students could select a favourite image or page from *The Arrival* and then talk or write about why it is significant for them or why it appeals to them (Cole, 2016).
- Teachers could strategically select a single image from the book and pose discussion questions such as: "How does this picture make you feel? What language can you use to describe it? How could you

Experimentations in Affective Reading 57

> a more dynamic and reciprocal engagement with the text over multiple affective reading events. Importantly, an affective reading pedagogy should not be limited to literal description of images or analysis of the text. Instead, it should invite both semiotic *AND* affective responses.

> **Socio-Material, Affective Connections**
>
> It is not necessary to read the book linearly. Excerpts or even single pages can be considered in isolation. A single image has its own affective powers, though they are likely to be quite different from the material assemblage of the entire text-body.

relate to this picture? What is the sensation of this picture?" (Cole, 2016). Then students could annotate a photocopy of the page using connecting lines, arrows, or creating speech or thought bubbles for characters (Arizpe et al., 2015).

- A lesson could focus on selected pages from the book such as the series of images in which the protagonist struggles to find appropriate employment, in part because of his inability to read print in the local language. Such a focus presents an opportunity to "examine real issues facing immigrants, such as nonrecognition of foreign credentials, racism in hiring practices, and accent discrimination" (Guo, 2015, p. 48). Similarly, a close study of selected images could open critical discussions about gender roles and shifting responsibilities within family structures.
- *The Arrival* could be used to link to other literacy practices that are essential for newcomers to become part of the community as they take the initiative to try to communicate and risk-take. For example, the protagonist's initial way-finding could provide a model and lead to reading an actual local city map. In this way, the pedagogy moves from the general to the specific in terms of the experiences of newcomer students.
- The powerful artwork of *The Arrival* could be used to create writing prompts (Danzak, 2011) requiring written expressions ranging from several sentences to a paragraph to a full essay in response to a key event in the book.
- *The Arrival* offers multiple opportunities for the exploration of shifting identities, more specifically, how identities are constituted through naming in language and documentation such as identity cards. For example, the students could read and discuss the scenes in Chapter II in which the protagonist undergoes a series of immigrant checks. Each check is very different from the other, but they all comment on

Socio-Material, Affective Connections

Guo (2015) observes that a focus on language skills is insufficient in newcomer language classrooms. She calls for teachers to take a critical multiculturalism approach that "makes explicit hidden or masked structures, discourses, and relations of inequity that discriminate against one group and enhance the privileges of another" (p. 43). Such an approach is very much aligned with the broader ethical and political exigencies of materialist theorizing that seek account for the workings of socio-political assemblages, those complex entanglements of people, cultures, language, and institutions.

Socio-Material, Affective Connections

What does the labelling of bodies do? What does it enable *AND* disable? How does it fix a body and stifle its potential for indeterminate becomings? How do students experience their identities, both as fixed and influx? How are identities dynamic and relationally constituted? What are the material consequences of labelling (e.g., as ESL learner, low literacy)? These are ethical questions underpinning a materialist teaching practice.

the process of codifying an identity with distinct labels and data on qualities such as physical health captured in official logs. It invites a reflection on the various, and culturally specific, ways in which human bodies are identified and not only in the immigration process (e.g., How are female bodies identified in relation to male relatives such as husbands and fathers?). This type of discussion could explore the identification process for *non-human* bodies as well through the study of the front pages of *The Arrival* that codify its text-body with copyright and publication data.

- Students could collaboratively read and analyze the visual grammar of the text by discussing the use of image size, color, and placement to tell the story (Arizpe et al., 2015).
- Advanced students might engage in Internet research about the author, Shaun Tan, an Australian of Malaysia decent, and compare his migrant story with the one depicted in *The Arrival* or with their own.

Critically Assessing *THE Arrival* as Materialist Teaching Practice

In sum, as a teaching material for use in adult language classrooms, *The Arrival* supports multiple language and literacy learning objectives: enriching vocabulary, developing multimodal writing skills, and providing meaningful oral practice. Even more important, it has the potential to support newcomers in the fraught process of integration by offering opportunities for critical reflection on experiences of migration (Arizpe et al., 2015). Given the unprecedented levels of migration that characterize global politics today, non-migrant teachers and learners can also appreciate *The Arrival* as one glimpse into this experience, even if it does not touch them deeply or directly on a personal level.

Despite these benefits, we also acknowledge certain drawbacks associated with an affective reading of *The Arrival*. First, the surreal nature of the world Tan has created in *The Arrival*—depicting fantastical beasts, imaginary foodstuffs, impossible urban infrastructure, and an invented foreign language—may pose challenges for some readers. Indeed, Arizpe et al. (2015) observed that often the teacher-researcher or "mediator had to encourage risk-taking as well as providing new vocabulary or helping to speculate about what the objects might be" (p. 186). Second, the migrant experience depicted in *The Arrival* cannot be assumed to resonate with *all* adult newcomers' experiences, and readers should be at ease to challenge the narrative or to offer counter-narratives if they wish. Anita noted this in her own reading as an immigrant to Canada commenting: "The events in the book move too quickly, and the happy ending is a disconnect for me. It assumes that children naturally adjust easily, and everything turns out in the end. That isn't necessarily the universal experience." Finally, care should be taken if reflections on migration stories shift from the general to the specific. Many adult learners' personal experiences of migration are traumatic, and retelling these stories whether orally, in writing, or in images can create highly emotionally charged moments in the language classroom. This is not necessarily something that must be avoided, but it is an important aspect of which to be aware when working with *The Arrival*. Students should never be obliged to share their own story of migration. Arizpe et al. (2015) propose one solution: they invited students to use drawing and photography with speech bubbles and captions to describe *a* journey but not necessarily their own.

Theory-Practice Encounters to Come . . .

Looking towards theory-practice encounters yet to come, we invite adult educators, and teacher-researchers in their own right, to create their own socio-material practice and to experiment with their students in affective reading. We assert that this kind of bold experimentation is ethically essential in our contemporary moment to enable language and literacy teacher-researchers push back against the detrimental effects of neoliberal thinking that pervade their classrooms: the artificial separation of subjective affect and objective cognition in learning, the subordination of relational becomings to individual outcomes, the denial of complexity and unpredictability in learning while imposing accountability measures, the undervaluing learners' competencies and ascribing deficit-labels to "illiterates," and the obscuring of an agentive material world in the shadow of human hubris. More specifically, in adult second language programs for newcomers, we view affective reading pedagogy as a way to temper the dominant employability orientations of these programs with an appreciation of the importance of the affective side of integration in a new socio-material milieu.

We have offered the text-body *The Arrival* as one potential teaching material that lends itself to diverse actualizations of affective reading pedagogy while acknowledging the power of the material world to intervene in our becomings. However, we caution that, from a materialist standpoint, any effort to unproblematically *implement* an affective reading pedagogy would be misguided. Every teaching-learning experience is singular because every classroom assemblage is unique in its composition and therefore in its functioning: a different place; a different language; a different teacher with his or her own particular positioning; different students, each with their own migration experiences and complex becomings; a different time of day; and so forth. Even if the text remains the same, it will be read differently each time by the teacher and students. We have offered articulations of how such a pedagogy *could* look, but these are not models to follow; rather, we hope they serve as inspiration for teacher-researchers to in turn invent their own socio-material, affective teaching practices.

Materialist teaching-learning involves continual experimentation, ongoing becomings in responses to problems emerging from classroom life. At the same time, literacy itself is a concept in becoming, continually transforming in response to shifts in the material world. The printing press resulted in mass literacy. Globalization created an appreciation of socially situated literacy practices. The World Wide Web demanded ever more complex, multimodal, and critical reading practices. Contemporary global problems—from environmental crises, to financial system failures, to terrorism—are destabilizing human hubris on multiple fronts. Non-human forces are exerting their powers to act, even beyond human control (e.g., artificial intelligence, intensification of meteorological events). The world is ripe for a resurgence of materialist and posthuman philosophies and a concomitant reimagining of the meaning of literacy and of what language and literacy education may entail.

Notes

1. Although we position ourselves as materialist, Nichols and Campano (2017) note that "a material stance is sometimes called *post-human* because it begins from the premise that humans never act in isolation, but rather in concert with changing networks of people, objects, histories, and institutions" (p. 246).
2. The term *newcomers* is used to signal both immigrant and refugee migrants settling in a new country.

References

Anwarrudin, S. M. (2017). Emotions in the curriculum of migrant and refugee students. *Curriculum Inquiry, 47*(1), 112–124.

Arizpe, E., Colomer, T., & Martínez-Roldán, C. (2015). *Visual journeys through wordless narratives: An international inquiry with immigrant children and the Arrival*. London, UK: Bloosmbury Academic.

Benesch, S. (2012). *Considering emotions in critical English language teaching*. New York, NY: Routledge.

Charteris, J., Smardon, D., & Nelson, E. (2017). Innovative learning environments and new materialism: A conjunctural analysis of pedagogic spaces. *Educational Philosophy and Theory, 49*, 8, 808–821. doi:10.1080/00131857.2017.1298035

Cole, D. R. (2016). *Affective literacy and TEFL*. Presentation slides. Retrieved June 12, 2017 from www.slideshare.net/dracle99/affective-literacy-and-tefl

Danzak, R. L. (2011). Defining identities through multiliteracies: EL teens narrate their immigration experiences as graphic stories. *Journal of Adolescent and Adult Literacy, 55*(3), 187–196.

Deleuze, G. (2004). Intellectuals and power (interview with Michel Foucault). In D. Lapoujade (Ed.), M. Taormina (Trans.), *Desert islands and other texts: 1953–1974* (pp. 206–213). Los Angeles, CA and New York, NY: Semiotext(e).

Deleuze, G., & Guattari, F. (1980/1987). *A thousand plateaus: Capitalism and schizophrenia* (B. Massumi, Trans.). Minneapolis, MN: University of Minnesota Press.

Guo, Y. (2015). Language policies and programs for adult immigrants in Canada: Deconstructing discourses of immigration. *New Directions for Adult and Continuing Education, 146*, 41–51. doi:10.1002/ace.20130

Masny, D. (2009). Literacies as becoming: A child's conceptualizations of writing systems. In D. Masny & D. R. Cole (Eds.), *Multiple literacies theory: A Deleuzian perspective* (pp. 13–30). Rotterdam, The Netherlands: Sense Publishers.

Nichols, T. P., & Campano, G. (2017). Post-humanism and literacy studies. *Language Arts, 94*(4), 245–251.

Tan, S. (2006). *The arrival*. New York, NY: Arthur A. Levine Books and Scholastic Inc.

Tan, S. (2010). *Sketches from a nameless land: The art of the arrival*. Melbourne, Australia: Lothian.

4 Planning-as-Burden, Planning-as-Gift

Shifting to Gift-Economy Approaches in Teaching and Learning

Jennifer MacDonald and Kevin M. Leander

When young children make crafts and work with paper, crayons, glue, and sometimes feathers, they routinely offer such work as a gift to someone else. Even if the creation is not *for* another at the outset, the question of who to give it to often comes up. It is only until sometime later on, and most often in a relationship to school, that a child's work steps out of this gift economy and becomes more commodity-like. As a commodity, the work enters into exchange of being traded—for school credit, for grades, for recognition or the avoidance of punishment, for "free time," and a whole host of other social goods. Over time, these schooled exchange relations become more distant from the child and teacher's awareness and become common sense to make schooling-qua-schooling possible. This logic persists even as the persistent and nagging problem of "motivation" continues to rise up, causing us to treat such issues as a quality of individual children or even teachers.

However, feeling resonance with Robin Wall Kimmerer's (2013) observation that "A great longing is upon us, to live again in a world made of gifts" (p. 32), we wondered how we could take inspiration from what appears to be a natural, early inclination toward gift giving. We asked ourselves if something could be recovered from that more innocent and joyful moment. What if we asked, along with Lewis Hyde (1979/2012), if an alternate economy is possible—one of *gifting*—alongside a more typical school economy? Andreas Weber (2017), writing of Hyde, speaks of a kind of "aliveness" in works that we do, as humans, that are not "subject to a dictate of performance or a compulsion to control" (p. 183). What if we worked to recover this feeling of aliveness from the compulsion, control, and ego-focus that seem, in large measure, to be necessary qualities of commodity exchanges in school? Such a movement could be described as a shift toward a *gift economy*. With gifting, abundance is normative, surplus is to be expected, and joy is found in generous movements towards the other.

In this chapter, we move to imagine schooling-as-gifting by engaging with a practice that we see as the bread and butter of teacher formation:

unit planning. Specifically, we use the conceptual and embodied space of unit planning to visualize how a gift ecology might come about in teacher education. Planning together can provide moments for reflection, to gather collective energy, and to explore possibilities that cross the boundaries of what is habitually done. While we believe collaborative planning can potentially offer genuine moments of creativity and sharing, we see how such practices can also become burdens to our student-teachers, as they face institutional drives for fixed endpoints, struggle with group work, or become anxious over grades. We hear some common feelings of *disenchantment*, including the lack of time, anxiety, blame on other group members, narrow focus, and low energy, to name a few. Planning becomes a burden, and these narratives commonly close off openings and invitations. Therefore, we wonder: what if our process of unit planning could be a process of *aliveness*? How might we invoke the reciprocity of the gift economy? In this manner, the purpose of this chapter is to imagine a shift in the ecology of planning and to explore alternative ways that might *breathe life* into the process.

Gifting, Posthuman Concepts, and Planning

To create a shift in the processes of planning as burden, we believe it is important to move these processes more directly into the body—our own bodies, and by extension, those of our students. Planning, we think, is too stuck in reason, in rationality. We want to find multiple entry points for planning as *gifting*—a process to encourage sharing, to embrace mystery and curiosity, and to evoke humility. To do so, we "assigned" ourselves the work of developing a unit plan for our own students or at least beginning the process of unit planning. In this process, we conducted a small series of experiments to open up space for tensions and possibilities.

As our creative process progressed, a few guiding concepts from posthuman theory informed our inquiry. The first concept was understanding and feeling "desire" as a type of flow of energy that is pre-personal. Deleuze and Guattari (1983) described humans as "desiring machines" because humans are, above all else, producing and being produced. For Deleuze and Guattari, desire is a productive energy that is subsequently organized either through its appropriation into social desires and expressions or that produces something unexpected and new. This constant movement of life's energy, catching up materials, humans, words, concepts, and other bodies into temporary "assemblages," describes an approach to life that "moves with" openings and rearrangements rather the shutting them down.

Central to Deleuze and Guattari's conceptualization of desire is difference. Life—the constant movement of and through assemblages—produces difference: "[D]esire is production and life itself a desiring flow towards ever-proliferating differences . . . a pre-personal and pre-individual germinal influx of intensity" (Fancy, 2010, p. 161). Difference, then, is our second key concept from posthuman theory, which, like "desire," has an everyday, folk meaning that is difficult to override—to think differently about. In this case, we do not mean "difference" as given in identity and recognized in either objects or subjects in a natural way (e.g., "the story is a different genre than the argument"). Rather, we mean "difference" or "differentiating" as differences in intensities (flows of energy) and differences produced *between* materials of all kinds coming into relationship. Thus, difference is always created in movement, in process, in proliferation. Difference is about what could happen—about what is unplanned and undesigned (Deleuze & Guattari, 1987; Massumi, 2002).

Our third related concept of relevance for planning as gifting is "emergence." From a posthuman way of being, "emergence" is a reorientation to time and activity as open, as not having fixed direction. (From a planning perspective, emergence may be seen as nearly an opposite in relation to time, but hence our experimentations that follow.) The idea of emergence in Deleuze and Guattari (1987) is about reality constantly producing itself, creating new becomings (Grossberg, 2003, p. 2). For Deleuze and Guattari, there are no endpoints, only centres.

For us, desire, difference, and emergence are posthuman ways of rethinking and re-feeling the relationship of gifting to planning. How might we open up to what both of these terms mean through experimentation that involves energetic movement (desire), wild juxtapositions (difference-production), and stay with the process of possibility (emergence)? Therefore, in what follows, we share two experiments as an attempt to unsettle common ways of being and doing and to invite other voices and beings into our conversations. We present our experiences, improvising and body storming, not as a how-to guide but wish to offer an invitation to others as we speak in a wider conversation of aliveness.

Given our common interest in outdoor activities and our shared feelings of loving natural over built institutional spaces, for our unit plan, we posed this initial topic of *How might inside learning spaces hold the kinds of enchantment that we feel with outdoor places?*

Improvising Toward Emerging Questions (Kevin)

In traditional practice, the central theme or question of the unit functions as a kind of motor to drive the feeling of student (and teacher) interest forward. If the question is interesting enough, we think, then answering it will also be interesting. But the problem with this logic is that it seals the question or theme off early on: everything we do after the moment of affirming the question (typically, very early on) becomes answer, becomes material to be found, becomes burden. We remake school for ourselves (as teachers) as filling in a giant blank—a blank that we have created.

To move towards questioning as gifting, we engaged in a practice of dialogue called "yes-anding." We borrow and adapt this practice from exercises for improvisational theater. "Yes-anding" is often an early type of activity that new improvisers will engage in as they learn to create improvised worlds between them. In our process, we simply gathered as a group of four (Jen and I recruited two of our colleagues—Candace and Barb) and had a yes-anding session. Each person in the group was asked to take a different "disciplinary perspective"—science (Kevin), physical education (Jen), visual arts (Barb), and music (Candace). In our activity, we kept the notion of "discipline" open and broad.

To engage in our yes-anding session, we stood up and faced one another. This embodied position is more active than seated in desks. Kevin led off: "Okay, our main question so far is: How could inside spaces for learning become enchanting like outside spaces?" The activity began like this:

KEVIN: This idea of bringing the outside in has to do with thinking about the qualities of light. I'm curious about white and yellow light, and I would like to think more about how light affects me.
BARB: Yes, and from a watercolor perspective, so much about watercolor is about tone variation, light and shade, so . . . people who know how to do this might paint the same place at different times of the day.
JEN: Yes, and tones and colors of light might affect the movements of our bodies.

Notice that even at the very beginning of the interaction, the yes-and structure is producing movement across the turns at talk. This is supported by the different disciplinary stances. From the original question, the line of connected thinking has moved across different qualities of light and their affects: from tone variations in watercolor, to the same place at different times of day, to the ways light tones and colors affect bodies and movement. The movement of ideas across the group is getting broader at moments already and also focusing in at times. (Jen's last thought in this sequence can be seen as a subtopic of Kevin's opening thought.)

Barb had to listen very carefully to Kevin's contribution in order to offer hers. This is difficult for many students at the outset because they are most used to topical chaining in classroom responses—when seven hands shoot up at once to response to a teacher's question and not to the person who spoke immediately previously. Close listening, in this sense, is a radically new practice of gift-like exchanges. Notice also that Barb's contribution and then Jen's comes with a bit of ritual: "Yes, and . . ." An important idea here is that Barb and Jen's contributions do not replace or exclude Kevin's gift in any way; they are rather added onto it. Together, the two gifts, and all of those following, become a connective web of gift giving, which itself makes up a new whole—the whole of the interaction becomes of gift of ideas.

Because of bad habits of burden learned over many years, there are a few traps to be aware of in this practice. The first trap is to offer a response (as gift) that doesn't relate to the one before it. You must attend to the gift—you must listen to the gift carefully. Note, for instance, the following exchange. Kevin is responding to Barb's offer that "many great artists attempted to paint what they heard in music":

KEVIN: Yes, and you're talking kind of about this relationship of the senses, and from a scientific perspective, I'm interested in this idea of synaesthesia, sensing one sense with respect to another—I don't know how that relates to this inside/outside relation
JEN: Yes, and I wonder how our senses of the body—indoor or outdoor—impacts, again, how we move or just how we are in space, and I am thinking about sound and how sound in my athletes makes them move faster or more efficiently or with more energy and with more life.

While Jen's response here uses the "yes-and" structure, the topic of her contribution really doesn't have much to do with the traversal of sensations in synaesthesia. Rather, it has more to do with the idea of sound affecting embodied movement, a topic she had brought up earlier in the interaction. This kind of return to one's own topic or commitment is very common for students who are learning to engage in yes-anding.

A second trap is to refuse the gift, responding with something like "no, but . . ." or a variation of that thought. In this case, you take up an either/or stance. You must choose between your group member's idea or yours—there is not space for both. The idea becomes a burden, and perhaps even your partner becomes a burden. Students often respond that they would rather just do work on their own rather than in a group; chances are these students have rarely experienced the idea of arriving at something much bigger than themselves.

The third trap is that you respond to the gift by making a demand. The most familiar way to make a demand is to ask a question. So, your partner says, "I am really interested in the problem of fake news and how there is too much bad information out there," and you ask, "Where have you seen fake news?" Your partner now has a burden—and it's *your* created burden, rather than hers. How could you instead bring a gift or offer with "yes, and. . . . "

Our session of yes-anding in relation to our initial question lasted just a short time yet was incredibly generative. Following is a partial list of the ideas that emerged in the process.

- Painters who paint the same place different times of day, such as Monet or Manet and the cathedral at Rouen
- How light might affect movements of our bodies
- Music and how certain tones and the clustering produce feelings of lightness.
- How does the body and our perception of our different surroundings impact how we move and our different space?

- How music is all around us.
- The moving of chairs and pencil sharpeners might make us feel light or heavy and how all of that works with the sound of a classroom.
- The sound of gravity on our bodies, how it's on a subconscious level, and how it impacts on how we move through sport
- Thinking about silence and how its generative, what happens as a teacher or music teacher, and how it offers permission for new compositions
- Wondering if silence exists
- Rhythms and how they are biological and natural but also technical—the science of rhythm
- What are the natural rhythms of music around us?

You will probably notice how the ideas in this reference the different disciplinary perspectives we took up. Yet as much as that happened, the disciplinary boundaries and binaries began to break down and sometimes in obvious ways. The gifts or offers in the interaction were no longer separate items as they came together:

CANDACE: So I'm thinking that what you're saying as a science person, and I'm thinking about music, is that we broke that binary or dichotomy, by saying that there's this science, and these sounds of nature, in our bodies—just hearing that together is how science, and nature, and music, and rhythm work together—what are the natural rhythms and music, you know, that are getting produced around us?

This chain of thoughts—a gift of idea movement across divergent and convergent ways of thinking—opens up our original question and breathed life into the demand of a group topic or question. Notice, however, that we arrived at some new questions not by being asked a entire series of new questions by our partners in the circle (a more conventional schooled practice) but by being given words, ideas, images, resources, and associations that are chained together in the act of listening, receiving, offering.

Body-Storming: Being Moved by Multiplicities of Place (Jennifer)

Unit planning is habitually negotiated in static settings. Tables, chairs, and fluorescent lighting all accompany a standard template used to map the coming hours, days, weeks, or months. A common collaborative practice Kevin and I notice in planning is to *brainstorm* strategic methods to deliver content, engage students, and how students will demonstrate their learning. Typically, in the first stage of a brainstorming session, *anything goes*; ideas around a topic are generated and recorded without critique. Once this initial expression of ideas is complete, the mess is *cleaned up*, so to speak, as group members deliberate options and move forward.

While this mode of planning may provide a sense of order and logic, we see it also assuming a one size fits all map, adaptable for all places and all people, and thus overlooks the ecological gifts that surround, infuse, and sustain life in a particular place.

To shift into planning as a form of gifting, we wish to go beyond human-centredness of learning to include the web of more-than-human relations that we find ourselves within. Places offer a series of interwoven gifts and relationships such as seasonal changes, human and more-than-human life, rhythms and patterns, connections, and stories (Massey, 2005). Reflecting on our initial inquiry, then, to bring the vivacity of the outdoor world into the indoor space, our second experiment led us to the unconditional gifts within our ecological surroundings. To engage with these gifts, we wanted to re-balance the body as a source of desire and emergence (over solely focusing on a cognitive way of knowing). To do so, we ventured outdoors and rested on a small area of grass as our site for inquiry. Surrounded by footpaths, buildings, large trees, and low-growing shrubs, we noticed people travelling by in a hurried way as other beings (e.g., squirrels, magpies, crows, rabbits and a variety of insects) went about their daily business. In this moment, everything between the afternoon sky and the ground we were sitting upon became an assemblage for us to be present with.

We began by questioning how enchantment is generated with these spaces and returned to the common process of *brainstorming* (as generative approach for inquiry). Metaphorically, as an aside, we pondered other uses of *storming* in relation to natural world and the unpredictability of natural phenomena—such as, snow, lightning, wind, rain, thunder, and so on. We saw how these occurrences often bring community together by way of sharing resources or stories of common experience. However, in the language of "brainstorming," we note that the *brain* is doing all the work—no *body* is present, active, or intra-active. So then, we came to consider the idea of *body-storm* to help us attend to the multiple voices, positions, and possibilities surrounding us.

This first required us to became present to our bodies and to feel the world by appreciate the gifts of our senses. We started to recognize the series of relationships we were already entangled in. We lingered on the ground listening, feeling, and observing. There were moments of silence between us, and then conversation would *emerge* again. This seemed to bring place and connection *alive* as a text of desire. I paid attention to what I was sensing in the moment and told Kevin how I enjoyed the earthy smell of the leaves on the ground around us. I explained how the leaves hold memory for me. First was the essence of home and playing outside during my childhood (a distinctive smell for this season), and this led us to a wider consideration of life cycle of leaves. In the spring, I feel joyful as the trees come to life after a long winter, and now, on this autumn afternoon, the leaves were gifting nutrients and minerals to the ground. Trees sustain life and give unconditionally. These offerings, we pondered, are often taken for granted. Our attention was led to the multiple bird songs coming from high in the trees and nearby shrubs—a language we do not understand, yet when given time and care, becomes rich in meaning.

Looking up, the sky offered another narrative. We talked about the clouds and the story they offered us. I took note of the thin-fibered cirrus clouds at high altitude, an indication of fair weather for several days. As we talked about the sky and I shared some knowledge from my work as an outdoor educator, we both suddenly commented on the warmth we were enjoying.

From here, the theme of the sun—the gifts of light and warmth—surfaced as a source of enchantment. Weber (2017) explains how both are gifts: "Light is the epitome of that which is given free of charge and without ulterior motives. It is also derived from an act that is completely void of intention: The sun bestows its warmth and wastes itself in the process" (p. 181). As we sat blissfully in the autumn afternoon sun, I felt a debt of gratitude.

As I reflect on our experience together, I understand that the earthy smell reminding me of my childhood, the generative conversation of the life cycles, hearing more-than-human languages, and embracing light and warmth were all expanding my understanding of this particular place and time. Yet these are only the small pieces of my experience that are accessible on the surface. I see that Kevin and I were trying to find something that is layered and highly subjective to get at. We both commented on the gift of being with our bodies in ways that allowed us to recognize and receive. With this, we felt resonance with Weber (2017), who states: "Many people who live in balance with the natural world feel that they receive gifts from it, and also feel prompted to give to it" (p. 183). Ultimately then, in the spirit of reciprocity, we then discussed how we give back to places that give to us. The unconditional offerings of the more-than-human inspire both the feeling of generosity we desire for our indoor space and signal deep considerations of cyclicality to overcome the common linear fashion of unit planning with a rush to the pragmatics of the end goal.

The practice of body-storming attunes us to the animacy of our inquiry in a deeply felt way. Instead of staying in our heads, we attempt to shift focus to our bodies. This process brings us into contact with materials that often go unnoticed in our everyday experiences (e.g., the texture of the grass, the sounds of the birds, the joys of conversation, the feeling of lightness while breathing in the fresh air and enjoyed the sun's embrace on our skin). At the same time, this practice comes with a sense of humility—affirmation that we are a small part of a larger web of relations. It is important to note that this was an unhurried process that required us to be quieter and more reflective than the typical brainstorm event characterized by group members spontaneously contributing ideas. We were called to listen and feel deeply to consider the *connections not seen*. While at times the practice seemed abstract, it points to the need to go beyond the surface level of knowing your way around. Places are highly integrated and do not disclose themselves straight away. Acquiring ecological insight through the body requires time and affective-laden ways of knowing to uncover mysteries, and even then, the mystery will likely come with multiple meanings. By being attentive to multiple beings that co-exist with us and discussing what emerges, we can allow new possibilities to be brought life.

Planning-as-Gifting: Improvising and Body-Storming

The process of gifting is participatory, personal, and dynamic. Largely, gifting requires us to give something of ourselves and allows us to receive something else—not always readily apparent—in return. Paying attention to the idea of the gift, as we see it, is a mode of promoting life in typical schooled conventions that generally centre human exceptionalism and commodity exchange. The two experiments from our collaboration—improvising and bodystorming—guide us to attune to the unique contributions of each other and all living entities in the places where we live and gather. A common theme that emerged through our experiments was the need to listen carefully (with our entire bodies) to arrive at a new whole. This listening exposed vibrancy allowing us to move with openings as they emerged.

Reflecting on our work with pre-service teachers, we imagine how our experiments might help generate spaces that build comfort following ambiguous leads. Both activities are nuanced in ways that pay attention and respond to the layered and connective webs of human and more-than-human gift giving, they promote fluidity and unfold in ways that require a certain level of vulnerability and trust. This level of openness pushes back against the often positivist mainstream perspectives of teaching and learning and might be difficult for beginners. Regardless, we see this work as necessary to bring a sense of aliveness to the process of teacher formation, and subsequently, to teaching and learning at all levels. From our perspectives, to live, teach, and learn in a world made of gifts supports living in ways honours enchantment (Bennett, 2001), generates kindness and tolerance, and promotes an ethic of responsibility to all that gives life.

Acknowledgements

While attending to gifts of place in this chapter, we acknowledged our gathering on the traditional territory of the Treaty 7 people, which includes the Blackfoot Confederacy (comprising the Siksika, Piikani, and Kainai First Nations), the Tsuut'ina First Nation, and the Stoney Nakoda (including the Chiniki, Bearspaw, and Wesley First Nations). The City of Calgary is also home to Métis Nation of Alberta, Region III.

References

Bennett, J. (2001). *The enchantment of modern life: Attachments, crossings and ethics*. Princeton, NJ: Princeton University Press.
Deleuze, G., & Guattari, F. (1983). *Anti-oedipus* (R. Hurley, M. Seem, & H. R. Lane, Trans.). Minneapolis, MN: University of Minnesota Press.
Deleuze, G., & Guattari, F. (1987). *A thousand plateaus: Capitalism and schizophrenia* (B. Massumi, Trans.). Minneapolis, MN: University of Minnesota Press.
Fancy, D. (2010). Difference, bodies, desire: The collaborative thought of Gilles Deleuze and Felix Guattari. *Science Fiction Film and Television, 3*(1), 93–106.
Grossberg, L. (2003). Animations, articulations, and becomings: An introduction. In J. D. Slack (Ed.), *Animations of Deleuze and Guattari* (pp. 1–8). New York, NY: Peter Lang.
Hyde, L. (1979/2012). *The Gift: How the creative spirit transforms the world*. Edinburgh, UK: Canongate Books.
Massey, D. (2005). *For space*. London, UK: Sage Publications.
Massumi, B. (2002). *Parables for the virtual: Movement, affect, sensation*. Durham, NC: Duke University Press.
Wall Kimmerer, R. (2013). *Braiding sweetgrass: Indigenous wisdom, scientific knowledge, and the teachings of plants*. Minneapolis, MN: Milkweed Editions.
Weber, A. (2017). *Matter & desire: An erotic ecology* (R. Bradley, Trans.). White River Junction, VT: Chelsea Green.

Gifting-giving is a dynamic practice that encourages sharing, embraces mystery, and evokes humility. Applying posthuman concepts of *desire*, *difference*, and *emergence*, we re-think and re-feel typical processes of unit planning to imagine approaches to promote schooling as a gift economy. In this spirit, some considerations:

- What are my gifts? What are the gifts of my discipline? What contributions are these gifts making to the collaboration? How am I listening to and giving life to the gifts of others?
- How will the unit plan come alive? Does the central question promote reciprocity? How do I honour other questions which emerge?
- What wisdom does my body hold? How can I give more of my whole self? How can my wholeness generate teaching and learning possibilities?
- What ecological offerings surround, infuse, and sustain life in this particular place? What goes unnoticed in my everyday life? How can I pay attention and give back to the often taken-for-granted gifts of life with(in) my learning space?

Orienting Map II

Opening Minds, Eyes, Ears, and Doors

Emergent Learning Opportunities for Literacy Educators Weaving Theory in Everyday Classrooms

Barbara Comber

Introduction

The everyday semiotic resources people access for imagining, meaning-making, representation, and taking action are increasingly vast and changing. Even young children demonstrate complex repertoires of diverse cultural, linguistic, and geographic knowledges. Right now, new public management in government and educational policy see standardization, competition, and big data rule. At the same time, educational workforces are facing massive intergenerational shifts with retirement of alienated and disappointed teachers leaving the profession. In this policy arena, sociocultural contexts, specificity, and particularity are dismissed in the face of demands for generic, and supposedly self-sustaining, school improvements. Sociomaterial approaches to literacy pedagogy can reignite educational imaginations and accomplish learning essential for engaging with the complex social, material, economic, and political problems of everyday life.

Theoretical resources are, as the products of human invention, wrought to explain phenomena which emerge in specific times and places. Consequently, different theoretical lenses bracket out or foreground different elements of literacy practices and pedagogies, forcing me to go beyond traditional language and literacy theoretical resources to pursue my research priorities. As Amanda Smith (2016) states, as literacy practices change, researchers may need to "access other aspects of the doing of literacies." She goes on to add that "affective, embodied and other non-cognitive domains of literacies are often more mercurial and difficult to unearth through traditional theoretical approaches" (p. 125). It may be that this has always been so but that the rapidity of change exposes how much we are yet to understand and also that }there is no unambiguous way to differentiate between the 'object' and the 'agencies of observation'" (Barad, 2007, p. 114; also see Kuby & Gutshall Rucker, 2016).

Through revisiting some of my previous research, I illustrate how I needed to supplement and adapt my theoretical repertoire over time to pursue the questions that continue to haunt me. These glimpses of earlier studies are fleeting as I spend longer on more recent and current work where I have brought place and space together with critical literacy, employing both social geographies and sociomaterial approaches. The question underpinning my program of research concerns the kinds of literate practices that schools make available to different young people and what they make of that, particularly young people growing up in relative poverty. The sociomaterial is important in my work as it focuses on the contingent and networked relationships among politics, people, places, power, and resources (following Edwards & Fenwick, 2015), all of which are entangled in literacy practices.

This ongoing inquiry relates to my own biography as I have discussed elsewhere (Comber, 2016a). While I do not intend to elaborate here, I note that my research problem and related questions first and foremost emerge from that history as a child, as a teacher, and much later as an academic researcher. My central question in its various iterations comes from lived experience rather than from theory. That is not to discard theory but simply to point out that I did not start with theory but from my everyday life as a learner and teacher, as a child growing up in a working-class, and sometimes poor, family in a culturally diverse neighbourhood located in a public housing estate. The research problem concerns the relationship between literacy and poverty and the extent to which education might become an empowering force for change. I started my research with unwavering faith in teachers, children, and literacy. As I discuss, that faith has been tempered not only be my ongoing research but also by wider world events, environmental and climate disasters, wars, education, and social policy. Yet I still believe we need radical optimism and hope to open our minds, eyes, ears, and doors to learn alongside front-line workers and students as we work locally to re-design critical literacies that are of our times and places. Doors because I believe we need to get out and about . . . and see and listen to what is going on. Minds because we need to be open to generative theories that offer explanatory power, so that we can open up to the possibility of negotiating "something new" (following Massey, 2005). For me, thinking and working with theory is as much an ethical matter as an academic matter. It is a key resource for an intellectual profession and educational institutions, as we have known them, increasingly under threat (Boden & Epstein, 2006). Most important, social geography and sociomateriality help me to better understand the dynamic relationships among people, poverty, places, and pedagogies. I wanted to be able to tell different stories of the work of teachers working in high-poverty locations that would represent more complex accounts of what was being accomplished (Comber, 2016b; Hirst & Burnett, this volume; Honeyford & Trussler, this volume).

Literacy, Place, and Pedagogies of Possibility: Imagining and Negotiating Dynamic Potential Over Time

As a researcher, I enjoyed the privilege of working and learning alongside teacher-researchers for more than three decades (Comber, 2016b). Here I highlight the work of just one teacher, Marg Wells, to give a sense of what she accomplished over time with different cohorts of students and colleagues. I highlight key projects and features of the curriculum and pedagogies she designed over time, which I believe were productive for me as a literacy researcher wanting to make a difference, particularly focusing on the sociomaterial relational aspects of her pedagogical practices. By looking at selected artefacts from Wells' and her students' oeuvre—as a retrospective gallery—I want to illustrate the ways in which her work is emblematic for me of the affordances of a sociomaterial approach to critical literacy. Just a quick list—neighbourhood walks and recording the condition and numbers of trees, researching indigenous flora and advising the planners about playgrounds, *A is for Arndale*, *Letters from Ridley*, *Windows*, embracing popular culture and ICTs, Grove Gardens, advising and participating in the new streetscape, the Superschool and Talking Walls, *Memories*, Literacy and Imagination, buying a block, house design, and new neighbourhoods. Wells embraced working with architects, builders, councilors, town planners, urban designers, children's literature, popular culture in various forms, drama, various hardware and software, and so on. She built her own knowledge of place and space, with built and natural environments, and treated her classroom and the neighbourhood as spaces and places open to construction and reconstruction, to imagining and reimagining.

Her students came from many different countries with different languages, faiths, and cultural heritages. Around 10% were Aboriginal, the preferred name for the Indigenous peoples of Australia. Many had recently arrived as refugees; others were migrants; others second-generation children of immigrants and refugees from China, Vietnam, Cambodia, Sudan, Afghanistan, and many other places frequently war torn. Wells made place the object of study by focusing on the common affordances of growing up together in a changing neighbourhood and the affordances of being together in a classroom. The key objective of her pedagogy was to foster a collective in which all students felt as though they belonged. By positioning the students as researchers of, and potential designers of, a changing material world, she positioned them as agentive with respect to urban renewal and school change.

On neighbourhood walks, children were invited to become active observers of both the built and natural environments—recording, for example, the conditions and numbers of trees, boarded up houses or empty blocks of land, whatever was salient to their inquiries at that time. During one of her projects in the 1990s, 5-, 6-, and 7-year-old children recorded their reflections after their walks. In the driest state on the driest continent, their observations about trees and water were telling. They noticed there were not as many trees in their neighbourhood as they would have liked. Their images and writing also conveyed that they also understood the micropolitics of people and place, such as the disposal of rubbish, noise regulations, and racial distribution. Wells' tasks critically framed their representations, yet she never leaves the critique without opportunities to imagine how things might be different (see also Appadurai, 1996; Greene, 1988). In the classroom, children constructed a range of "belonging spaces"—both real and imagined (e.g., designing and making the habitat for a pet they wished they had).

Wells showed children how to read maps of various kinds, from the urban renewal project, to Google Maps, to aerial maps, and how to construct their own maps of the area surrounding the school. Elementary school children were inducted into the world of texts designed for adults. They went to neighbourhood parks to investigate the ways that the grounds had been landscaped and the different surfaces, structures, and plantings. They learned how to problematize every day and authorized texts in terms of colonial representations of race and place, including the ways in which Indigenous Australians had been typically portrayed in books for children. Additionally, she introduced them to brilliant counter-stories and artefacts, including Jeannie Baker's work on *Belonging* (Baker, 2004) and Elaine Russell's work on the stolen generation (Russell, 2000). In the alphabet book for children constructed by one of her year 3/4 cohorts, we see the artefactual traces of her enabling pedagogies in action. Children are introduced to new semiotic resources, those of Aboriginal artist and storyteller Elaine Russell. Following a number of field trips around the local area, the whole class put together their own alphabet book, *A is for Arndale* (the nearby Westfield shopping mall) and, in so doing, grappled with the current places and spaces nearby and those in the planning or rejuvenation stages. She helped the class work together to produce something none of them could have done alone. The book demonstrates a mix of old and new, critique and celebration, and fear and familiarity, as the multiple authors construct their alphabet book for children in South Africa. They also put together another book, called *Letters from Ridley*, to introduce themselves to children in Attridgeville. When Wells and her principal later visited the school in Pretoria, they were inspired by the food gardens growing at the school.

On return, this led to another more ambitious project, about which I have spoken and written a great deal, *The Urban Renewal From the Inside-Out* project, which Wells came to call the *Grove Gardens* project. This collaborative research and development project involved architects, journalism and education academics, and university students working together with the children, school, and the wider community. The project was designed to involve the children and their families in re-designing and building a space within the school grounds as a garden for parents dropping off young children at the Childcare Centre or waiting for their school-aged children. It was to be a welcoming place that offered comfort, shade, and pleasure to adults and children alike and connected the pre-school with the school.

In that study, Wells and Trimboli built their own knowledge of architecture and design through their engagement with the architects. The journalism academic and students helped the teachers and children consider how they would document and publicize the processes of material change. The architecture academic and his students helped us all develop the spatial literacies associated with landscape design. That project resulted not only in the research and the usual publications but also a garden, which is the only thing left now of Ridley Grove Primary School.

Fast forward to 2015: 74% of the school students were from families on an income below average, with 48% in the bottom quartile. That year, Wells embarked on what turned out to be her final research project titled *Literacy and the Imagination: Working with Place and Space as Resources for Children's Learning*. That year her inquiry questions to investigate with her class were:

- How do people and environment influence one another?
- How do people influence the human characteristics of places and the management of spaces within them?

She took her inspiration from the recently written national curriculum learning area of geography. Their neighbourhood walk undertaken early in that year revealed many empty blocks of land. Interestingly, the urban renewal project was still dragging on, more than a decade after it began, with state-owned blocks remaining empty and fenced in.

That year turned out was to be her last as a teacher-researcher as she retired from teaching in 2016. In describing her enabling pedagogical practices, I first want to note how on this occasion she found the space for imaginative curriculum in the geography learning area. I had seen her select similar cross-curricular opportunities previously, as what constituted literacy was increasingly the subject of whole school planning. I had seen her work in science, design and technology, drama, and arts to create extra time and space to explore critical literacy. In 2015, the theme developed from the idea of housing, blocks, homes, and good neighbourhoods. Again, it involved extended inquiry from February to July. Again, Wells led the children in learning how to notice change and to find out what was happening and why and what was planned for the future. They wrote a class letter to the council to find out why so many blocks remained empty. Again, she invited the children to play with what they had learned and what they imagined. They started by bidding for empty blocks; to bid, they needed to have a strong written rationale for their choice. They then had time to design their house/home, starting with empty milk cartons and gradually designing both the house and garden as part of the re-imagined neighbourhood. They were invited by the urban planners to share their work on Renewal South Australia's website (see https://renewalsa.sa.gov.au).

One of Wells' crucial pedagogical moves was to build children's knowledge of how things work in the built environment. This kind of knowledge was rarely available to children through their everyday lives because most lived in cheap public rental accommodation. Wells did not keep things hidden from children. She assumed that they would be interested in how things were organized, and they were. Another crucial pedagogical move was to make complex relationships concrete through embodied experiences—moving through the neighbourhood, learning to read maps, photographing buildings and blocks from various angles, and so on. A further crucial move was her task design and related student activities.

Wells' pedagogy across her oeuvre was considered. She imagined her students doing specific things and designed curriculum to position children as co-researchers. A sociomaterial reading of Wells' practices helps me to focus on the ways in which she made the dynamics of the everyday neighbourhood and school worlds the object of study. Her practices enabled young people, as a collective group of researcher-learners, to come to a more sophisticated understanding of how things are put together and how they might be otherwise. She worked with theories of social and spatial justice, belonging, place-conscious pedagogy, and critical literacy; these theories, amongst others she assembled across her career, were adapted and improvised in situ in response to the changing world of the neighbourhood and the school.

Literacy, Learning, and Leadership: Beyond Pedagogies of Poverty

Like Wells, I gradually added to my theoretical and design toolkit across my career, and one of my most recent studies was a four-school ethnography investigating the relationships among leadership, literacy teaching, and learning in high-poverty schools. I did not have any prior relationships with any of the participants in any of these schools, but again, the research took me back to sites of contemporary poverty in the northern suburbs of Adelaide and to a regional mining town. The material and intergenerational histories of poverty along with newer versions of hardship were palpable as we drove in and more so as we embarked on a process of work-shadowing the school principals. And perhaps because I was flying back from Queensland, where I was living at the time, it made a deep impression on my psyche. Along with Deb Hayes, who was flying in from Sydney, I experienced a kind of ethnographic exhaustion as we absorbed the sights and sounds of everyday school and neighbourhood lives on our commuting visits. There is much more which could be said about this experience (Hayes & Comber, 2017). Here, however, I simply want to show how sociomateriality gave us extra resources for understanding literacy pedagogies in these schools.

Just one brief example will suffice here. All four schools were invited to join the project by the Department of Education because they had shown positive signs of improvement in school culture, leadership, and literacy pedagogy in a recent departmental evaluation. Our task was to document that leadership (as it pertained to literacy in particular), investigate how it was being taken up and applied in classroom practices, and check the effects on students. Each school had a literacy policy, mostly described as a "literacy agreement," in which the staff had decided on particular approaches to literacy pedagogy that would be consistent across the school. Such ensembles might include Jolly Phonics, Guided Reading, and weekly spelling, for example. In two of the schools, a key element of the literacy agreement was *Accelerated Literacy*, an approach to close and repeated readings of a text as a whole class experience and the explicit teaching of various genres, such as information reports. This approach originally grew from the work of Brian Gray in Aboriginal communities focusing on how the teacher might scaffold children's early reading and writing through demonstrations of the ways in which texts were constructed and meanings made. The approach was underpinned by Vygotskian theory (Vygotsky, 1978) and Hallidayan functional grammar (Halliday, 1978) and was found to be effective in the contexts where he worked. A couple of decades later, David Rose and other colleagues of the systemic functional linguistic school in Sydney have popularized the approach through a range of professional development offerings across Australia.

In one school, where Deb Hayes was the ethnographer, the teachers agreed that to supplement her observations, they would video record typical Accelerated Literacy lessons so that she could view them later. Without going through the full analysis here (but see Hayes et al., 2017; Hayes & Comber, 2017), in viewing the lessons conducted by the year 5 teachers, one focusing on a fiction text, *Tanglewood* (Wild, 2012) and one focusing on an information report on the problem of childhood obesity of Australia, we began to see how the "same pedagogy" was constituted very differently in each classroom even though both teachers aimed for fluent reading for deep understanding. Both lessons clearly involved repeated readings, modelled whole-class reading, and deconstruction of the sequencing and structure of the text. There was evidence of the teachers' active take-up of the key moves recommended in the Accelerated Literacy Pedagogy. In one class, students volunteered commentary as they recollected their previous readings; they were seated close to the teacher on the rug, and she recorded their enthusiastic brainstorming on a whiteboard in handwriting (when the Smartboard would not work). Later we watched them discuss and order the copied pages of the book using memory and logic and then re-reading it aloud to the whole class in their groups. In the other classroom, students took it in turns to read aloud a sentence each from the information report using a microphone to ensure they could be heard. They sat at their seats to perform this task.

A sociomaterial analysis illuminated how the engagement of the teacher and students was low in this second classroom. The second teacher stood and directed from the front. The students did not move except to pass on the microphone. They did not speak except when nominated. When the teacher reminded them of the text, she began by observing that there were words that they probably did not know, that were not in their vocabulary, namely *obesity* and *dietician*. After reading their sentence, a number of students slumped on their folded arms across their desks. It was as though the oxygen had been sucked out of the room. Everyone appeared to be going through the motions (such as they are), including the teacher. We recognized again how much of the work of teachers is embodied, how much is emotional, how much is pragmatic, how much involves stuff—copies of texts, furniture, paraphernalia, whiteboards, microphones, spaces for students to work, alone and together, and that it is beyond discursive work (Comber, 2006). Sociomaterial analysis shows how things are regulated and organized beyond the actions of the individual (Smith, 2005) and yet how profoundly teachers' different engagements with literacy theory had led to very different enactments of the pedagogy.

Current Questions: Daring and Defiant Research Imaginations

In a current project with my colleagues Annette Woods (project lead investigator), Lisa Kervin, and Aspa Bouritsis, we are employing sociomaterial approaches to conduct a study of young children learning to produce texts in a school in a poor neighbourhood of Wollongong in NSW and a school in a poor neighbourhood in Queensland (see Kervin, Comber, Woods, & Bouritsis, 2017). We are exploring:

1. How, when, where, with what, and with whom are children writing in early childhood classrooms?
2. What are the implications for teaching and learning, when writing and other text production is understood to involve collaborative practice; and tools, resources, and devices that are print and digital?

Sociomaterial theory has impacted on the ways in which we have co-produced the data with teachers and children and invited them to produce data that gives a sense of their experiences. For example, we have invited young children to tell us about how, where, when, and with whom they are learning to write and to show us what this looks like in a drawing. We surveyed all teachers across both schools about their beliefs and reported practices concerning text production. We have invited teachers to take us on virtual tours of their classrooms, particularly focusing on how they go about teaching children to produce texts. One teacher volunteered to have his classroom video recorded over an extended period with a range of devices. In an attempt to capture longitudinal-style video data and to remove the obtrusiveness of a research team in the space, an observation system comprising portable cameras, a networked base station, and a digital audio recording system was installed. We have invited teachers to embark on collaborative inquiries using design-based experiments and to wear GoPro cameras to record children's responses. Some children are also wearing the GoPro cameras to record classroom actions, bodies, materials, and talk from their perspectives. We have just started the student case studies and thinking about what we might do; so far, we have done one-on-one chats and classroom observations and collected their products, listened to their conversations, and so on. The one-on-one interviews have forced us to think differently about how children report their experiences of learning to write. Lisa recently invited two students to take us on a virtual tour of their classroom.

Already we are learning about which students are those that their peers commonly turn to. We are learning about children who see themselves as under the teacher's gaze. We are learning what children believe writing is and what they believe constitutes good writing. We are learning where children believe that they are learning to write and people who they believe are good writers. We are learning that there are big differences between the ways in which children view their families and homes in terms of writing and what teachers believe. We are learning that teachers' practices emphasize skills and drills, paper and pencils, desks and individuals. Children tell us they are learning to produce texts at home, in kindergartens, inside and out, with parents, aunties and uncles, cousins, siblings, and friends on computers and video games. These young children remained highly positive about learning to write and produce texts of various kinds. Writing has not yet become a problem for most.

We know that the capacity to write and to communicate more broadly is a key practice not only for academic success at school but also in everyday life and in workplaces (Brandt, 2015). However, it is also the domain of literacy where students in poor areas of Australia consistently perform badly, and their performance deteriorates rather than improves as they *progress* through the school system. How and why does this happen, and how might it be otherwise? Using a sociomaterial approach is forcing us to examine what we have taken for granted or ignored, such as the reported important role of families and friends for children when learning to write, and teachers' semi-reluctance in incorporating information and communication technologies (ICTs) in the processes of teaching and learning literacies. If writing is constituted only as an individualized skill, it may well be that it becomes an increasingly alienating experience for some children, perhaps not unlike the oral reading of the childhood obesity text referred to earlier.

Conclusion

I end by returning to the idea that sociomaterial approaches may reignite educational imaginations. By working with creative and committed teacher-researchers for extended periods, I have become even more convinced of the potential of learning and working in collective and collaborative ways. Such teachers notice and take account of everyday, immediate stuff. They notice who their students are and recognize the specific resources they bring. They tackle new inquiries and are not intimidated by fear, change, and regulation. They make their teaching and their students' learning the continual object of study. They demonstrate both daring and defiant research imaginations (Boden & Epstein, 2006).

Let me finish by being very specific in terms of sociomateriality. Marg Wells taught children how to observe, how to listen, how to record, how to translate, how to interview, how to produce collective and collaborative texts and artefacts often with aesthetic beauty—how to make the familiar strange. She also taught them new words, phrases, concepts, games, and designs. Her classroom was a place of pleasure and challenge. It was a space of belonging and learning. Her students reported that they were becoming researchers and journalists. They engaged in imagining and designing and making. They also learned about the politics of people, places, and spaces through negotiating, imagining and constructing various texts, structures, models, gardens, art installations, and books.

Importantly, children walked, designed, collected data, took photographs, interviewed, transcribed, analyzed, negotiated, followed maps, made maps, conducted experiments, produced multimodal collaborative texts, and presented to peers and adults. If we think about the "doings" of literacy in and out of Wells' classroom, it is easy to see that it involved movement, working together over time, being in and outside, using a range of materials and media and more. Children are able to genuinely learn from and with each other. The classroom is simultaneously negotiated as a place of belonging as well as a space of complex learning and pleasure. An enabling critical pedagogy of place exposes how relationships between people, places, and things are made and how they can be re-made in inclusive ways.

It is important for those of us who are privileged to be researchers that "new theories" force us to remember who and what we have forgotten or bracketed out. While new theories act as a corrective to the forgotten, they also push the remembered dimensions into the foreground as they help us to explain what is going on. For instance, people (in terms of race, ethnicity, sexuality, gender, class) insist on their presence; places (bushfires, floods, earthquakes) demand we take note, animals (plagues of rodents, too many foxes), refuse to be ignored, and so it goes. However, it is front-line practitioners, people, places, flora, and fauna that are actually experiencing what it is we are trying to understand and make sense of it and live with or change the realities as they encounter them. Theory can only go so far in its explanations because it is always catching up or running ahead.

References

Appadurai, A. (1996). *Modernity at large: Cultural dimensions of globalization.* Minneapolis, MN: University of Minnesota Press.

Baker, J. (2004). *Belonging.* London, UK: Walker Children's Paperbacks.

Barad, K. M. (2007). *Meeting the universe halfway: Quantum physics and the entanglement of matter and meaning.* Durham, NC: Duke University Press.

Boden, R., & Epstein, D. (2006). Managing the research imagination? Globalisation and research in higher education. *Globalisation, Societies and Education, 4*(2), 223–236. doi:10.1080/14767720600752619

Brandt, D. (2015). *The rise of writing: Redefining mass literacy.* Cambridge, UK: Cambridge University Press.

Comber, B. (2006). Pedagogy as work: Educating the next generation of literacy teachers. *Pedagogies, 1*(1), 59–67.

Comber, B. (2016a). Poverty, place and pedagogy in education: Research stories from front-line workers. *Australian Educational Researcher, 43,* 393–417. doi:10.1007/s13384-016-0212-9

Comber, B. (2016b). *Literacy, place and pedagogies of possibility.* New York, NY: Routledge.

Edwards, R., & Fenwick, T. (2015). Critique and politics: A sociomaterialist intervention. *Educational Philosophy and Theory, 47,* 1385–1404.

Greene, M. (1988). *The dialectic of freedom.* New York, NY: Teachers College Press.

Halliday, M. A. K. (1978). *Language as social semiotic: The social interpretation of language and meaning.* London, UK: Edward Arnold.

Hayes, D., & Comber, B. (2017). Researching pedagogy in high poverty contexts: Implications of non-representational ontology. *International Journal of Research and Method in Education, 40.* doi:10.1080/1743727X.2017.1395409

Hayes, D., Hattam, R., Comber, B., Kerkham, L., Lupton, R., & Thomson, P. (2017). *Literacy, leading and learning: Beyond pedagogies of poverty.* London, UK: Routledge.

Kervin, L., Comber, B., Woods, A., & Bouritsis, A. (2017). Towards a sociomaterial understanding of writing experiences incorporating digital technology in an early childhood classroom. *Literacy Research: Theory, Method, and Practice, 66,* 183–197. doi:10.1177/2381336917718522

Kuby, C., & Gutshall Rucker, T. (2016). *Go be a writer! Expanding the curricular boundaries of literacy learning with children.* New York, NY: College Press.

Massey, D. (2005). *For space.* London, UK: Sage Publications.

Russell, E. (2000). *A is for Aunty.* Sydney, Australia: Australian Broadcasting Commission.

Smith, A. (2016). Bare writing: Comparing multiliteracies theory and Nonrepresentational theory approaches to a young writer writing. *Reading Research Quarterly*, 52(1), 125–140.

Smith, D. E. (2005). *Institutional ethnography: A sociology for people*. Lanham, MD: AltaMira Press.

Vygotsky, L. (1978). *Mind in society: The development of higher psychological processes*. Cambridge, MA: Harvard University Press.

Wild, M. (2012). *Tanglewood* (V. Goodman, Illus.). Parkside, Australia: Omnibus Books.

Plateau II

Becoming Worldmakers With Ethics and Difference

Mairi McDermott and Kim Lenters

The chapters in this plateau re-orient us to literacy as a worldmaking process through ethical entanglements with difference. We are interested in what kinds of world(s) are being made possible, for whom, and in what ways through our literacy practices/approaches/pedagogies. So, we ask, what are the histories and legacies of particular literacy pedagogies, and who do they serve and in what ways? How do our literacy emphases produce particular worlds and possibilities for becoming (for students and texts—inclusive of curriculum as text)?

Literacy education thus becomes a practice of relationality with others, to the unfolding *assemblages* of bodies, texts, histories, materials, policies that emerge moment by moment. This attention to the in-the-moment uncertainties, or "literacy desirings" (Kuby & Gutshall Rucker, 2016), shifts our emphases from what can become an over-determined focus on end products deemed easily "assess-*able*" through literacy benchmarks. These "literacy desirings" re-attune us towards the incommensurable processes that assemble literacy possibilities. What about the embodied-material literacy enactments that are beyond measure, indeed, beyond noticing? How might we open ourselves to being attuned to the different ways in which literacy manifests or takes shape, however fleetingly? Who or what do we need to pay attention to?

Posthuman Ethics

In this plateau, posthuman ethics "is also about affirming difference and the production of the new. Rather than limiting the future to what has already been done or what is already known, ethics involves opening up the potential for the unknown" (Hickey-Moody & Malins, 2007, p. 4). This is an ethics that is reminiscent of Kumashiro's (2002) and Ahmed's (2000) cautions against repetition; it requires that we open ourselves and our literacy practices to the yet-to-be rather than remaining solely in the what is. As we have noted throughout this volume, while we believe that tried-and-true literacy practices have much to offer, we are curious by what we haven't yet tried; this curiosity takes courage. As Hargraves

(2019) animates, "An ethical act is understood to emerge with the connections and productions which increase a body's *capacity for action*" (p. 187, emphasis added). The courage to allow our curiosity and pedagogical wonder to propel us to act, to do things differently, to centre different ways of being, knowing, and doing literacy, is, in this way, an ethical act.

This approach to ethics in literacy education asks us to pause and draw out some of the conundrums frequently faced in literacy teaching and learning to ask how we might differently orient ourselves to the "problem," as Aukerman and Jensen (this volume) do in their chapter. In some regards, ways of being-doing literacy education have become sedimented as "just the way things are done," and as Aukerman and Jensen amplify, this causes us to miss the "hundred languages" or "a hundred, a thousand creative and communicative potentials" (Rinaldi, 2006, p. 175) of our students. This is ever-more important for those who have historically been dis-recognized as literate bodies through the disciplinary regimes of literacy instruction that focus on visible and recognizable outputs and postures of learning (Luke, 1992; Siegel, 2016).

The question of where knowledge resides is critical here, "Much contemporary schooling is contingent on reinforcing the notion of the teachers as she who 'knows' (as classroom manager, curriculum implementer, sociologist, even adolescent psychologist) and of students as knowable" (Gannon, 2009, p. 70). In a strange move, this location of knowledge(able subjects) objectifies students while simultaneously dis-recognizing the role of objects and materials in literacy education beyond how they can be leveraged for literacy learning but rather as agential entities within the literacy assemblage (Barad, 2007; Bennett, 2010). So the question arises: How do we take up literacy as a way to "shift the boundaries of the familiar," as an ethical encounter that holds open the potential for surprising realizations about "what [and who] we assume we know" (Ahmed, 2000, p. 7)?

Difference

Spring and Huddleston's chapter (this volume) in this plateau takes up questions of identity work in literacy education in their re-reading of Rosenblatt's reader response theory (RRT) through a posthumanist ethics. Whereas RRT often focuses on the connections readers make to the texts they read in identity work (thus centring sense-making agency in the human), posthuman ethics shifts attention to the effects of the text on **differenciation**. This repositions texts with **thing power** (Bennett, 2010) or agency to act upon the assemblage of identity. Texts matter. What texts do we bring in, and put on offer, for our youth to read? What texts are sanctioned or promoted in the curriculum or approved reading lists? Who are the authors? What are their positions? How do they interpellate, or call, students/readers into being? How might the texts offer alternative becomings, or for those who are more often misrepresented or essentialized in texts (see, for example, Morrison, 1992), how might the texts shift recognizability?

When thinking with difference, ethics, and relations with human and non-human others, we must recognize the histories of common usage haunting these concepts. In Deleuze and Guattari's (1987/2004) work, difference and the other are reconceptualized. Rather than conceptualizing *difference* as ways that a student (as a discrete entity) differs from another student or departs from a socially constructed idea of what that student should know or be able to do at a particular point in time (externalizing difference as out there in some *other* body), students, literacy practices, and texts are continually becoming something new, something different, through intra-activity in a literacy learning assemblage.

Indeed, while repetition of ways of being-doing-knowing literacy certainly make it seem as though things are naturally as they should be, that there is an essential identity to individuals (again human and non-human), we are urged to notice slippery moments when these boundaries seem to fall apart, when boundaries are (un)ruly. This is what Thiel and Pelling (this volume) take up in their chapter through their focus on space and boundaries as a constitutive force in shaping literacy possibilities. Like the other chapters in this plateau, they call for necessary transformations in our literacy relationships and as such a shift in worldmaking through recognition of the porosity of seemingly stable boundaries (among humans, nations, texts, objects, materials).

Worldmaking

Merchant and Devender-Kraft's chapter (this volume) takes us into the role of literacy in (un)making boundaries for/of belonging through global flows of bodies (human, knowledge, capital, and so on) in so-called postcolonial times. Here literacy practices open spaces for making worlds of difference-and-belonging. How one comes into and through various school assemblages fraught with uncertainties around the language, culture, texts, and postures becomes a central ethical issue in this chapter. How these assemblages and the critical role of human-human relations as well as (con)text(ual) connections is amplified. This chapter offers a pedagogy of hope, a future-oriented belief that we can do better by our trans-national students that is grounded in the politics of the present, a notion that Nichols and O'Sullivan (this volume) call mutual flourishing in their chapter in this plateau. If "the world and its possibilities for becoming are remade with each moment" then "Meeting each moment, being alive to the possibilities of becoming, is an ethical call, an invitation that is written into the very mater of all being and becoming" (Barad, 2007, p. 396). Thus, being open to each literacy moment becomes an ethical practice of worldmaking for mutual flourishing.

Literacy as worldmaking through ethics and difference, then, asks about what comes to **matter** through our literacy practices and what is excluded, muted, or denied from mattering. In posthuman ethics, we have a responsibility to acknowledge the ways the world—our classrooms, our communities, our literacies, our identities, our texts—are always in-the-making through moment-by-moment **assemblages** of human and non-human others. We also have to engage critically with the habitual literacy practices that we repeat without question; we must ask what these ways of being and doing literacy do, what they open and what they foreclose? Furthermore, and of utmost importance is questioning who/what is included as agential in the becomings of these literacy practices. How might we unbound the fixed meanings embedded in and through our literacy approaches? As we have noted throughout the volume, we believe this critical engagement ought to be generative rather than dismissive; perhaps our tried-and-true practices do hit the mark? How might we allow ourselves to be open to the different literacy possibilities both within what we already do as well as beyond that?

How do we retune ourselves to the not-yet-imagined/surfaced within literacy? What role has literacy played in disciplining bodies (of students, of communities, of knowledge, of text)? How might we re-orient ourselves to what "counts" as recognizable literacy? Who or what fits in our conceptualizations of literacy?

References

Ahmed, S. (2000). *Strange encounters: Embodied others in post-coloniality*. London, UK: Routledge.

Barad, K. (2007). *Meeting the universe halfway: Quantum physics and the entanglement of matter and meaning*. Durham, NC: Duke University Press.

Bennett, J. (2010). *Vibrant matter: A political economy of things*. Durham, NC: Duke University Press.

Deleuze, G., & Guattari, F. (1987/2004). *A thousand plateaus: Capitalism and schizophrenia* (B. Massumi, Trans.). Minneapolis, MN: University of Minnesota Press (originally publishedas *Mille Plateuaux*, volume 2 of *Capitalisme et schizophrenie*. Paris, France: Minuit, 1987).

Hargraves, V. (2019). The posthuman condition of ethics in early childhood literacy: Order-in(g)be(e)ing literacy. In C. R. Kuby, K. Spector, & J. J. Thiel (Eds.), *Posthumanism and literacy education: Knowing/becoming/doing literacies* (pp. 187–200). New York, NY: Routledge.

Hickey-Moody, A., & Malins, P. (2007). Introduction: Gilles Deleuze and four movements in social thought. In A. Hickey-Moody & P. Malins (Eds.), *Deleuzian encounters: Studies in contemporary social issues* (pp. 1–24). London, UK: Palgrave Macmillan.

Gannon, S. (2009). Difference as ethical encounter. In B. Davies & S. Gannon (Eds.), *Pedagogical encounters* (pp. 69–88). New York, NY: Peter Lang.

Kuby, C. R., & Gutshall Rucker, T. (2016). *Go be a writer! Expanding curricular boundaries of literacy learning with children*. New York, NY: Teachers College Press.

Kumashiro, K. (2002). Against repetition: Addressing resistance to anti-oppressive change in the practices of learning, teaching, supervising, and researching. *Harvard Educational Review*, 72(1), 67–92.

Luke, A. (1992). The body literate: Discourse and inscription in early literacy training. *Linguistics and Education*, 4, 107–129.

Morrison, T. (1992). *Playing in the dark: Whiteness and the literary imagination*. New York, NY: Penguin Random House.

Rinaldi, C. (2006). *In dialogue with Reggio Emilia: Listening, researching and learning*. London, UK: Routledge.

Siegel, M. (2016). Inscription, erasure, embodiment: Literacy research and bodies of knowledge. In G. Enriquez, E. Johnson, S. Kontovourki, & C. A. Mallozzi (Eds.), *Literacies, learning, and the body: Putting theory and research into pedagogical practice* (pp. 20–38). New York, NY: Routledge.

5 What Nose Hill Taught Us About Boundary-Making, Boundary-Knowing, and Boundary-Becoming

Jaye Johnson Thiel and Melody Pelling

As I (Jaye) stood at the bottom of Nose Hill (Figure 7), my body began to feel anxious. Eyeing the walking path upward to where the earth meets the sky, the road to the top seemed endless. "I'll never make it," I thought to myself as my mind quickly provided a list of all the possible physical limitations standing in my way. At some point, this list materialized as spoken words to Melody (my writing partner for this project), "WHEW! That is a big climb," to which she replied in agreement.

Melody had shared with me that she often walks Nose Hill after her long days as a Canadian school administrator. Power walks even. So, I knew she was familiar with the space and her body knew how to engage with the bodies around her in ways that felt very foreign to me. As an American academic who does not power walk anything, I started to feel very nervous about the climb we were about to embark on together. But being who I am, I did not want to be too fearful. I did not want to be too vulnerable. I did not want to be too defeatist. Taking a deep breath, I walked forward.

I knew in the first few yards or meters that I would lose the group, as they seemed to be jaunting upward at a pace of conquest, while I, on the other hand, felt Nose Hill might conquer me. I shared with Melody that I would need to walk very slowly, that I understood if she wanted to go ahead. I did not want to hold her up. (All things women seem to learn to do as to not be a bother to the world around them.) Melody assured me that a slow pace was fine and that she planned to stick with me the entire way.

As we travelled upward, the group melted into the horizon—gone as sunsets often do—lovely, bright, becoming one with the horizon, and then suddenly there is no trace that one was once 2 or 3 or 4 or in this case approximately 32. They were all—just gone.

Retrospectively, this moment, when the other bodies melted into earth, was the exact moment when the body of Nose Hill, the constraints of my body, and the willingness of Melody's body gave me something very precious. The space gave me time to wander and wonder with Nose Hill and Melody in a way that our assigned writing room in the Werklund School of Education could not. It gave us time to become more than writing partners. It gave us a chance to become friends.

Figure 7 A view of Nose Hill

Standing in the Shadows of Diffractive Light

It was not until later that evening, once Melody had returned to her home and I to my hotel room, that it became clear to me how climbing Nose Hill had offered a different kind of boundary-making practice (Barad, 2007) than our meeting room could or would ever be able to provide. Something different had been produced there. Something that seemed a bit magical in a way. Something that distinguished Nose Hill as a new way of knowing-becoming in the wild "throwntogetherness" (Massey, 2005) that had occurred on this particular week in space and time.

When Melody and I spoke the next day, she felt the same. Something beautiful had taken place on Nose Hill. Melody confessed that although she had accepted Kim Lenters' invitation to be part of this project, she had been a bit nervous and apprehensive by this same throwntogetherness when the workshops commenced. As Melody explained in our writing sessions:

> From the onset, the "throwntogetherness" of the group was felt by many of us. This throwntogetherness was not in the form of disorganizing as we often refer to it but rather a sense that the group of people brought to this time, this place for this event were all present but from such diverse backgrounds and experiences. I wondered if I were in over my head? Was I capable of this kind of work? Did I have anything to contribute?
>
> (written reflection during workshop, October 2017)

As we gave testimony to our fears, we laughed. There was something very serious and very absurd about the preconceived expectations that we had

What Nose Hill Taught Us 93

placed on ourselves to perform a certain way during that week. Like dotted lines on a trail map, Nose Hill (Figure 8) offered us a new path with open boundaries into an unknown that we were willing to follow. Is this what Barad (2007) means when she speaks of diffractive grates, when random places, people, and things are pushed towards one another to see what differences get made from just being in the same space and going through the same openings at once? Perhaps. One thing is for certain:

Figure 8 Path on Nose Hill

putting Nose Hill in that grate sure changed things. But it is always easier to see how the rays dance when we are standing in the shadows of diffractive light rather than starring into the beam head on.

We use this chapter as a way to explore that light, to pay attention to the way it dances—the images, boundaries, and realities it creates as "stuff" (specifically the "stuff" of literacy classrooms) gets pushed through the grate. Like our time on Nose Hill, we use the terrain of these pages to wander and wonder how it is that space can serve as a boundary-making apparatus shaping both small and big things. But we also reach for the unruly edges (Tsing, 2012) of boundaries, where unexpected things proliferate and where potentialities reside if only we were to tug and pull at those edges and shift the lines a bit. For as Tim Ingold (2016) asks us, "What do walking, weaving, observing, singing, storytelling, drawing, and writing have in common? The answer is that they all proceed along lines of one kind or another" (p. 1).

We invite you (the reader) to come wayfaring with us—to proceed along the lines as we try our hand at orienteering the boundaries and unruly edges of the literacy classroom, the embodied literacies those boundaries produce, and look for potentialities in the markers along the way.

Following the Breadcrumbs

Standing at the top of Nose Hill Park, one can see its physical boundaries, where dirt and grass meet human-made concrete streets. But the residual boundaries are not as easy to spot. It is not lost on us that Nose Hill is sacred ground that continues to give much more than we venture to say it has received over the years of colonization, which is one of the reasons our group brought gifts for the earth. We are also aware of the way schools served as a colonizing mechanism for the Indigenous peoples in what is now called Canada. It is sometimes very easy to forget that we need to remember the situated histories of the more-than-human bodies around us (sea, earth, land, and so on) as we craft new histories and stories in the world.

Colonizing land is an awful lot like colonizing humans—both bodies under siege and certainly inextricably entangled. Retrospectively, we considered the boundaries of place—both the ones that are easily visible (like the physical lines of Nose Hill) and the ones that are not (like the boundaries created through complicated histories). All of these boundaries accumulate the past, present, and future to create potential realities that ultimately have consequences for all people, places, and things. The absence of the Plains bison, the remnants of tipi rings, the glacial erratics carrying stones and debris from one place to the another—all serve as residue of a people who continue to receive the gifts of this place, the encroachment of a city upon the land, and any subsequent push back to being usurped. Today, Nose Hill remains a thriving endangered grassland that serves as a habitat for many different species, including human ones.

A mutualistic relationship rumbles through Nose Hill, reminding us of our ethical obligation to the places we move in, out, and through.

> Our co-presence, that is to say the simultaneity of our being in the world together, sets the tune for the ethics of our interaction. Our ethical relation requires us to synchronize the perception and anticipation of our shared, common condition. A collectively distributed consciousness emerges from this—i.e. a transversal form of non-synthetic understanding of the relational bond that connects us. This places the relation at the centre of both the ethics and the epistemic structures and strategies of the subject.
> (Braidotti, 2013a, p. 22)

If we are to turn our attention to our relational bonds with people, places, and things, then it seems sensible to say that these ethical obligations do not end where Nose Hill meets concrete. They extend well beyond these lands, into our homes, our places of worship, businesses, and schools. With each new boundary comes a new set of ethical considerations and new potentials. And given that boundaries offer potentialities, we wondered, what then, does it mean to create spatial boundaries, both imaginary and real, and who and what interests are those boundaries serving?

What the Beaver Already Knows About Boundaries

Inevitably, space is a boundary-making-knowing-becoming apparatus shaping possibilities and the stories that get to unfold in those spaces. Exploring borders and boundaries is not a new concept, as Anzaldúa (1987) crafted an eloquent and powerful theory around the concept years ago. Similar to Anzaldúa, the theories of feminist new materialism (Barad, 2007; Bennett, 2010; Braidotti, 2013b) attempt to look at boundary-making practices and understand what those boundaries produce or what materializes after boundaries have been constructed and how these productions might shift with new boundaries. As Barad (2010) writes, "apparatuses are the material conditions of possibility and impossibility of mattering; they enact what matters and what is excluded from mattering" (p. 148). This means when a boundary is created by humans or otherwise, the creators of these boundaries are getting to know the space as it is being created. Collectively, boundary-makers tussle with decisions about what a space and its inhabitants will be. Take, for instance, the beaver.

Time and again humans have cursed beavers as they dam up waterways such as ponds, rivers, and deep streams. But the beaver is a keystone species. A keystone species is defined as "a species on which other species in an ecosystem largely depend, such that if it were removed the ecosystem would change drastically" (Google dictionary, n.d.). Keystone species work with their surroundings to create entire ecosystems. This means that when a beaver creates a dam for its own habitat, it is also creating a new habitat for others—others who can only exist if the beaver creates the dam. While the beaver makes decisions about where to build the dam and its construction, it is also learning about the space itself—what resources are there (trees, stones, wind, water, mud) and what predators might be lurking. The beaver does not make the dam without contemplation. In part, the beaver is deciding what gets to enter the space, how the space is used, and what gets to be part of the space. Changing the flow and boundaries of water makes new things possible, crafting new possibilities for dozens of species, including fish, birds, and other mammals while also filtering water naturally.

However, the beaver does not live within a boundary alone, nor does it create the only boundaries. A historical look at this keystone species tells us the story of how beavers, like land, were once colonized and monetized, too, playing a key role in Northern expansion. They were killed for their fur and for their castoreum. Wherever pioneers went in North America and the bigger their boundaries became, they killed every beaver they could find even though the habitats beavers create were part of humans' survival as well. So, beyond the beaver's boundary-making practices, other boundary-making proliferated, overlapped, and usurped. These new boundaries made new possibilities—ones where some folks were profiting economically and through political power but all the while making it impossible for a whole host of other creatures (and humans) to subsist.

Perhaps as educators, we have much we can learn from the beavers and much we can unlearn from the colonizers.

Schools as Habitats and Boundary-Making Apparatus

When we think about habitats, we often think of the more-than-human—other living things around us in the grasslands, forests, and ponds. But people craft and take up residence in habitats, too. Our homes, our places of work, our places of worship, our places of learning are all habitats that require different ways of being and knowing to survive. Human habitats are places where boundary-making is prolific, defined by social, political, and economic constructs. Space, time, and capacity are all forces we wrestle with and against while settling into our habitations and schools have been no exception to boundary-making-knowing-becoming practices.

Space in schools is clearly defined by physical boundaries. Fences around buildings and land, locks on doors, and entryways operated through intercom systems all serve as boundaries to who and what can come inside and who and what can leave. Boundaries can also include tree lines, gardens, parking lots, ad so on because boundaries are sneaky things and are often hard to notice. Sometimes outdoor spaces are further defined by areas that only certain age groups of children can access or certain places where particular games can be played (e.g., how paved spaces are often used as a priority space for certain games such as four-square or handball). And boundary-making does not stop once indoors. In classrooms, teachers spend copious amounts of time during school start-up and throughout the school year speaking to children about defined boundaries and the expectations within each. Students know where they can and cannot go. They can write here—but not there. They can eat here—but not there. They can sit here—but not there, except for *some*times, for *some* people, in *some* instances, when these boundaries become permeable. Boundaries can get really, really confusing. Clearly, if we are serious about crafting equitable literacy classrooms and communities, an attention to the precarity of spaces and the boundaries that percolate, persist, and profuse in their making is needed.

As we continued our rapid conversation the day after our visit to Nose Hill, we were filled with questions about boundaries and the possibilities and potentials that placemaking by educators and the educators before all of us fabricate. It was clear to us even before our throwntogetherness that schools create an expectation of what one is to do once inside the grounds. Our walk together just made it less of a taken-for-granted theory and more of a reality—a realization that expectations are also historically situated in a way that becomes so embodied, that we often fail to notice they are even there. Perhaps this is why we felt the need to be so serious and the profound pressures to produce writing while working at the university together even though no one ever demanded or complained about our progress. We felt an internal *need* to produce.

As Melody writes in her reflections:

> As a school administrator, I had spent extensive time and energy thinking about how space is best utilized and also about the aesthetics of physical space, but I had not spent the same level of time or energy thinking about the impact that the material had on students, staff, and community members who come to the school.

After taking a quick inventory of her school, Melody listed several incidences of boundary-making that could shift possibilities in the classroom. We discussed the "teacher space"—a space clearly delineated for the teacher only—as a possible problem for the literacy classroom. Something as small as a desk, table, or cabinet produces boundaries around accessibility. We lamented over students needing permissions to use a classroom sink, and we wondered about the artifacts that are often off limits—such as not touching the walls with their bodies while moving through the school. Often referred to as "hallway hands" (hands clasped behind the back while walking), this decree to not touch physical spaces surely indicates something about who the space belongs to and who it privileges. Items such as water bottles and coats and lunches are only to be stored in certain spots with the risk of an item being confiscated if it is placed elsewhere. While many of these boundaries are often drawn under the guise of teaching respect for self and space, as well as for ease or organization, do we spend time thinking about how each of these routines are permissive or restrictive? Does it matter? Should we care? Whose interest is put first in a place designed for children?

Going from room to room, we continued mapping these potentialities and their unintended consequences. Collectively, we wondered, what other boundary-making practices in the everydayness of school-knowing-becoming were threaded throughout its physical borders and how were we complicit in proliferating those boundaries? What did the boundaries of schools make the students in our care feel they needed to produce?

These are questions that our time on Nose Hill begs us to consider when thinking about literacies, particularly the literacies of space and the ways these literacies become embodied (habitual practices and responses) and how these embodiments enter into relationships of power.

Questions to Consider as You Think About Your Own Boundary-Making Practices

- Why are boundaries constantly being drawn around the physical spaces in schools?
- What other boundaries (social, political, emotional, economic) do these physical boundaries produce?
- Are we worried young people are at risk of using the space "wrong" or worried about the supervision in each space? Who is worried? Why are they worried?
- What are the risks?
- Once a space is prioritized for children, how are they limited by this?
- Who defines what is best done in a particular space?

Moving More Like the Beaver While Making Boundaries

Physical boundaries create habituated understandings and responses—or embodied literacies—connected to people, places, and things. As Jaye has written elsewhere (Thiel & Jones, 2017), these embodied ways of knowing teach us something about how to perform, how we are read by others, and who we are allowed to be in any given space at any given time. Just as Nose Hill brought our attention to the university's power to make us feel as though we *must* craft writing there, things serve as "actants" (Bennett, 2010) in our lives, too. They make us respond—do something—and sometimes these responses yield unintended consequences (like us being nervous about finishing a draft of this chapter before the workshop concluded). With this in mind, something as simple as a notebook has the potential to open someone up to a world of writing as well as limit their willingness to write, predicated on the different ways boundary-making also makes the people within these boundaries.

If we are to move like the beaver, we know that some boundary-making opens up an opportunity for others to thrive. But if we move like the colonists, we know that boundary-making can also limit opportunities and limit who gets to thrive. In a way, we must think of ourselves as a keystone species when we create boundaries. We must think of ourselves like the beaver. Or at the very least, we must see ourselves as playing a role in how keystone species are able to freely move about the physical and virtual lines of borders, margins, and edges. We are not making these boundaries alone nor for only ourselves. To illustrate this point further, we look to the book.

Text serves as a kind of keystone species for a school. Text most certainly serves as a keystone to traditional literacy practice. Most often, text in schools is situated within the bounded space of books that are also situated in the bounded spaces of libraries. But these boundaries are semi-permeable. Books are carried in and out. Therefore, where books are located matters. How access to those books is granted matters. Who has access to those books matters.

Books also carry readers near and far. They take readers to unimaginable worlds and grant us the ability to take a long look at what is happening in our own backyards. Books have the potential for exploring, crying, learning, crafting, thinking, clarifying, dawning, emerging. Clearly, books are powerful, powerful actants/things with the ability to make someone feel large. Which also means, they have the potential to make someone feel small.

Take the leveled reader—both bound and binding. Leveled readers operate within boundaries—bound by number and types of words, bound by the little alphabetic letter or number written in the corner of the cover (i.e., Level A, Level B, Level C, and so on), bounded by formulaic programming. At the same time, leveled readers (a type of book) serve as boundaries: binding people into groups, categories, and labels, such as "struggling readers," which in turn becomes embodied as its own literacy, sticking around well into adulthood. Who among us has not had a conversation at some time or another where an adult announces themselves as a "nonreader" adding, "I always struggled with reading in school."

Alas,

> The entanglement of the discursive and the material implies continuously mutating and enacting boundaries so that words and things become provisionally constructed and mutually distinct. Individuations occurs through boundary-making practices whereby the superposition of construed or mutually distinct entities, such as dead or alive, are seemingly cut out of the fold and separated.
>
> (De Freitas & Sinclair, 2014, p. 49)

The word, "struggling" falls out of adult mouths as easy as breath, as if that way of knowing has become a part of the body, a self-knowing that is as fluid as water and sticks like sap. An embodied literacy of being a struggling reader. These are the unintended consequences of boundaries, the ones that do harm. The ones that look more like the colonizer than the beaver.

If we are to move like the beaver, we know that denying someone a book because she failed to return the last book she borrowed just would not do. If we are to move like the beaver, we know that leveling books and labeling young folks as a "type" of reader just would not do.

If we are to move like the beaver, we understand that there are an infinite number of ways to think about and know the world in which we live, and our relations almost always limit the possibilities within it. If we move like the beaver, we understand that "relations of thinking and knowing require care" (Puig de la Bellcosta 2012, p. 198). To move with care is to move like the beaver.

Carefully Making-Knowing-Becoming With Boundaries

The earth makes all kinds of boundaries such as rivers, oceans, mountains, and plateaus. People make all kinds of boundaries within the earth. We will never NOT make boundaries. We make them with every move we make and with every word we utter. Like the beaver, we are a boundary-making species. It is the way we engage with the power-relations that emerge through those boundary-making practices that we must pay close attention to. We recognize how difficult this work is in an educational world where we are told to make quick decisions and complete a multitude of tasks daily. As Melody reflected,

> As a goal-oriented person, who rushes too often, who does not often pause to consider how seemingly everyday occurrences impact both the human and the non-human in our environment, I was struck with the notion that this venue, this workshop, this experience had led me to a place that I had not gone before and in all likelihood, had previously purposely avoided. School administrators, with their endless list of things to do, may be easily led away from taking the time and energy required to consider how space, place and being impact the students in their buildings and ultimately how children spend their time and energy while at school.
>
> (Reflective notes, 2017)

Perhaps if we are to make boundaries more care-fully, we must slow down and notice how we are relationally engaging in and always entangled with people, places, and things and that our pedagogical decisions as literacy educators are no exception. It seems this is our ethical responsibility as teachers, as researchers, as humans. But how do we start with such an overwhelming task?

Start With a Diffractive Mapping

Take a large sheet of paper. Draw or write the thing/action, creating boundaries in the middle of the paper/space. Collaboratively think of all the possibilities and potentialities this particular boundary may create and ask yourself who or what is being served by this boundary. Is it worth it? You might be surprised at what you find.

There is much we can learn about boundary-making from watching keystone species like the beaver. And there is much we can learn from walking in places like Nose Hill. The earth knows things our bodies have forgotten, and we believe it is high time we got back to those ways of knowing. As Shiva (2009) writes,

> For centuries, the human mind has been shaped by education that treated the universe as a machine, and humans as cogs in the machine. We have to begin again, with a new education for a new imagination. We have to imagine our way forward at a time when the present trajectory is closing the future for humans. And with that new imagination we have to act to generate a future—with care and compassion, with hope and courage.
>
> (p. ix)

If the earth has taught us nothing else, it has taught us that boundaries are not static, which means we do not have to keep doing things the same ways we have always done them or the ways colonizers did before us. We have the ability to redraw boundaries and redraw the ways we engage in something as seemingly small as placemaking in the literacy classroom because like the beaver, the size of something does not always mirror its impact.

So, go forth teachers, and make-work like the beaver.

References

Anzaldúa, G. (1987). *Borderlands/La frontera: The new mestiza*. San Francisco, CA: Aunt Loot Books.
Barad, K. (2007). *Meeting the universe halfway: Quantum physics and the entanglement of matter and meaning*. Durham, NC: Duke University Press.
Bennett, J. (2010). *Vibrant matter: A political ecology of things*. Durham, NC: Duke University Press.
Braidotti, R. (2013a). Becoming-world. In R. Braidotti, P. Hanafin, & B. Blaagaard (Eds.), *After cosmopolitanism* (pp. 8–27). New York, NY: Routledge.
Braidotti, R. (2013b). *The posthuman*. Cambridge, UK: Polity Press.

De Freitas, E., & Sinclair, N. (2014). *Mathematics and the body: Material entanglements in the classroom*. Cambridge, UK: Cambridge University Press.
Ingold, T. (2016). *Lines*. New York, NY: Routledge Classics.
Keystone species. (n.d.). *In google dictionary*. Retrieved from www.google.com/search?q=what+is+a+keystone+species&oq=what+is+a+keystone+species&aqs=chrome.69i57j0l5.5303j0j4&sourceid=chrome&ie=UTF-8
Massey, D. (2005). *For space*. Los Angeles, CA: Sage Publications.
Puig de la Bellcosta, M. (2012). "Nothing comes without its world": Thinking with care. *Sociology Review*, 60(2), 197–216.
Shiva, V. (2009). Forward. In M. McKenzie, P. Hart, H. Bai, & B. Jickling (Eds.), *Fields of green: Restorying culture, environment, and education*. Cresskill, NJ: Hampton Press.
Thiel, J., & Jones, S. (2017). The literacies of things: Reconfiguring the material-discursive production of race and class in an informal learning center. *Journal of Early Childhood Literacies*, 17(3), 315–335.
Tsing, A. (2012). Unruly edges: Mushrooms as companion species. *Environmental Humanities*, 1, 141–154.

6 The Literacy Is in the Listening

Honouring Multiplicity and Interrelatedness as Early Grade Teachers

Maren Aukerman and Krista Jensen

Contemporary literacy education frequently treats children as empty vessels, seeking to fill them up with the right knowledge and strategies. Our discussion here aims to trouble models of literacy education in which children are viewed as isolated minds to be filled up. Instead, we see literacy—as well as the teaching of literacy—as fundamentally an act of relating. We argue that teaching and learning literacy can become more meaningfully relational when educators honour *multiplicity* and *interconnectedness*. What could it mean to re-envision classroom literacy with multiplicity and interconnectedness at the centre?

We use multiplicity to refer to the wide range of creative ideas, perspectives, and possibilities generated by diverse thinkers who bring their unique relationships with the world around them into the reading and writing that they do—readings and writings that cannot be predetermined by even the most thoughtful teacher. *Interconnectedness*, in turn, refers to the relations humans forge with the material world around them and with each other—connections that some have described as posthuman, in recognition of the key ways in which humans act "in concert with changing networks of people, objects, histories, and institutions" (Nichols & Campano, 2017, p. 246).

In this chapter, we describe three teaching dilemmas: for each, we highlight how a transformation that takes multiplicity and/or interrelatedness seriously can deepen literacy teaching to better meet children where they are. We imagine these transformations as ways of supporting students towards developing a fuller sense of identity as readers and writers as well as a sense of belonging within a classroom literacy community. We close with several teaching applications as examples of how classroom practice might, concretely, embody these transformations.

> ### Considerations for Honouring Multiplicity in Student-Teacher Relations
>
> We do not believe that honouring multiplicity and highlighting interconnectedness lie in a fixed set of procedures. Instead, as teachers, we have found it most useful to pose ourselves questions that set us on the

> path to more fruitful kinds of relating and interrelating. A sampling of such questions:
>
> - What is the most unexpected thing a child said today? Did I invite that moment? How did I follow up? How could I learn more about that child's perspective?
> - Which child bores, unsettles, offends, or annoys me? What I could do to move towards seeing and understanding what that child brings, notices, and understands?
> - What was I afraid might happen the last time I corrected, ignored, or glossed over a student idea that sounded wrong to me? What would it mean to embrace that fear? How can I use such a moment to demonstrate courage and to offer deep listening?

Teaching Dilemmas and Transformations

Dilemma: Lack of Belonging

The first dilemma we highlight is by no means unique to literacy instruction. As a grade 2 student, my (Maren's) child said: "I feel like I'm trapped inside a box" at school. Like arguably many children, she did not have a sense of belonging and purpose there. While a variety of experiences can contribute to such alienation, one common aspect is feeling unseen or unheard (my daughter: "No one listens!"). Children's individual stories, histories, and identities are part of the inevitable fabric of a classroom's multiplicity, yet children often do not feel these have a place in school, and they have little reason to listen to feel connected to peers, whose stories they never get to learn. They may feel that their teacher does not understand or even care about them. While educators sometimes do talk about ways to build classroom community, those efforts are not necessarily connected to the multiplicity of meanings children assign to their worlds, much less to the things they as individuals find meaningful.

Transformation: A Classroom Culture of Belonging and Dialogue

Through opportunities to make sense of each other's ideas, emotions, and histories, students can join together in an ongoing, collaborative dialogue—one that depends on the teacher establishing meaningful platforms for personal sharing about children's experiences and perspectives and for student-driven dialogue.

Establish Meaningful Platforms for Personal Sharing About Children's Experiences and Perspectives

Teachers can create opportunities for students to share and hear personal stories. The resultant sharing, whether in writing, talk, or some other medium, provides glimpses of the humanness that we need to see in each other, stories that highlight both our multiplicity and our interconnectedness. These glimpses may initially be small, but they enable those in the classroom community to become curious about each other, to pose questions, to engage differently. Across time, the platforms for sharing could become generative spaces for a sense of classroom belonging.

Establish Meaningful Literacy Platforms for Student-Driven Dialogue

For children to believe their voices matter, they must have things to talk about that matter to them—and they must have things to discuss where divergent ideas can emerge in the first place. This is where stories and other more traditional written texts come in: these are places for children to bring themselves into their reading and have those selves become visible and important during classroom talk. Teachers might facilitate this process by highlighting different student ideas and by regularly posing authentic questions—those where there is no correct answer. But establishing meaningful platforms, we believe, depends equally on listening for what ideas children bring to the table and allowing these, whatever they are, to meaningfully shape the dialogue. This brings us to our second dilemma.

Dilemma: The Privileging of "Right Answers"

Upon learning that I (Krista) would be writing a chapter with Maren, a University of Calgary professor whom I had not yet met, I read up on some of her published work. Over the past two decades, Maren has researched ways in which teachers can facilitate dialogue that makes space for children to share their textual perspectives and engage with each other's perspectives more deeply (e.g., Aukerman, 2007, 2008; Aukerman, Johnson, & Chambers Schuldt, 2017). What I read struck a chord. She wrote that "[e]very meaning a child constructs for a text is, in some important way, a reflection of who s/he is. And valuing children for who they are and for what they bring . . . means respecting and welcoming the full range of knowledge and practices they draw upon, including their meaning-making repertoires" (Aukerman, 2015, p. 55). As a Calgary-based elementary teacher with 17 years of experience, it was a moment of embarrassed enlightenment. I had always given all students voice, but too often it was insincere, I realized upon reflection. Many children had the chance to answer, but it was the child's answer that matched my own that I often lingered on. I had missed out on moments of learning and valuing the ideas of the rest.

I (Krista) may not be unique in my struggle to fully honour the multiplicity of divergent student interpretations. Indeed, both teachers and students often associate being a "good reader" with getting right answers or at least with having a textual understanding matching the teacher's interpretation (Aukerman & Chambers Schuldt, 2015). Students whose ideas about stories do not easily conform can inadvertently be labeled or silenced (Hall, 2009; Lewis, 1993). Over time, students may come to see themselves as part of an intellectual hierarchy rather than as valued thinkers (cf. Aukerman & Chambers Schuldt, 2015).

Transformation: Honouring the Multiplicity of Children's Perspectives

Valuing the multiplicity of ideas depends, first of all, on a shift from being the primary arbiter of truth, as a teacher. This shift might begin with an acknowledgement: "In our classroom community, we don't all think the same. We all learn from seeking to understand and responding to each other's perspectives." To invite this idea to become reality as classroom interaction unfolds, we suggest that teachers avoid evaluation and invite elaboration (Aukerman, 2008).

Avoid Evaluation

What is possibly the hardest part of building a community centred in student ideas is for the teacher to steer clear of telling the students they are right or wrong or indirectly favoring certain ideas. While it may not be possible at all times, having a teacher who is non-evaluative for substantial stretches of time can play in critical role in allowing students to see their own and each other's ideas as important and worthy of consideration (Aukerman, 2007). Trusting students is key here: it is easier not to evaluate if teachers trust students to work things through. Teachers can still express interest in student ideas—"I never thought of that!"—but must remember to offer such encouragement to every student, not just to students whose ideas align with those of the teacher.

Invite Elaboration

To be valued intellectually is to have others genuinely believe one's ideas are worth fleshing out, developing, and further discussing. This is particularly important with students whose ideas may seem less conventional or even difficult to understand. While requests to elaborate can be posed fruitfully in many different ways, never underestimate the power of a simple "Tell me more." Of course, such invitations only matter if one is prepared to listen, and to listen deeply, to what a child says next.

Dilemma: Everyday Sensemaking Is Not Valued

Every child is engaged in a lifelong process of "reading the world" (Freire, 1985), making sense of the world according to their interest (Kress,

1997). Everything they encounter—a sunset, a smile, the sound of a distant train—becomes a text at the moment the child constructs, shares, or even ponders possible meaning(s) for it. Kress offers the example of a 4-year-old girl who observes her father biting out of a piece of toast, looks at the resulting shape, and then announces, "You made it like a crocodile!" (p. 87). Often, as in that case, sensemakers assign *words* to the texts in their world, but certainly that is only one possible dimension in everyday sensemaking; sometimes texts evoke emotion or provoke action—also ways of constructing meaning.

Yet the varied and vibrant sensemaking in which children engage during their everyday lives is not routinely considered reading at all, and perhaps because reading is seen as disconnected from everyday sensemaking, students may not connect story reading to their everyday lived experience of making sense of the world. Their enormous competence as sensemakers is often rendered invisible when they are asked to make sense of a classroom text, particularly when that text is culturally, linguistically, or thematically unfamiliar (Hull & Rose, 1990; Lewis, 1993; Moll & Whitmore, 1993).

Transformation: Engage With Children's Everyday Sensemaking

If every child comes into the classroom a sensemaker, teachers can build upon this resource by encouraging everyday sensemaking (Warren, Ballenger, Ogonowski, Rosebery, & Hudicourt-Barnes, 2001) and by highlighting its interrelationship with reading as we more commonly think of it.

Make Space for Everyday Sensemaking

Teachers can make time for children to read the world—to notice and discuss their observations of people, places, things, sensations, emotions, and so much more—and the possible meanings they assign to these. One of the classroom rituals that struck me (Maren) most when I heard Kristin talk about her teaching was her commitment to taking her students regularly to a beautiful place on campus where they could consciously notice, explore, and talk about the natural world. Simple questions may be all that are needed: "What do you notice?," "What does that mean to you?," "How did you decide?"

Relate Everyday Sensemaking to More Traditional Literacy Practices

Teachers can help children—particularly those who may be less confident as readers—become consciously aware of the ways in which they are already making sense of the world. Because this sensemaking is reading, children are reading already, even those who haven't mastered decoding yet. Rather than treating reading as something different, we should treat children's reading of the words in traditional stories as an interconnected part of a greater whole. Children should have opportunities to discuss how reading and writing might be similar to, and occasionally different from, other strands in a grand reading tapestry of everyday sensemaking. With opportunity, children can even take note of these resonances themselves: one of Krista's students recently said, during an outdoor experience in which they looked for evidence of spring, "Hey, this is like we are reading nature!"

Classroom Applications

Preamble: The Gut Check

We believe that enacting the transformations above depend, in part, on the spirit of the teacher. First, there is a need for *vulnerability* (Johnson & LaBelle, 2017). Are you willing to share authentically with your class? Can you bring forward, into the classroom, stories that bring a lump to your throat, that make you pause mid-sentence to take a quick breath?

Second, there is a need for *authentic curiosity* (Aukerman, 2008). Are you truly interested in the ideas your students share? Do you genuinely want to better understand what they see and experience?

Finally, there is a need for *trust* (Zittoun, 2014). Can you let go of full control of the conversation? Do you believe that children learn things of value from each other that you have not directly sculpted and predetermined? Are you able to let go of the "teachable moment" when it would interfere with children's collaborative sensemaking, trusting that, across time, they will still learn what they need to know?

Here are several concrete suggestions for bringing these transformations to life, with this disposition of vulnerability, authentic curiosity, and trust in your mind. Except where noted, "I" and "we" will refer to Krista and her students in the next sections.

Belonging Through Belongings

Everyday sensemaking can flourish when children have the opportunity to talk about physical objects—artifacts—that matter to them. I ask my students to decorate and bring in a "Bag of Belonging" filled with items that are important to them (See Figure 9). Stories, the ways that children (and grown-ups) make sense of the world, often dwell within the mementos we keep. When asked to curate items, the children and I sift through our trinkets, holding them in our hands and remembering, something like the elderly Miss Nancy Alison Delacourt Cooper does with objects in *Wilfrid Gordon McDonald Partridge* (Fox, 1989). Other rich texts that explore the stories of objects include *Shi-shi-etko* (Campbell, 2005) and *Yard Sale* (Bunting, 2015).

When I first began doing this activity, I called these collections "important bags." I changed the name to Bags of Belonging, though, to highlight *why* we were engaging in the sharing. First, the objects are not just things that are important in the abstract—they are belongings, things that have a particular, meaningful interrelationship with the child who chose them. It is this "belongingness" to which we need to be listening, as we hear each other's stories. Furthermore, we are not conducting a simple "show and tell" of items—the work we do together around the bags and their contents is all about building a sense of belonging amongst ourselves.

Each day, a few bags at a time, the belongings are laid out, their original curator unspecified. The children look carefully at these representations of a classmate's life and then read the belongings to anticipate to whom they may belong, for example, "I think this set belongs to Thomas because he said he has a dog, and I know he likes hockey." This everyday sensemaking of the objects also shows a listening to and a reading of each other. Even if the set does not belong to Thomas, Thomas may feel seen by his peers. And the conversation takes off from there, as students ask questions about one another, and as they say, "Hey! Me, too!" to someone who might have seemed too different to care about the day before. There is an intentional space for us to make sense of one another.

And then, after the sharing and the layering of same-nesses, after the moments of "I've never heard of that before," the students write. Some children describe a treasured belonging, some students tell stories about their belongings, some students sketch and label and caption. Through intermingling and relating objects, images, words, and selves, we broaden our collective understanding of what we understand text to be.

As we share these student-composed pieces, we continue to build our sense of belonging. Students are asked to describe how they think their objects and stories connect with those of others. They usually start out with the obvious—"Jana brought a shell, and I brought a shell, so ours go together." "Thomas and I both wrote about hockey." But, when given time, the connections can deepen. "Abuk and I both told sad stories." "Amar and I both had to move far away from home." (Such comments reveal that where we are does not feel like home yet.) By illuminating interconnectedness between our stories and our belongings and each other, we build a kind of commonplace within our multiplicity, described more in the next section.

Commonplaces

For the past several centuries, readers have engaged in "textual marking, re-marking, and response activities" (Sumara, 2002, p. 241), writing and adding materials, ideas, and jottings as they read. Such writing/response transforms the initial text being read into a new hybrid text, called a commonplace book. A commonplace text developed as a class can become a touchstone of personal and collective selves: multiple ideas from multiple people come together to form the extra/ordinary.

In my classroom, I begin by sharing and re-sharing multiple rich, layered picture books, so my students become familiar with a wide variety of books. As a class, we then decide on one or two favorites. We dialogue about why a particular book—which will become our commonplace book—is our favorite. What makes a book a favorite? What do you feel when we read it? What stories do you have that come from or relate to this one? This part can take time; I need to sit and listen, trusting the students and the process. In the past, I have sometimes been too restrictive (expecting everyone to connect with one book), hurried ("Do you have story yet? Think of a story!"), or judgmental (urging students to develop a "better" story to connect). I have found that such well-intended efforts can crush the purpose of the project and am learning to give more space.

Eventually, a child, often someone unexpected, shares that a certain page makes them feel something. It might be the picture, it might be the words, or most likely it is both. Often there are some beautiful "Me, too's." The remembering begins; my learning and deep listening are essential. The children tell stories that connect to the published text we are sharing, enabling me broaden my own understanding of what has been read and shared.

The children compose stories (in a variety of multimodal ways, through pictures and words), and we physically add these (think tape, staples, glue sticks, and improvised pockets!) to the published book, yielding layered stories. The commonplace book can create a space for sensemaking that honours all the ways of knowing that come through the door each year. It also publicly illustrates how a text/commonplace is transformed by the voices that we hear and the multiplicity of voices that we bring—that which is at the very heart of reading.

While picturebooks can serve as one kind of commonplace, other rich possibilities include options that are differently multimodal. For example, Maureen Boyd, Christopher Jarmark, and Brian Edmiston (2018) describe a second-grade classroom practice in which, over the course of a year, the children and their teacher developed a class handshake. Every week, a different child would add a new movement to the handshake, and children would pair off to practice the entire collaborative repertoire, adopting the actions suggested by peers but embodied with their own forms of expression. The students developed a shared history across time through their enactments (and even the inevitable missteps!) with each other. In short, whatever is built together as a space for sharing and for reflecting on each other's perspectives and experiences can become a commonplace—a place in which our multiplicity is both celebrated and brought together.

TAHQ Time

I (Maren) once heard an animated discussion among grade 2 students discussing the fairy tale "The Elves and the Shoemaker." What was most interesting to them was a question never directly addressed in the text: "How did the elves get into the shoemaker's house?" Their teacher, wisely, let the children talk at length about this question—one he confessed he would never have thought of himself—and the students developed all sorts of ideas, drawing on the words and illustrations in the version they were reading, as well as their own ideas about how elves and houses work. This teacher allowed the conversation to be driven by ideas the students offered and was genuinely curious about those ideas.

Children can thrive in such conversations, yet genuine dialogue of this sort remains rare in classrooms (Applebee, Langer, Nystrand, & Gamoran, 2003; Gallas, 1995; Nystrand, 1997). One way to make space for it is to deliberately set aside time for discussion that highlights the multiplicity of student ideas, an idea I (Maren) call Text/Artifact/Hypothesis/Question (TAHQ) Time. During TAHQ time, students are actively encouraged to explore their own and each other's ideas without the conversation being steered toward a predetermined learning outcome related to the content of the talk. Instead, the time is fully oriented toward uncovering, elaborating, and juxtaposing children's varied ideas about the text, artifact, hypothesis, and/or question on the table.

As the name suggests, TAHQ time can go beyond talking about traditional print-based texts. Children might talk about artifacts, whether the classroom silkworms or an assembled set of objects that beekeepers use or about geographical locations that trigger thinking. Karen Gallas (1995) discusses how first graders talked together to make sense of scientific phenomena, such as the question, "What is blood for?" In another example, a math teacher encouraged discussion prompted by a child's (Sean's) hypothesis that the number 6 could be both odd and even. Rather than correcting Sean and moving on, the teacher made space for the class to dialogue about his hypothesis (see https://deepblue.lib.umich.edu/handle/2027.42/65013 for the video and transcript).

TAHQ time is pan-disciplinary, and integrating it could happen in a variety of ways. It might arise organically, in response to moments when the teacher senses such talk could enrich children's collaborative sensemaking. One danger with this *ad hoc* approach, though, is that daily classroom practices might not provide enough openings for such talk, especially when curricular pressures are high. For this reason, teachers can set aside a time each day or at least each week for TAHQ time. In the classroom where "The Elves and the Shoemaker" conversation took place, students instigated TAHQ time on the fly throughout the day with their teacher's encouragement. But typically, there were also several days a week where the teacher set aside half an hour for deliberate, student-centred discussion about a text being read by the class; he found time for these discussions despite considerable curricular constraints because he saw them as so important (Aukerman & Chambers Schuldt, 2017).

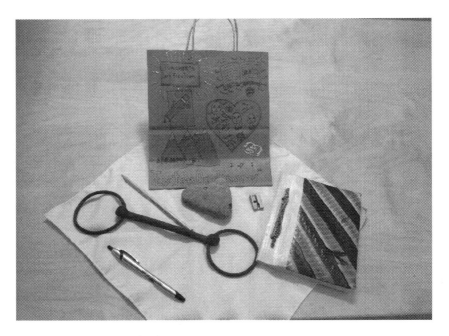

Figure 9 Krista's Bag of Belonging.

Beyond Formulas

We (Maren and Krista) do not offer these illustrative examples as a specific how-to manual, and what we have provided as potential classroom applications is certainly not an exhaustive list. We hope, however, that these suggested classroom applications can help flesh out the imperative to transform education in ways that honour multiplicity and highlight interconnectedness as children make sense of themselves and the world around them. We argue that educators owe it to all children to build a culture of belonging-in-multiplicity, not just in the name of their literacy but in the name of their humanity as growing readers, writers, and observers of the world with one another.

My (Krista's) Bag of Belonging. The bag itself is decorated with visual representations, both drawn and collaged. The horse's bit, which was found rummaging through my grandparents' barn (a story in itself!), is an example of an artifact that holds many of my stories—riding horses as a child, time spent with my grandparents, and the family history of settling the land in 1906, to name a few.

References

Applebee, A. N., Langer, J. A., Nystrand, M., & Gamoran, A. (2003). Discussion-based approaches to developing understanding: Classroom instruction and student performance in middle and high school English. *American Educational Research Journal*, 40(3), 685–730.

Aukerman, M. (2007). When reading it wrong is getting it right: Shared evaluation pedagogy among "struggling" fifth grade readers. *Research in the Teaching of English*, 42(1), 56–103.

Aukerman, M. (2008). In praise of wiggle room: Locating comprehension in unlikely places. *Language Arts*, 86(1), 52–60.

Aukerman, M. (2015). How should readers develop across time? Mapping change without a deficit perspective. *Language Arts*, 93(1), 57–64.

Aukerman, M., & Chambers Schuldt, L. (2015). Children's perceptions of their reading ability and epistemic roles in monologically and dialogically organized bilingual classrooms. *Journal of Literacy Research*, 47(1), 115–145. doi:10.1177/1086296x15586959

Aukerman, M., & Chambers Schuldt, L. (2017). Bucking the authoritative script of a mandated curriculum. *Curriculum Inquiry*, 47(4), 411–437. doi:10.1080/03626784.2017.1368353

Aukerman, M., Johnson, E. M., & Chambers Schuldt, L. (2017). Reciprocity of student and teacher discourse practices in monologically and dialogically organized text discussion. *Journal of Language and Literacy Education*, 13(2), 1–52.

Boyd, M. P., Jarmark, C. J., & Edmiston, B. (2018). Building bridges: Coauthoring a class handshake, building a classroom community. *Pedagogies: An International Journal*, 1–23. doi:10.1080/1554480X.2018.1437731

Bunting, E. (2015). *Yard sale*. Somerville, MA: Candlewick Press.

Campbell, N. (2005). *Shi-shi-etko*. Toronto, ON: Groundwood Books.

Fox, M. (1989). *Wilfrid Gordon McDonald partridge*. Brooklyn, NY: Kane and Miller Book Publishers.

Freire, P. (1985). Reading the world and reading the word. *Language Arts*, 62, 15–22.

Gallas, K. (1995). *Talking their way into science: Hearing children's questions and theories, responding with curricula*. New York, NY: Teachers College Press.

Hall, L. A. (2009). Struggling reader, struggling teacher: An examination of student-teacher transactions with reading instruction and text in social studies. *Research in the Teaching of English*, 43(3), 286–309.

Hull, G., & Rose, M. (1990). "This wooden shack place": The logic of an unconventional reading. *College Composition and Communication*, 41(3), 287–298.

Johnson, Z. D., & LaBelle, S. (2017). An examination of teacher authenticity in the college classroom. *Communication Education*, 66(4), 423–439. doi:10.1080/03634523.2017.1324167

Kress, G. (1997). *Before writing: Rethinking the paths to literacy*. London, UK: Routledge.

Lewis, C. (1993). "Give people a chance": Acknowledging social differences in reading. *Language Arts*, 70, 454–461.

Moll, L., & Whitmore, K. (1993). Vygotsky in classroom practice: Moving from individual transmission to social transaction. In E. A. Forman, N. Minick, & C. A. Stone (Eds.), *Contexts for learning: Social dynamics in children's development* (pp. 19–41). New York, NY: Oxford University Press.

Nichols, T. P., & Campano, G. (2017). Post-humanism and literacy studies. *Language Arts*, 94(4), 245–251.

Nystrand, M. (1997). *Opening dialogue: Understanding the dynamics of language and learning in the English classroom*. New York, NY: Teachers College Press.

Sumara, D. (2002). Creating commonplaces for interpretation: Literary anthropology and literacy education research. *Journal of Literacy Research*, *34*(2), 237–260.

Warren, B., Ballenger, C., Ogonowski, M., Rosebery, A. S., & Hudicourt-Barnes, J. (2001). Rethinking diversity in learning science: The logic of everyday sensemaking. *Journal of Research in Science Teaching*, *38*(5), 529–552.

Zittoun, T. (2014). Trusting for learning. In P. Linnell & I. Markova (Eds.), *Dialogic approaches to trust in communication* (pp. 125–151). Charlotte, NC: Information Age.

7 On Being Thrown Together
Living and Learning in Diversity

Guy Merchant and Divya Devender-Kraft

Population mobility is not a new phenomenon. In fact, human history is patterned by movement, by responses to changes in the more-than-human environment—to drought, famine and other disasters—as much as to the upheavals of human conflict, economic necessity, and ambition. Throughout the 20th century and into the early part of this century, technological developments, both in transport and communication, have had the effect of "shrinking" the world so that now mobility is more of a global phenomenon than ever before (Evans, 2017). Such mobility is both material and social, and it leavens contemporary living through the many different ways in which people carry their histories with them. In post-colonial settings, these histories come into contact with one another to create complex intersections, referencing different senses of being, different senses of belonging, and of place (Massey, 2005). Negotiating these intersections gives texture to generational interactions and to family life, as well as to local and national politics and policies (Barley & Merchant, 2016). This negotiation also produces particular kinds of places; schools, as we shall see, are often on the front line in this respect.

Diversity in Schools

In the contemporary world, children from a wide range of cultural and linguistic backgrounds are "thrown together," helping to produce very particular places such as schools and classrooms which as a result become an important meeting place or contact zone. Students from "elsewhere" are identified in particular ways—as newly arrived, as ELL students, or as children with limited formal schooling and they come into contact with each other, with teachers, specialist teachers, and various resources. They are brought into relation with these things, in place, and with one another in the process of becoming a classroom community using the materials at hand, governed by teaching approaches, routines, lesson plans, and other technologies. Their varied histories and memories entangle with those sedimented in host communities, dominant social practices, and institutions, in the human as well as the more-than-human, adding richness and depth.

But this process of entangling is not frictionless; in fact, it is fraught with tension and challenge. Alongside all the potential of becoming, there are also uncertainty, confusion, and sometimes deep feelings of dislocation, loss, sadness, or pain. Yet at the same time, diversity in all its forms is a formidable resource, weaving together different identities, perspectives, and cultural practices which all add to the liveliness of the everyday.

As educators, we are committed to the positive benefits of this intermingling, to what has been called an asset model (Fishman, 1980), but we are also mindful of the everyday challenges of learning and teaching "on the front line." In this sense, the pressing questions for us are:

- How might we better understand these processes of becoming and provide support for teachers and learners who are on the front line?
- How do we help teachers to bring out the best in students and to help them to realize their potential?
- How do we equip teachers with resources and support to use literacy teaching and learning to draw out, uncover, access, and empower students?

There are no easy answers, but we work from the basic premise that *all* students have significant cultural resources. Helping students to share *who* they are is a process of being and becoming empowered participants in classroom communities and society at large. This underlines the importance of creating caring environments in which students can trust in the fact that teachers and other adults respect and value what they bring and where they feel safe enough to share who they are.

In what follows, we explore some key themes relating to identity and diversity, following the life story of one particular student who became part of numerous social and cultural congeries, moving between South East Asia, the Far East, the Middle East, the Caribbean, and North America. From the very start, though, we must acknowledge and underline that students have many different histories and trajectories—there are no set patterns. Nevertheless, we hope that some of the key themes we identify here will resonate with the experience of others. We use this material to illustrate how shifts of identity happen over time as a result of interactions with materials, texts, educators, and other students in surprising and often unpredictable ways. These shifts can help students to realize who they are, their place in this world, and how to use literacy to their advantage. In particular, we underline the role of teachers and the nature of the established relationship with students and the classroom contexts that they help shape. We focus on four specific, but overlapping, themes:

- the affective textures associated with change and mobility;
- the influence of different encounters with texts;

- the role of teachers and the importance of building relationships where students feel respected and valued for what they bring; and
- students writing themselves and their experiences into the texts they produce and the therapeutic power of this process.

These themes are not exhaustive, nor do they directly address the key questions we identify; they simply arise out of the material we are working with and in so doing begin to shed some light on those questions, opening up areas for discussion and further exploration.

Affective Texture in the Contact Zone

As we think through the educational implications of population mobility through one telling case, we use narrative fragments from a first-hand account to illuminate experience, particularly, the experience of school and of schooling. Of course, one story cannot ever speak for all the diversity of circumstances, things, and personal responses that pattern experience, but it is our hope that its themes might speak to some important issues that practitioners grapple with on a daily basis.

The story begins at home:

> She was born in Southern India where the regional language is Tamil, but although her Grandma would talk to her and tell stories in Tamil her parents would always speak in English. Her mum taught her to read. She remembers a book called 'Penelope Strawberry'. Later on, she enjoyed reading Enid Blyton. Growing up she wanted to be George from the Famous Five, eating cake and biscuits, going camping and solving mysteries! Things you just wouldn't do in India. She had no idea at that time that she would end up living in Canada.

Pratt's notion of a *contact zone* is useful to reflect on here, as we see how the beginning of this story weaves together a number of different cultural reference points. The contact zone is realized in the way in which the regional language and geographical context are inflected with the traces of a colonial history (in this case, the British in India) and the way that these are then overlaid with the post-colonial influence of the English language, as well as with a very specific version of Englishness, captured by Blyton's Famous Five (2011) eating cakes and biscuits. However, there is no sense of conflict in the narrative, merely a complex backstory of things coming into contact. In defining the contact zone, Pratt (1991) explains how she uses the term:

> to refer to social spaces where cultures meet, clash, and grapple with each other, often in contexts of highly asymmetrical relations of power,

such as colonialism, slavery, or their aftermaths as they are lived out today.

(p. 34)

And in a sense, although power asymmetry and language politics haunt this particular narrative, they are not directly caught in the gaze of the storyteller but remain in the background as reminiscences of the joy of reading and the desire to partake in particular activities like those described in the book.

Perhaps for young children the affective texture of events is more salient than it is for adults—it would be hard to say—but, certainly, as we see here, it remains in memory and adds depth and specificity to what is recalled, as the following extract suggests.

> *She remembers kindergarten when she was sitting with 45 other children at wooden desks in rows facing forward—the boy beside her was pinching her while they were doing a spelling test on lined paper. And she remembers bawling her eyes out when she went to school for the first time.*

Here physical discomfort and anxiety are interlaced with memories of the school as a *place*, the materiality of the wooden desks, the lined paper, as well as with the rules and routines of classroom life. These disparate elements combine to give specificity to the lived experience.

Later on, following a move to the United Arab Emirates, recollections centre on different feelings—those of anxiety and alienation.

> *The teacher didn't like her. She thought she was strange. Once she called her parents to complain that she was nasty to other children when she was playing. She felt shame. In school she didn't understand what was expected of her. She was with 10 other kids—Australian, English. She felt alone. They had to learn Arabic—that caused her a lot of anxiety and stress. She didn't understand it all. She learned the alphabet, but that was about it.*

In this new contact zone, the complex of relations and emotions takes precedence over any curriculum content, which in this description becomes peripheral. For a Tamil speaker with a strong background in English, Arabic seems to be an additional, and perhaps unnecessary, burden, and the experience of schooling is a source of unease and confusion.

These recollections help to underline the complexity of educational experience, a complexity that defies any attempt to simplify it in terms of language or ethnicity. Of course, we are not the first to note this—when Miller (1983) set out to investigate the language histories of London school children, she encountered something very similar, often coming face to face with feelings of vulnerability and loss. This led her to suggest experiences of mobility and migration could be painful and unpredictable for children and young people, but more than anything, they were ungeneralizable, always unique as students entered into the contact zone.

Encounters With Text

Encounters with textual material pattern our experiences of schooling, and they are often quite vivid. In this account, the very early experiences of reading in English were a powerful influence. Not only did they involve enjoying *Penelope Strawberry* (Fisher, 1979) and Enid Blyton (2011) but also included particular approaches to literacy instruction in school—specific pedagogies such as rote learning, memorizing, and repeating poetry.

However, as time went on, the texts encountered in school began to play a more significant role. Literature, in particular, provided important messages, which in times of turbulence and uncertainty seemed to offer a sense of stability and purpose. Here, perhaps rather surprisingly, it is Charlotte Bronte who is identified as a key influence:

> *In Grade 8 she read Jane Eyre. She read that book over and over again for many reasons. Believe it or not she could identify with this English girl—alone—carving her way through a hostile environment. That gave her hope—a vision. She understood her feelings. It gave her hope and inspiration.*

Maybe as a result of finding some solace in this English literature classic, a new-found academic confidence began to emerge. Opting to remain silent in class—always a preferred position—was now no longer necessary:

> *Her confidence to speak up came in English . . . . there was one time when a Hardy book, probably Tess, resonated with her, she felt comfortable enough to share it. She just said what she was thinking out loud and the teacher was amazed. As was the rest of the class. The book brought it out of her.*

What at first sight might seem rather like a gradual, even familiar, journey through English language texts, is not actually so straightforward. The texts are replayed through very different experiences, standing out here in contrast to learning Arabic and the student's earlier contact with Japanese language and culture.

It is worth returning to this here because whilst the experience of the Arabic language was not particularly positive, a certain curiosity patterns the less formal exposure to Japanese.

> *She remembers learning a bit of Japanese and numbers—she's not sure how she learned them. In Japan she watched cooking shows on TV. They said "Oishi!" which she knew meant delicious.*

Here it seems, there was no particular pressure to learn another language—Japanese—but being immersed in the culture, making friends with children of the same age, and encountering language through media seemed to constitute a more meaningful experience. And, of course, all these language experiences combine to create a very particular *textual fingerprint* fashioned from the specific cultural artifacts and the social and linguistic practices that were encountered. We are reminded of the work of Gutiérrez and her colleagues. In commenting on the lives of children of Mexican descent, they observe something similar. The children's experience was:

> textured with Spanish, English, and African-American dialect, as well as hip-hop vernacular; and multimodal signs ranging from familiar cultural artifacts to popular culture and school-related icons adorn their notebooks, backpacks, and drawings.
> (Gutiérrez, Bien, Selland, & Pierce, 2011, p. 235)

The hybrid and multimodal meaning-making practices described in the studies the authors report on interweaves to create rich and complex contexts for identity. Recognition of this complexity invites an approach that acknowledges how cultures and identities intersect with both formal and informal learning in specific contexts or contact zones, and in so doing, they underline the role played by a variety of texts.

Teachers and Schools

In the formal context of school, children are regularly plunged into a dense world of materials, discursive practices, and relationships that may be challenging for them to interpret. The same is evident here. In this particular story, the earlier description of rows of wooden desks facing forward and spelling tests on lined paper redolent of school life in India in the 1980s exemplifies this. But teachers, their pedagogy and practices can create equally strong impressions.

> *In India they used to rank kids—and she was very aware of her position in the class. Her mum used to teach her at home. She was never number 1 but she was always number 2 or number 3.*

Here, a school culture and ethos that instills individual competitiveness is described, with the account suggesting an aspiration to achieve—to attain that illusive number 1. But although such a system is enacted by individual teachers, their institutional behaviour is given force through the use of the plural pronoun *they*.

On Being Thrown Together   121

Considering school's approach to discipline evokes a similar theme. A later description of schooling in India, for instance, refers to school practices rather than individual teachers:

> *Punishments were strict. If your shoes weren't clean, you would have to walk around barefoot for the rest of the day on rocks and pebbles between classes.*

Memories of a harsh and uncompromising approach to discipline are reiterated:

> *When they were in class, they weren't allowed to speak unless the teacher called their name, and if they caught you speaking, you would be sent outside—which was humiliating—or you had to stand on your chair in front of the whole class.*

But there were other sources of conflict, too, mainly because this school was run by Catholic nuns, and their practices ran counter to local family traditions. The tension between home and school culture were stark. For example:

> *Each day started with The Lord's Prayer. It wasn't her religious background. Her grandmother thought the Christians were trying to brainwash them, so she filled her head with traditional Indian religious stories.*

It is only later, in an international school in South America, that individual teachers became an important influence in this particular student's life. Here, as we will see in the final section, a strong relationship was forged with a guidance counsellor and an English teacher who seemed genuinely interested and caring.

Making Texts—A Sense of Identity

Taking hold of the dominant language and developing an ability to express oneself in it can be empowering. For this student, as we have seen, speaking out in class was always a challenge—and this is perfectly understandable given the earlier injunctions not to—and in fact, remaining silent may have become an act of resistance as well as one of self-preservation. As we see here:

> *She never spoke out in any of her classes, because she didn't want to be exposed. It took 4 years, at an International School in South*

America—initially, she communicated herself through writing and in private conferences with the teacher.

Over time, though, what began to emerge was an important exploration of belonging, of culture and identity, which attracted encouragement and praise from teachers who honoured and respected the student. Some of this writing was intensely personal, including an exploration of being alone and feeling afraid—and at times depressed—which invited written dialogues with the teacher. These written dialogues and ensuing conversations with caring adults (a teacher and a counsellor) affirmed the student's identity, who as a result felt valued and "heard." At the same time, these conversations encouraged the student to reveal more, and through that process helped her to realize her own potential—what she could do and was capable of doing.

Writing produced at this stage drew on childhood memories of India, evoked, for instance, in descriptions of a vegetable vendor, puja, and household cooking smells. Another unfinished story describes Tirupati, a famous hilltop pilgrimage site in Andhra Pradesh in Southern India. Growing confidence spilt over into other areas of the curriculum, too, including an exploration of what it is like to be a woman in India (written in Spanish). All that had previously been suppressed came to the surface in a climate of acceptance as the richness of first-hand experience was written into the texts. This new-found confidence was reflected in achievement, with the student eventually winning a place at a top-ranked U.S. university, gaining a master's degree and eventually embarking on a successful career.

Reflections

By no means do all stories of migration have happy endings like this one. In some cases, poverty, prejudice, and adversity construct insurmountable barriers, or the trauma of conflict, separation, and suffering becomes impossible to overcome. But understanding something of how caring and respectful environments can help is a hopeful starting point. Through the narrative extracts in this chapter, we have described some of the ways in which classrooms are contact zones (Pratt, 1991), and these ways are refracted through one student's experience and identity. They have been presented as four overlapping themes—but as we said at the start, they are not exhaustive or in any way definitive.

Vertovec (2007), writing in the British context, coined the term *superdiversity* to describe the "new, small and scattered, multiple-origin, transnationally connected, socio-economically differentiated and legally stratified immigrants who have arrived over the last decade" (p. 1024). The description fits many different contemporary contexts and suggests how it may be crucially important to think—or perhaps to re-think classrooms as contact zones—contexts in which a multiplicity of phenomena become entangled. Classrooms, from this perspective, are very particular places in which humans and non-humans in all their diversity are, in various ways, thrown together.

As Massey (2005) underlines:

> what is special about place is not some romance of a pre-given collective identity or of the eternity of hills. Rather, what is special about place is precisely that throwntogetherness, the unavoidable challenge of negotiating a here-and-now (itself drawing on a history and a geography of thens and theres); and a negotiation which must take place within and between humans and non-humans.
>
> (p. 140)

Classrooms, in conditions of superdiversity, may well be these very special places marked by a crucially important meeting up of material, social, and discursive practices.

Summary

Population mobility: Increased mobility and migration is a key feature of life in the early 21st century. The resulting social and cultural diversity has been associated with larger metropolitan areas but has recently become a wider phenomenon. This has important implications for education at all levels.

Classrooms are contact zones: Cultures meet, clash, and grapple with each other, often in contexts of highly asymmetrical relations of power, such as colonialism, slavery, or their aftermaths as they are lived out today.:

(Pratt, 1991, p. 34)

- If classrooms are contact zones, the linguistic and cultural diversity of the community should be represented in the classroom environment.
- Teachers need to understand that students may experience acute feelings of dislocation, loss, or pain and that these may interfere with their ability to engage and learn.
- Students relationships with each other and with teachers and other adults are vitally important in creating a sense of belonging.
- Well-chosen texts can promote enjoyment and help students to understand their personal journeys.
- Students can be encouraged to produce their own texts through which they can explore their own sense of identity.

Coda

The ideas that give shape to this piece emerged out of our work together in Calgary in October 2017. And because place—or what Massey (2005) refers to as the *event of place*—was an underlying theme in this initial work and indeed in this chapter, we return to this place of contact, Canada.

> Canada—a post-colonial country whose cities are amongst the most ethnically diverse on the planet, and where the rate of environmental change has pitched us all into unknown territory.
>
> (Thien, 2017, p. 17)

To visit, to stay for a while, to remain, no matter what, you are part of it. You are part of it just because—just because "what unsettles the world must also unsettle Canada" (Thien, 2017, p. 17).

True as that might be, this project is not just about Canada even though it was where it all began. Instead it is about shared concerns and an attempt to find common ground. And this is because different trajectories led into the collaboration, pathways that crossed in the Nose of the Buffalo, in Calgary, epicentre of the Canadian energy industry, in the Prairie ecozone, in the russet autumn of 2017.

In our own ways, we were thrown together, bringing our personal experiences to bear. Divya, who works as a literacy specialist with the Calgary Board of Education, has a longstanding interest in linguistic and cultural diversity. Guy, a visiting academic, now at Sheffield Hallam University, previously worked in a similar capacity in England as an adviser to schools facing the challenge of responding to cultural and linguistic diversity. Our shared experience cut across spatial and temporal separation, and our personal and professional histories and experiences were temporarily woven together as we worked to produce our own very particular contact zone.

References

Barley, R., & Merchant, G. (2016). "The naughty person": Exploring dynamic aspects of identity and children's discourses before and during the Libyan Uprising. *Childhood*, 23(4), 477-491.

Blyton, E. (2011). *The famous five short story collection*. London, UK: Hodder.

Evans, R. (2017). *The pursuit of power: Europe 1815–1914*. London, UK: Penguin Books.

Fisher, J. (1979). *Penelope strawberry*. London, UK: Penguin Books.

Fishman, J. A. (1980). Bilingualism and biculturism as individual and as societal phenomena. *Journal of Multilingual & Multicultural Development*, 1(1), 3–15.

Gutiérrez, K. D., Bien, A. C., Selland, M. K., & Pierce, D. M. (2011). Polylingual and polycultural learning ecologies: Mediating emergent academic literacies for dual language learners. *Journal of Early Childhood Literacy*, 11(2), 232–261.

Massey, D. (2005). *For space*. London, UK: Sage Publications.
Miller, J. (1983). *Many voices: Bilingualism, culture and education*. London, UK: Routledge and Kegan Paul.
Pratt, M. L. (1991). Arts of the contact zone. *Profession*, 33–40.
Thien, M. (2017, Autumn). Introduction. *Granta, 141*, 16–17.
Vertovec, S. (2007). Super-diversity and its implications. *Ethnic and Racial Studies, 30*(6), 1024–1054.

8 Classroom Cosmopolitics
Worldbuilding for Mutual Flourishing

T. Philip Nichols and Brianne O'Sullivan

In this chapter, we explore literacy teaching as an act of worldbuilding—a coming-together of instructor, students, materials, and histories to shape and reshape a shared classroom world. Such a perspective reframes the work of schooling, from a transmission of information or an unfolding of activity to the collective negotiations among the humans and nonhumans that constitute the classroom space. We begin by considering the classroom as a *cosmogram* (Tresch, 2007), a social world that materializes teachers' ideas and beliefs about students, literacy, and learning. We argue that these cosmograms are powerful but not uncontested: students, administrators, local and national policies each graft additional layered worlds onto those imagined by the teacher. What results, we suggest, is a kind of *cosmopolitical* (Stengers, 2010, 2011) friction, as teachers and students are made to reconcile the competing—and, at times, contradictory—worlds that circulate in their classrooms. In taking such a perspective, we suggest that literacy teaching and learning can be understood as a recursive process of shaping worlds for mutual flourishing—and that educators and students who engage in this work carry these worlds with them in their future trajectories of literacy instruction, learning, and practice.

We come to the subject of classroom worldbuilding from different perspectives and locations. Phil is a literacy researcher, teacher-educator, and former high school English teacher based in Texas, United States. Brianne is an educator in Calgary, Alberta, Canada, with a background in science who has worked in a variety of roles and contexts in public education. However, in what follows, we write from a joint perspective, weaving together our voices, stories, and experiences to consider how thinking-with-worlds reframes the teaching and learning of literacy as a patient and ethical act of collective creation. By braiding together theory and practice as such, it is our intention to show how the two are entangled. Educators may, at times, seek out external guidance from researchers to inform their instruction, or they may make in-the-moment decisions, rooted in experience. Neither of these is more or less theoretical than the other—and both can serve as generative inspiration as teachers work with students to shape a classroom world worth sharing. To illustrate this, we have structured this chapter as a progression through a school year, interweaving classroom vignettes and theoretical explorations that gradually converge through the passing of seasons. In doing so, we consider how the work of worldbuilding positions the classroom as a space where theoretical knowledge is generated, enacted, and refined through the lived dynamics of teaching and learning.

Key Terms

Cosmogram: A materialized or spatialized social world. Where "worldviews" are locked away in people's heads, cosmograms bring these ideas and beliefs to life by representing them in physical space—for instance, in the configuration of a classroom.

Cosmopolitics: The political process of shaping a shared social world out of multiple competing ones. Teachers, students, and other stakeholders may understand the meaning and purpose of a classroom space differently; cosmopolitics names a means by which these points of friction might be reconciled through the collective work of instruction and practice.

Summer: Imagining Worlds for Learning

Reading Robin Wall Kimmerer's *Braiding Sweetgrass* (2013), I find myself poring slowly over her words, savoring them. She describes a grove of pecan trees, detailing the ways it is less a cluster of individual trees than an interdependent collective. Its component parts do not thrive in isolation; its flourishing is mutual. She gives me language for my own experiences as a student of science, as a teacher of children, as a human being in this world. I have found a new mentor within the pages of this text.

I am grateful to have found this book in the summer. When time slows. As a teacher, summer brings the opportunity to pause, to reflect, to imagine new possibilities. I find myself returning to Kimmerer's words. *Mutual flourishing.* I imagine my classroom and the children I will soon welcome there—the collective we, as teacher and students, will form. I wonder: what might it mean to build a learning community where flourishing is mutual? Where individuals feel not only that they belong but that they are also necessary to the thriving of the group? Where they see themselves in the learning space and in the content we take up together? How might we come together as a collective, to see and hear one another, to know and understand our differences, to strive for justice and equity in all that we do? I know the key to building a world of mutual flourishing lies in building relationships. This is where we will begin. This will guide us. We will come to know one another.

*****

To be a teacher is to be a builder of worlds. We are not just charged with developing learning communities in our schools but with cultivating the world of the classroom that will allow such communities to grow and thrive. The worlds we imagine and bring into being are as integral to instruction as the content we teach and the lessons we plan. It is for this reason that many scholars and practitioners have theorized space as a pedagogical resource (Leander & Sheehy, 2004). Loris Malaguzzi, founder of the Reggio Emilia preschool method, famously referred to the child's physical environment as—"the third teacher"—after adults, and other children—to denote its capacities to guide and instruct (Rinaldi, 2006). Paulo Freire, likewise, stressed the import of space for literacy learning. "Reading the word," he argued, was always preceded by "reading the world"—and, importantly, both of these were preceded first by acts of "writing or rewriting the world" (Freire & Macedo, 1987, p. 35). Such perspectives suggest that teaching and learning are context-dependent: the classroom is less an empty container to hold students, desks, and books than it is a permeable presence that conditions what can be said and done and known (e.g., Lenters, 2014; Stornaiuolo, 2014).

In this way, the classroom-world is both physical and ideological—composed of objects, artifacts, and arrangements, as well as the substrate of assumptions and histories that animate these component parts. It is what Tresch (2007) calls a cosmogram—a material representation of an ordered universe. While a cosmogram can be a literal map of the universe—a mandala, for instance, or the Hebrew Tabernacle—more often it is an artifact that asserts a particular vision of the world, not as it is but as it might be. Ford's assembly line, for example, forged a social world that, for better or worse, celebrated mechanization and efficiency. Mark Zuckerberg's Facebook, likewise, shaped a social world where human connection is facilitated through an attention-economy of *likes* and *shares*. In the same way, our classroom cosmograms materialize our ideals and beliefs about teaching, learning, and literacy—and spatialize them into a social world that we and our students inhabit together. The cosmogram of a teacher who believes education is principally for preparing students for a job will be different than that of one who believes it is for cultivating civic engagement or social mobility. Such a perspective invites us to ask: what is the world of our classroom meant to produce? And how does its material configuration support or upset this ideal? Do our cosmograms privilege competition and personal achievement—or are they arranged in a way that can cultivate and sustain mutual flourishing?

Fall: Negotiating Shared Worlds

The first day of school has come to an end. Sitting in the stillness of the classroom, I take a moment to pause and reflect. I am in awe of how a group of children brings the classroom to life. Over the past months, I have been thinking about the kind of learning community I hope to build—and I have arranged furniture, organized materials, and planned lessons to create a space for sustaining that sort of community. But today, I was reminded that each child who walked into this space also plays a role in shaping this world we share. We each bring our own stories and histories. These are the tools we will use to negotiate this space together.

This morning, I asked students to draw lines and shapes and then invited them to turn these designs into monsters. I watched and listened as they joyfully completed their transformations. They captioned these monsters with things they were excited about and things they were nervous about for this school year. During a gallery walk, students placed stars on any monsters whose captions echoed their own sources of excitement and anxiety. And afterward, students voiced their relief to know they were not alone in their feelings. A sense of belonging was emerging—it was only our first hour together, but already, connections were being forged.

Now, sitting at my desk and looking back over the students' creations, I begin to see more than just monsters and captions and stars—these are pieces of each student's story. I know who is hesitant about math or writing. Who is worried about finding friends or being bullied? Who is nervous about report cards and standardized tests? I also know what they perceive to be their strengths. What their passions are. And now it is my responsibility to carry this knowledge forward, to ensure that each child's gifts and passions are nurtured and that they feel supported amid their fears. Perhaps this is the beginning of our work, together, of creating a world where flourishing is mutual.

* * * * *

The worlds we build are not ours alone. The cosmograms we shape with the refractory components of our classrooms have real consequences for all who are asked to inhabit them, to abide by their logics and rules. But neither are these worlds uncontested. As surely as teachers materialize their beliefs about learning and literacy, students do as well. In the space of a single classroom, there may be multiple cosmograms in circulation. Each student brings with them their own histories of identity and education, their fears and aspirations, their image of what a learning environment is or ought to be. Teachers, from this perspective, are not just responsible for designing an ideal classroom-world to impose, by fiat, on others; they are in a position to recognize how learning environments are "pluriversal"—a world in which many worlds coexist (Mignolo,

2018; Simon, Nichols, Edwards, & Campano, 2018) The work of the classroom, then, is the precarious negotiation of competing cosmograms: the collective, tentative efforts of teachers, students, objects, and unseen actors working with, for, and against one another to determine what sort of world they will share.

Importantly, such negotiations are never neutral. As Mignolo (2018) cautions, "A pluriverse is not a world of independent units . . . but a world entangled through and by the colonial matrix of power" (p. xi). It is for this reason that the philosopher Isabel Stengers (2010, 2011) refers to the work of worldbuilding as cosmopolitics, that is, a process of political deliberation within and across different worlds. In the context of the classroom, this means educators have an ethical responsibility to use their positions of power to learn about the worlds students bring with them into the community and to make room for these worlds as the pluriverse of the classroom is collectively shaped. And as rich traditions of teacher research remind us, the work of inquiring into our practice and allowing it to be shaped by the needs, concerns, identities, and histories of our students is always eminently *political* (Cochran-Smith & Lytle, 1990; Lytle, 2008). Engaging in this cosmopolitical process is how we shape the contours of the classroom-world to support equitable learning for all who share it.

Winter: Reconciling Contested Worlds

As a teacher, my goal is to inspire students to truly want to learn, to take risks and push boundaries for what they think might be possible. I know this only happens when they feel safe and respected. At this point in the year, I am proud of the learning community we have co-created. Joy lives here. Students are willing to take risks. They support each other. They are open to learning with and from one another. There are days when it feels like we have arrived at what teaching and learning could and should be.

And then there are days when I am reminded that teaching and learning are bigger than what exists within the four walls of this classroom. Bigger than myself and these children. After a string of sleepless nights when I've found myself waking in a panic and unable to quiet my busy brain, I have to acknowledge that the looming standardized tests are taking their toll. I'm worried about being too far behind with curriculum and not doing enough to ensure that each child will be successful.

The pressure finds its way into our classroom, as we make time for exam prep. Time that takes away from our authentic and joyful approach to learning. I work to overcome the urge to skip our read-aloud or independent reading time. I try to resist the temptation of replacing experiential, hands-on tasks with more direct forms of teaching. Students know the exams are nearly here. Many begin to voice concerns about not doing well enough, asking questions about what to expect. A tension is mounting that did not exist in the first half of the year.

I am reminded that the learning community we are building is also shaped by factors beyond our control. And when those external pressures threaten to unravel what we have worked so hard to create, I do the best I can to remember what is important. So, on test day, I greet each child with a smile, leave notes of encouragement on each of their desks, read a timely picture book, and lead them through a mindful breathing exercise. I assure them that this is just one moment in time, a minor interruption of what we have come to know as teaching and learning. I remind them of my hope that they will become lifelong learners driven by curiosity and a thirst for knowledge, something that cannot be measured on any standardized test.

* * * * *

In the day-to-day worldbuilding of the classroom, it is easy to forget that the cosmograms we mold into a shared learning environment are not just ours and our students': the pluriverse of the classroom is nested within and conditioned by the pressures of other, outside worlds. It would be comforting if this were not so—if the communities we cultivate could be shielded entirely from those forces that might undermine or upend them. But the walls of our classroom-worlds are porous, and the cosmograms of school and district policies, national mandates, and guidelines circulate widely, enabling and constraining how teaching, learning, and relating unfold. At times, these pressures are so subtle that they are almost invisible to us, but at other times, the friction between these worlds and our own make them all too apparent. During standardized testing, for example, we may feel the discomfort—perhaps even physically, affectively—as a cosmogram ordered by quantitative metrics for sorting and ranking students is grafted onto a world we have collectively structured to define worth otherwise and locate success elsewhere.

Such tensions show the importance of the *cosmos* in cosmopolitics: the political work of worldbuilding is not bounded by the walls of the classroom but extends outside as well. A true politics of the cosmos draws our attention to the ways we live environmentally, as the residues of distant policies and activities inflect the day-to-day, lived practices of teachers and students. In doing so, cosmopolitics provides a pathway for articulating a "poetics of space" (Glissant, 1989) that unearths from our transparent surroundings the artifacts, ideologies, and labour that give them shape and hold them stable. Just as Ellison's "invisible man" was not really invisible but was rendered as such by the landscape of his time, the perceived discernibility of our classroom worlds may, too, elide histories of inequity, domination, or neglect that should be attended to as we work, with our students, to shape a new, collective cosmogram.

This also means considering what worlds we invite into our classrooms alongside practices and artifacts that, likewise, appear to us as transparent. Forms of instruction, evaluation, and assessment that we take for granted as "best practices" may carry with them ideologies that sit in uneasy alignment with the classroom-worlds we are trying to build. A computerized learning management system, for example, may provide a means for more efficiently delivering feedback to students, but the interface and protocols of the platform may also change the fundamental character of that feedback in ways that work against our stated ideals for supporting student growth. Similarly, such devices also introduce to the classroom the cosmogram of educational technology companies whose profit motives may be at odds with the underlying principles of our own, and our students', worldbuilding. In other words, while actors and techniques may serve as what Brandt (1998) calls "sponsors of literacy"—enabling artifacts that underwrite and support literacy learning—it is necessary to interrogate the conditions of this sponsorship because it may not be strictly benevolent and is certainly never neutral (Brandt, 2015).

How are we to navigate so many cosmograms, with so many competing aims? The answer will look different for different educators, in different contexts, and at different times. An early-career teacher in an under-resourced school may not have the same leeway to reshape outside pressures in the image of the world they envision with their students as a veteran teacher in a similar situation. However, for each of these educators, the process will involve a similar form of reflexive creativity—what Campano (2009) calls "systematic improvisation" (p. 112)—that carves out, from a cosmos of external demands and constraints, the space necessary for humanizing praxis. There are no innocent positions, free from the entanglements of near and distant worlds—and as such, it is crucial that we reflect on both where we are located in this pluriverse and what levers might be available to shape it into a common world worthy of our students.

Spring: The World We Have Made and the Worlds to Come

I'm reminded of David Eagleman's (2009) vignette *Ineffable* as I walk through the classroom, surveying the empty walls and boxes of resources packed away for the summer. He describes soldiers whose paths diverge at the end of a war, actors who part ways after a finale performance—collectives, once part of something larger than themselves, now disbanded and travelling their separate ways. It is June, and the school year has come to an end. I have said goodbye to each of my students and watched as they exited, for the last time, the classroom we've shaped and shared together. In my years as a teacher, Eagleman puts words to the strange sense of loss that I feel at this time each spring, that I've never quite been able to name. The students and I have spent the past 10 months building a world within these walls. We have brought our stories, our histories, our experiences together, allowing them to circulate and be braided into practices that have sustained our learning together over the year.

Of course, this world that we built does not really go away. In the months ahead, this world and the experience of building it will help me to imagine what sort of world my classroom might become next year. And the year after. My students, too, will carry this world with them as they enter spaces imagined and designed by other teachers. We may find that the worlds we carry with us into new environments align, or we may find our histories colliding with the new worlds we are asked to inhabit. The only certainty is that we will be changed in the process—which invites us to ask, always, how might the resources available to us aid in the building of more just and equitable worlds?

Conclusion

The process of worldbuilding reframes the classroom as a space of possibility, where humans and non-humans, materialities and immaterialities, work with and against one another to shape a shared world for learning. As Stornaiuolo (2014) suggests, such a stance offers teachers and students "new ways to imagine the relationships between and among worlds that [they] might create, inhabit, and transform" (p. 568). This is especially true for literacy educators, whose purview is not only the relationships between students and the classroom-world but also the worlds of text—written and read—that circulate in and beyond the walls of the school. From this perspective, Freire and Macedo's (1987) observations about the interdependence of reading *the world* and *the word* take on new meaning: while these remain central to the practice of literacy education, teachers must also attend to the spaces where such relations are nurtured, negotiated, and at times, negated. It is here, in this layered, cosmopolitical labour, that educators and students collectively configure the sort of world they will share—one that reproduces power differentials and social hierarchies; one that reduces learning to test scores and numbers of school improvement charts; or, perhaps, one that provides a foundation for equitable education and mutual flourishing for all.

References

Brandt, D. (1998). Sponsors of literacy. *College Composition and Communication*, 49(2), 165–185.

Brandt, D. (2015). A commentary on literacy narratives as sponsors of literacy. *Curriculum Inquiry*, 45(3), 330–333.

Campano, G. (2009). *Immigrant students and literacy: Reading, writing, remembering*. New York, NY: Teachers College Press.

Cochran-Smith, M., & Lytle, S. L. (1990). Research on teaching and teacher research: The issues that divide. *Educational Researcher*, 19(2), 2–11.

Eagleman, D. (2009). *Sum: Forty tales from the afterlives*. New York, NY: Vintage.
Freire, P., & Macedo, D. P. (1987). *Literacy: Reading the word and the world*. Westport, CT: Bergin and Garvey.
Glissant, E. (1989). *Caribbean discourse: Selected essays*. Charlottesville, VA: University of Virginia Press.
Kimmerer, R. W. (2013). *Braiding sweetgrass: Indigenous wisdom, scientific knowledge, and the teaching of plants*. Minneapolis, MN: Milkweed Editions.
Leander, K., & Sheehy, M. (Eds.). (2004). *Spatializing literacy research and practice*. New York, NY: Peter Lang.
Lenters, K. (2014). Just doing our jobs: A case study of literacy-in-action in a fifth grade literature circle. *Language and Literacy*, 16(1), 53.
Lytle, S. L. (2008). At last: Practitioner inquiry and the practice of teaching: Some thoughts on "better." *Research in the Teaching of English*, 373–379.
Mignolo, W. (2018). Forward. In B. Reiter (Ed.), *Constructing the pluriverse: The geopolitics of knowledge* (pp. ix–xvi). Durham, NC: Duke University Press.
Rinaldi, C. (2006). *In dialogue with Reggio Emilia: Listening, research, learning*. New York, NY: Routledge.
Simon, R., Nichols, T. P., Edwards, W., & Campano, G. (2018). "There's really a lot going on here": Toward a cosmopolitics of reader response. In P. P. Trifonas & S. Jagger (Eds.), *The Routledge handbook of cultural studies in education* (pp. 175–189). New York, NY: Routledge.
Stengers, I. (2010). *Cosmopolitics I*. Minneapolis, MN: University of Minnesota Press.
Stengers, I. (2011). *Cosmopolitics II*. Minneapolis, MN: University of Minnesota Press.
Stornaiuolo, A. (2014). Literacy as worldmaking: Multimodality, creativity, and cosmopolitanism. In K. Pahl & J. Rowsell (Eds.), *The Routledge handbook of literacy studies* (pp. 561–571). New York, NY: Routledge.
Tresch, J. (2007). Technological world-pictures: Cosmic things and cosmograms. *Isis*, 98, 84–99.

9 Ways of Being and Becoming in the Adolescent Classroom
An Invitation to Consider the Possibilities of Throwntogetherness

Erin Spring and Amanda Huddleston

Amanda did not read many books in her school-age years, but she does remember being a pre-teen and meeting Anne and her journey to Green Gables (Montgomery, 2008) and imagining the Lake of Shining Waters. Prince Edward Island (PEI) sounded like the furthest possible place from her prairie home. Amanda's grandmother gave her a handmade Anne doll in her teenage years, which sat on her shelf with other handmade gifts for decades. Montgomery's story *Anne of Green* Gables, in this case, not only belongs to Amanda but to her grandmother as well.

Just last summer, Amanda travelled to PEI with her family. Seeing the land Lucy Maud Montgomery lived on and wrote from was at the top of her wish list. She re-read the book before she went and thought about how, back then, she did not imagine herself as being an English and creative writing teacher; she just loved words (like Anne does). As an adult, she responded to how emotive Anne is. Re-reading the text through the lens of adulthood was like reading a new story, set in a different place. She asked her husband and two teenage boys to explore and be together at Green Gables for 1 hour. They (somewhat reluctantly) agreed. The doll sat with her as she encountered the Lake of Shining Waters, and Amanda realized for the first time that Montgomery had looked at this landscape and wrote about it through the eyes of Anne. As a young reader, Amanda had imagined, and mentally configured, the landscape similarly despite having never been there. Now she was physically standing where Anne and Lucy had stood. She saw the house and Haunted Wood and was grateful to share this place and memory with her family and her grandmother's doll. Amanda's children may not read Montgomery's novel, but Anne's story is now woven into their literacy histories through their great grandmother's doll and their visceral experience of standing in this place.

When Amanda and Erin sat down to write, Amanda shared her story about Anne and her doll after a discussion of meaningful stories and of the importance of place, reading, and artifactual literacies, particularly in childhood. We recognized that both of us had stories that were woven through and between generations, stories that blurred the boundaries of real and fictional places. Erin's childhood reading identity was similarly shaped by Montgomery's novel, prompting her to write about Anne for her MA thesis. She focused on the role of place on Anne's emerging adolescent identity. Last summer, Erin visited PEI for a Montgomery conference, just 5 weeks before Amanda's family had been. Like Amanda, visiting Green Gables brought Erin back to her childhood self and to the place she had repeatedly imagined through reading. In July 2017, Erin got a job in Calgary. Having lived 3 years in transience as a precariously employed academic, all of her belongings were stored in her parents' basement in Ontario. When she bought a house, her parents happily shipped her belongings across the country, including her childhood Anne doll.

Throwntogether Through Childhood Reading— A Road Map

While we were throwntogether as strangers in an unfamiliar place, for this writing project, we quickly recognized how our trajectories aligned, even if momentarily. Not only did our conversation highlight our shared love of reading and our history as English teachers, but we soon were also swapping photographs of our Anne dolls and stories of our visits to Green Gables as adults. The conversations we had, as a whole group, about materiality, embodiment, affect, and place, within the context of critical literacy, emerged organically in these moments of throwntogetherness. While the theory was there to support our understanding, we did not *need* the theory to explain our shared encounter or our assemblage with this particular story and place. There were tangible overlaps in our trajectories and histories that created a space of familiarity, synergy and possibility for pedagogical and theoretical imaginings. We also recognized that our professional identities and learning epistemologies aligned: how our learning spaces are configured, how we engage with texts within the classroom, how we interact with young readers, and how we privilege their stories and the places they come from.

Within this chapter, we focus on some of the materials and methods we draw on as literacy educators to foster critical and creative moments of throwntogetherness. The methods and materials we share prioritize throwntogetherness and fluidity over singularity and stasis. Prior to delving into these pedagogical examples—which have implications for both research and practice—we provide an outline of several key terms that are woven throughout this chapter. We then share examples of some of the ways in which our teaching pedagogies, practices, and philosophies shape our work with young people's texts and identities.

The Adolescent Classroom 137

Figure 10 Erin and Amanda's Anne dolls

Framing Key Terms

Adolescent Identity

Rather than conceptualizing identity as a linear or static process that is achieved in stages, we understand it to be something that changes over time and across space. Our pedagogies are grounded in the understanding that our students' identities are continually informed, for example, by their cultures, histories, communities, families, peers, and places beyond the local. All of these varying facets of their identities are continually interacting with one another within and beyond classroom walls, resulting in ongoing change. Each student is part of Massey's (1991) time-space compression: their identities are temporally and spatially situated in the moment of throwntogetherness. Through the process of reading and discussing texts, adolescents' identities are developed—that is to say, reading (and literacy, more broadly) is identity work (Moje, 2004).

We believe that conceptualizing identity as fluid and dynamic is particularly urgent for work with adolescent readers. Their own identities are in question: who do I want to be, and where and who will I become? What stories define me, and how do I want those stories to be told? With these learners, making room for varying trajectories to become possible creates a true connectedness between learners in a time in their lives when the focus is often on the individual rather than the collective.

Reading as a Social and Spatial Practice

Drawing on the work social and critical literacies scholarship, we position reading as a social event that is prompted by a "transaction" (Rosenblatt, 1994, p. 16) between reader and text. Rather than thinking about reading as a solitary pursuit, we conceptualize reading as active, exploratory, multiple, collaborative, and non-linear. Similarly, texts do not have pre-set, fixed meanings, nor do our interpretations of them stay the same over time. In a classroom setting, readers' identities are continually being renegotiated and challenged by other readers. Texts and stories similarly accumulate new meanings as they come up against the varied histories and identities of their readers who are throwntogether in a momentarily shared space. As teachers, we have found that it is possible to elicit adolescent's identities through their responses to and creation of a range of texts, examples of which we provide next.

Texts

We use the term *texts* broadly—not just in reference to novels in traditional form. Our classroom spaces are filled with a variety of texts, including poetry, novels, short stories, graphic novels, science fiction and fantasy, comedy, essays, non-fiction, fan fiction, wordless texts, oral stories, intergenerational stories, photographs, and maps, all of which feature real and imagined as well as local and global worlds.

We also reflected on our shared belief that place (a city or the land, for example) is a text that can be read. As with our conceptualization of reading, both texts and places are active and transactional; all stories move beyond the page and across/through both place and time. Introducing our students to a range of texts not only increases the possibilities for response, but it also provides students with breadth and choice to respond in a way that feels most suitable to their varied experiences of the world. Similarly, grounding the texts that we share with our students within a local framework ensures that connections can be drawn between their identities and varied understandings of the world. Margaret Mackey (2016) highlights the physicality of reading by returning to her childhood texts and the places she read from. Mackey argues that reading and exploring place are intricately interconnected. We come to this work with the appreciation that as we learned to read, as children, we were simultaneously beginning to explore the places where we lived and were reading from. As adults, visiting Green Gables, a place we had vicariously visited through the written word, transported us not only back to our childhood selves but also to our childhood-reader selves. Spatial approaches to literacy privilege these connections.

Place

Much like reading, texts, and identity, it was important for us to find a theorization of place that resisted a linear or singular approach. We are drawn to the work of Massey (2005), who writes about place as a "simultaneity of stories-so-far" (p. 9) or as sites 'throwntogetherness,' a concept also taken up by Barbara Comber (2013, 2016) in her work on place and critical literacies. Our classroom practices have been informed by David Gruenewald's (2003) work on the critical pedagogies of place; he similarly writes resisting the "isolation of school's discourses and practices from the living world outside the increasingly placeless institution of schooling" (p. 620). For these scholars, and indeed for us, places are meeting points where various trajectories (real and imagined) encounter or collide with one another in a shared space, where ideas are constantly being exchanged and therein renegotiated. Rather than seeing our classrooms as static rooms with four walls, Massey would encourage us to conceptualize these spaces as dynamic, as being formed by the encounter of different trajectories, stories, histories, and identities. Like reading, then, place is dynamic, non-linear, multiple, and transactional.

Throwntogetherness: An Assemblage of Places, Stories, and Identities

Our chapter is centred on Massey's concept of throwntogetherness as the underlying thread to our shared understanding of reading, texts, place, and identity. As educators, our approach is to *embrace* the messiness, or throwntogetherness, of classroom spaces: where readers and texts collide in a momentarily shared place. Converging in this place are people coming from various communities, with different cultures, memories, homes, histories, and epistemologies. In this space, students must "negotiate a common place where they all belong . . . reach out from their sociocultural, familial and personal experiences and interactively make a place of multiplicity, of diverse experiences and perspectives" (Comber, 2016, p. x).

Throwntogetherness explicitly shapes our work with texts, broadly speaking. As English teachers, we agree that privileging one text or a particular set of stories (the canon, for example) or a particular *form* of storytelling (written, for example) within a classroom is artificial. Rather than seeking out the similarities in our students' stories and identities, we should capitalize on and celebrate the throwntogetherness and distinctiveness of their varying, often divergent, histories and trajectories. If this is our guiding principle, then we should also embrace the multiplicity of texts and forms that can support us in this endeavor.

Throughout this chapter, we posit that focusing on the throwntogetherness of classroom assemblages is when real learning (and identity work) takes place: where the world of the student, teacher, author, and text bump up against each other, creating moments of discomfort, repositioning, and rebalancing. Students will organically find moments of commonality and shared experience, just as we did when throwntogether. But students will also come to understand their world in more complex ways when their stories are read alongside others. We ask: how have we, as critical literacy scholars, negotiated throwntogetherness *in practice*? In the forthcoming section, we highlight several methods or materials that have, or have the possibility of, prioritizing throwntogetherness and fluidity over singularity and stasis in our work with young adult readers and their texts.

Working with a Posthuman Reader Response Theory

- Reading, place, texts, and identities are dynamic, non-linear, multiple, and transactional as opposed to static or linear
- Through reading, adolescents do identity work. They come to understand themselves, their world(s), and the experiences of others in new ways. This can be fostered through discussion groups, visual methods, artifactual literacies, and so on.
- Through a variety of approaches, teachers can provide opportunities for students to create and share their stories.
- Classrooms are sites of throwntogetherness, where multiple identities, texts, objects, places, and stories engage with one another.

Enacting Throwntogetherness

Throwntogether Through the Stories We Encounter

A shared aspect of our classroom design is our understanding that the joy and curiosity of reading vary immensely among readers. Erin wants to read books about familiar places because they offer a mirror of her own experience of the world. Amanda chooses to read books unfamiliar to where she is from as a way to imagine what it might feel like to be otherwise or to live in other ways. Readers have different preferences. In a classroom, the availability of varied texts is essential. As an example, within her own practice, Amanda does not rely on one common class text. She provides her students with non-fiction and fictional novels, images, and poetry, some with a focus on ideas, others with characters at their choice. Students then read multiple pages of various books to make an informed decision of what they would like to add to their reading history and identity. Similarly, she provides examples of student and published work that purposefully break and follow conventions of personal, critical, and creative voice and structure to expose students to a variety of non-traditionally crafted texts. This opportunity allows students to understand that there is no singular way of creating a narrative of any form. Rather, the emphasis is on: what kind of story would allow you to express yourself and your experiences authentically?

Throwntogether Through Our Encounters With One Another

Responding to stories in the throwntogetherness of the classrooms is a way of articulating and highlighting our differences alongside our similarities. We both draw on informal reading discussion groups as a way of centring learning on students' voices and expertise. Reading discussions, either in pairs or small groups, allow students to think of and ask their own questions while responding to a text. When students can articulate their individual wonderings as they read independently to others or share the most important passages from a text, authentic and meaningful conversations happen that are inevitably intertwined with their own experiences and identities beyond and within the classroom. In other words, the text *as well as* the conversation are alive: dynamic, shifting, and part of the unfolding process of place and identity-making. Students, too, are throwntogether in these groups, inevitably prompting the creation of new classroom trajectories and dynamics. Readers come to recognize that their worldviews and histories often do not match up with others; while they are throwntogether in a shared classroom space, their entryways are as diverse as their imagined journeys. Without the opportunity to share their stories, readers' identities never bump up against the ideas of others to foster classroom identity assemblages. Discussion groups prompt the development and re-articulation of ideas, therein enacting change.

Throwntogether Through Various Methods of Response

Show Me What You Know

Beyond shared conversations about texts, a series of tasks can be designed for during or after the discussion. These approaches prompt students to find connections between texts in addition to one other. For example, Amanda has introduced a "Show Me What You Know" project into her secondary English curriculum. Students are encouraged to choose any format that they think would help them best represent their text-related learning and strengths. Students are offered the opportunity to paint, draw, sculpt, design a stage or robot, soundtrack, write self-help advice, or make a puppet show, for example. Alongside their creative piece of choice, students write or verbally explain their choices and learning processes to others in the class. Show Me What You Know Projects give students the opportunity to respond in a way that feels most suitable to their experience of the world. Creating a range of multimodal texts foregrounds the complexity and multiplicity of students' experiences, identities, and ways of being in the world, situating them as the experts of their stories with the power to tell them.

Artifacts as Texts

When artifacts move among home, school, and community spaces, students have the opportunity to develop their identities. Carol Shields' short story "Dressing Up for Carnival" (2001) is a text Amanda uses in the classroom to explore the idea of clothing *as* text or as response *to* text. In the spirit of throwntogetherness, Amanda wears her Stampeders football glasses, hat, and jersey and uses a noisemaker to tell a particular narrative of self. Students are often shocked by her "beyond the classroom" identity coming into contact with her "teacher identity." In this moment, Amanda's dynamic, multiple identity is illustrated for the students. She then challenges the students to do the same. Bringing home and community artefacts into the classroom enacts a meeting of histories and texts in a common place, therein creating an opportunity for story-sharing and identity work that transcends the four walls of that singular classroom.

Visualizing Reading Identities

Drawing on Massey's (2005) concept of place as a "meeting up of histories," reading scholar Gabrielle Cliff Hodges (2010, 2016) writes about the Rivers of Reading incident collage methodology she has used with adolescent readers. Students begin by tracing the outline of a river onto a page and then plotting different reading events onto the river, such as texts, stories, and memories. The river comes to represent the ways in which their reading identities are spatially and temporally located in a specific place. The method requires students to "think about readership not only in terms of the space created by their interconnection with others through reading—families, friends, classmates, authors, fictional characters for example—but also, simultaneously, in terms of time—past, present and, in some cases, future" (Cliff Hodges, 2016, p. 188).

Similarly, both Amanda and Erin encourage their students to ground their reading in the local. Amanda often introduces the idea of metaphor to represent a learning journey through texts. For example, the students begin with a prompt such as: "What have you learned in this course/high school through reading?" For example, "My learning is a wardrobe/spider web/candy store/and so on." Other times, students receive a common metaphor, such as a bookshelf, and are asked to describe the itemized texts on their shelves (or perhaps the shelves of a family member or an author). Not only then do the students' representations operate on a personal level, but they also invite the readers to draw on intergenerational stories and histories to consider their own positioning within both time and space. One might ask: if a story influenced my mother or grandmother, it is also part of my reading history? Has it informed my sense of self? How might the story be different for me?

Local Literacies

To reiterate the intersections among place, reading, and identity to her students, Amanda often shares her *Anne of Green Gables* story. She uses the pictures taken on her PEI trip to highlight the ways in which the material objects of this space and text are vital to its telling and retelling in her reading history. After a discussion of the relationship of the real and the imagined, Amanda asks students to write about a place in their history that is framed around a series of questions, such as: what does that place look like, feel like, sound like? Who is with you? What happens in this place in this moment, in the past, and after you have left? When and how do you remember this place after you have left it? As a further step, students are then prompted to consider the following: "If you could go to the world of a text (book, song, tv show, conversation), where would you go?"

Erin has used the strategy of asking young people to draw maps of meaningful places in response to reading. She worked with students in Toronto who were reading a novel set on the streets of Toronto. She wondered: how might reading about a known place prompt these students to reflect on their own relationships and navigations of the same place? While describing the maps to Erin, she found that the students slipped between reflections of the text and memories and stories from their everyday lives to explain their wanderings through the city, demonstrating that reading, identity, and place are intricately woven together. It was not possible for the students to separate their reading encounters with the city from their experiences beyond classroom walls. The maps prompted a discussion about the permeability of place, particularly around representation. Similar to the questions noted earlier, one could question: how might this map change? How might my particular view of the world as an adolescent, at this particular time and place, shape how I've read this story or chosen to represent the city where I read from? How might the *map* change with each telling? Through articulating and sharing snapshots of these different places, feelings, and memories, students are again thrust into the throwntogetherness of the literacy classroom.

The Possibilities of Throwntogetherness

The different transactions explored above—text to text, text to self, text to reader (Rosenblatt, 1994)—lead to a deeper and more meaningful encounter with the text, with each other, and with self. Importantly, through these inquiry-based approaches, students become knowledge-producers rather than simply receivers: their stories, identities, and areas of expertise are explicitly located and given a voice within the throwntogetherness of the classroom. In doing so, celebrating throwntogetherness in the reading classroom fosters inclusivity and celebrates diversity. All students believe that they have something to share when we move away from thinking about stories or identity as linear or static. In this space, all stories and experiences are valid of being told and re-told.

Each child and class has its own trajectory. A teacher can bump up against/nudge/redirect to some extent by intentionally bringing in varied voices and formats of text (in genre, style, craft, tone, content, authorship). Teachers can design tasks that provide students with opportunities to communicate their knowledge of the world and develop their identities in a safe space of throwntogether learners. Thinking about classrooms and the role of students and their stories in this way has tremendous potential for literacy educators.

When teachers conceptualize identities and texts as dynamic and transactional, in this way, there is the potential to privilege place as something beyond where the setting unfolds but rather as an assemblage of throwntogether stories. Anne does not just exist in PEI. She lives in Calgary, intricately interwoven into Erin, Amanda, their classrooms, and their students' trajectories.

References

Cliff Hodges, G. (2010). Rivers of reading: Using critical incident collages to learn about adolescent readers and their readership. *English in Education*, 44(3), 181–200.

Cliff Hodges, G. (2016). *Researching and teaching reading: Developing pedagogy through critical enquiry.* New York, NY: Routledge.

Comber, B. (2013). Schools as meeting places: Critical and inclusive literacies in changing local environments. *Language Arts, 90*(5), 361–371.

Comber, B. (2016). *Literacies, place, and pedagogies of possibility.* New York, NY: Routledge.

Gruenewald, D. (2003). Foundations of place: A multidisciplinary framework for place-conscious education. *American Educational Research Journal, 40*(3), 619–654.

Mackey, M. (2016). *One child reading: My autobibliography.* Edmonton, AB: University of Alberta Press.

Massey, D. (1991). A global sense of place. *Marxism Today, 35*(6), 24–29.

Massey, D. (2005). *For space.* London, UK: Sage Publications.

Moje, E. B. (2004). Powerful spaces: Tracing out-of-school literacy spaces of Latino/a youth. In K. M. Leander & M. Sheehy (Eds.), *Spatialising literacy research and practice* (pp. 15–38). New York, NY: Peter Lang.

Montgomery, L. M. (2008). *Anne of Green Gables.* London, UK: Puffin Classics.

Rosenblatt, L. (1978/1994). *The reader, the text, the poem: The transactional theory of the literary work.* Carbondale, IL: Southern Illinois University Press.

Shields, C. (2001). *Dressing up for the carnival.* New York, NY: Penguin Books.

Orienting Map III

Knowing/Be(com)ing/ Doing Literacies

(Re)Thinking Theory-Practice With a Personal Narrative Game Board

Candace R. Kuby

This chapter begins with an invitation—an invitation to think and to create. I am asking you to think with me about theory and practice, specifically the definitions, etymology, and the two quotes shared below, in relation to your work as an educator.[1] Take a moment to think, write, sketch, and respond to them; go ahead—get out a pencil or pen and write down your thoughts.

Theory[2]

A supposition or a system of ideas intended to explain something, especially one based on general principles independent of the thing to be explained.

Comes from Greek meaning "contemplation, speculation," from *theōros*, "spectator"

Practice

The actual application or use of an idea, belief, or method as opposed to theories about such application or use.

Comes from Late Middle English meaning "perform, carry out"

* * * * *

You cannot put a theory onto a practice. What is needed is a kind of encounter between the theory and the practice, where neither has the right to function as a highest organizing or defining principle.
(Olsson, 2009, pp. 97–98)

148 *Candace R. Kuby*

> *Practice is in fact continuously and* already *doing and practicing educational theories, whether we are aware of it or not.*
> (Lenz Taguchi, 2010, p. 21)

* * * * *

My research partnership since 2010 has been with an elementary school teacher, Tara Gutshall Rucker.[3] It is often our thinking, reading, talking together about literacies in her classrooms[4] that prompts our theorizing about literacy *and* our reading-theorizing prompts pedagogies. Theory-practice[5] is relational and mutually constitutive of each other; in other words, they make each other or are entangled in each other's be(com)ing.

In conversation with the rest of the chapters in this book, my writing aims to provoke you to (re)think theory-practice. I share an example from Tara's classroom of Billy[6] creating a personal narrative game board. I invite you to wonder with me. How might educators notice the ways humans, non-humans, and more-than-humans are already producing literacies? How might educators foster spaces for intra-active[7] pedagogies inspired by posthumanist theories? I hope educators will imagine ways, as they read examples from Tara's classroom, to invent various pedagogical practices for/with children that honour posthumanist ways of knowing/be(com)ing/doing literacies.

Billy is a second grader in Tara's classroom. I share from his composing during Writers' Studio, a time of the day that Tara invites students to "go be a writer" with a range of artistic and digital tools. He is creating a game board (i.e., a baseball field) for a writing unit on personal narratives. I focus my writing-thinking around two video clips that have been combined together (see Figure 11: QR code for video and endnote 8). The first clip is me having a conference with Billy as he drafts the game board design. You'll hear Tara's voice in the background in the first part of the clip; she is not talking to Billy but another child nearby, and then you'll hear my voice asking Billy some questions about the draft. The second clip is 3 weeks later and includes the voices of peers playing and experiencing the game board to learn of Billy's personal narrative related to a baseball game. (Billy is recording this clip, so you'll hear his voice and experience his movement while holding the camera.)

As you watch, jot some notes, sketch your thinking, find someone to talk with about how the definitions and quotes at the beginning of the chapter, scholarship you've read, and the video work together to produce new ideas about literacies. Mainly, I want you to think about how theory and practice aren't separate or binaries. Rather, they are a togetherness, a force, a flow—perhaps best written as theorypractice or practicetheory. Or perhaps we need another word altogether. What if we take the definitions and etymology for the words *theory* and *practice* and merge and (en)fold them with/in one another? Instead of theory being independent of the "thing" (i.e., practice) being explained or applied as stated in the definition provided earlier, what if we (re)think and (re)define theory and practice as relational or mutually constitutive of each other?

Theory-practice *or* practice-theory *or* theorypractice *or* practicetheory as:

> Contemplating and speculating from with/in/while/carrying out/performing
>
> *or*
>
> Carrying out/performing/with/in/while contemplating and speculating

Consider these rethought definitions, definitions that join body/mind and doing/thinking as you engage with the video and this chapter.

As the chapter title indicates, my writing plays with words and symbols. As I've read more and more theories about how humans, non-humans, and more-than-humans come into being together (see Davies, 2014; Lenz Taguchi, 2010; Murris, 2016; Olsson, 2009 for examples of education scholars), I have found myself needing to play with language and (re)presentation to try to (re)present theoretical concepts in my writing—to not only *think with theory* but to also *write with theories*; to try to convey through (re)presentation with language philosophical and theoretical ideas.

> Take a moment to think, write, sketch, and respond to this section; go ahead—get out a pencil or pen and write down your thoughts.

Coming to Know/Be/Do Posthumanist Theories-Pedagogies

I began reading work inspired by Gilles Deleuze and Pierre-Félix Guattari, poststructural thinkers, when an article by Kevin Leander and Deborah Rowe (2006) was first published. I felt lost, unsure, and completely

Figure 11 QR Code for video[8]

confused by what I was reading and yet invigorated, inspired, and yearning for more. I ordered *A Thousand Plateaus* (Deleuze & Guattari, 1980/1987) and began by reading the first plateaus titled, "Introduction: Rhizome." Again, I felt lost and confused, but my thinking felt new and went in a thousand directions. I kept returning for more.

Since then, I have read the work of early childhood scholars who not only think with poststructural thinkers such as Deleuze and Guattari but are also inspired by posthumanist, feminist "new" materialist, and/or Indigenous ways of knowing and being (e.g., Davies, 2014; Lenz Taguchi, 2010; Murris, 2016). While engaging these, I was also learning-with Tara, her students, the writing materials, and school discourses about literacies. Tara and I began to read together and think about what was coming to be in Room 203.

We were also intimately familiar with literacy scholars who write about New Literacy Studies, multimodality, and multiliteracies (e.g., New London Group, 1996; Pahl & Rowsell, 2012; Wohlwend, 2011). The work of these scholars is heavily influential in our thinking as we began to reimagine a traditional Writing Workshop curriculum into what became Writers' Studio (e.g., Kuby & Gutshall Rucker, 2016). However, our reading of poststructural and posthumanist theories ruined us (in a good way). We cannot *not* think with post-concepts. The theories have changed the way we understand the world, and all the lively relations, coming to be, including literacies. The literacy scholarship on multimodality and multiliteracies seemed too human focused for what we noticed coming to be in Writers' Studio. We needed theories to help us think-with and understand the *togetherness* of students, teacher, paint, yarn, iPad, tissue paper, pipe cleaners, paper, and, and, and. . . . Not as separate bodies but as relational bodies. Not solely theories about humans (subjects) mediating tools (objects) for meaning making. Thus, the human is still a part of how we conceptualize literacies and pedagogies but not the sole focus and origin of producing knowledges, realities, and relationships—nor literacies. This is how poststructural and posthumanist theories became pedagogies *and* how pedagogies of Room 203 became theories. As Elizabeth St. Pierre (2011) states, people produce theories. We would also say that people (and non-human and more-than-human bodies) produce theories *and* theories produce people (and non-human and more-than-human bodies).

Tara and I didn't have a preset research question to guide our thinking together. Rather, thinking-problems-questions emerged as we entangled[9] in the literacies coming to be. Generally, we were interested in opening up Writing Workshop by inviting children to compose with a range of materials (not just lined paper with pencils and crayons). Our ways of inquiring were inspired by Maggie MacLure's (2013) discussion on data glowing. In other words, we focus our thinking on intra-actions in the world that grab us, so to speak (and we are a part of), that we can't let go of and live with/in us. Our publications have focused on literacies coming to be or, as we've conceptualized, literacy desirings.

> the concept of *literacy desiring* [is] to focus on literacy processes (the becoming of artifacts such as books, movies, dramas, 3-D models, wall murals, puppets, and so forth) and to emphasize the fluid, sometimes unintentional, unbounded, and rhizomatic ways multimodal artifacts come into being through intra-actions with humans and nonhumans (i.e., time, space, materials, environment).
>
> Literacy desiring is oriented toward the present (ever-changing) needs, wishes, and demands of students-with-nonhumans, but also with possible users of literacy artifacts in mind.
>
> (Kuby & Gutshall Rucker, 2016, p. 4, emphasis in original)

In our book, we also discuss how we see theory, research methodology, and pedagogy as all intertwined in a mutually constitutive relationship. Meaning while we initially thought that theory would become our research methodology—or that we'd think with theories and with data—what happened was that the lines or boundaries or definitions between theory, methodology, and pedagogy were blurred and not easily distinguishable. This relates to the opening two quotes of this chapter and how we thought-with Billy's literacy desiring(s) with materials. We do not believe this idea of literacy desiring(s) is a thing or a fixed (even definable) concept. It would not look the same in the spaces you work, as it did in Tara's classroom. Rather, literacy desiring(s) are constantly being made and unmade (see Gutshall Rucker & Kuby, forthcoming).

Inspired by Posthumanism and Feminist "New" Materialisms

It is important to begin a section on what inspires my thinking about posthumanism and feminist "new" materialisms with an acknowledge to the ways Indigenous peoples have thought of/with/from knowing and being as intricately tied together. Scholars such as Eve Tuck and Wayne Yang (2014), Linda Tuhiwai Smith (2012), and Robin Wall Kimmerer (2014) remind us all to consider the content and processes we undertake in our research and for what purposes. People in literacy education are beginning to read and think-with more-than-human theories from various bodies of scholarship, such as socio-material, posthuman, Indigenous, and feminist "new" materialism. While there are some overlapping philosophical concepts in these areas, it is important to note that labels, and the ideas behind them, are not synonymous and

152 *Candace R. Kuby*

come from specific traditions with nuanced assumptions. When I read across these theories, I ask myself questions about their "grids of intelligibility," a phrase as Michel Foucault used. Mainly, what assumptions (or grids) on knowing (epistemology), realities (ontology), and relationships (axiology) hold the theory together? What makes the paradigmatic assumptions of the theory? Said another way, theories each have underlying beliefs on "language; discourse; rationality; power, resistance, and freedom; knowledge and truth; and the subject" (see St. Pierre, 2000, p. 477).

Posthumanism is a philosophical orientation that states "things" don't pre-exist their relations but rather come into being through/in relations (Barad, 2007). Posthumanism is situated within a relational ontology that believes ontology (reality) cannot be separated from epistemology (knowing) and axiology (ethics, relationships). Therefore, posthumanist scholarship is deeply and integrally a justice-oriented, ethical philosophy of how we are all already entangled—in everyday moments—with humans, non-humans, more-than-humans, and discourses. Therefore, it is our responsibility (or our ability to respond as Karen Barad and Donna Haraway write) with/in entanglements that produce the world and makes changes. In posthumanism, there is an effort to shift the focus from the human—*not to rid the human or create a binary of human versus non-human* but rather to look at the relationships *between* or *among* humans, non-humans, and more-than-humans. Therefore, *posthumanist scholarship is not a theory on materiality and to(solely) focus on materials I believe doesn't honour the writings*. Focusing on materials continues to reify a binary of material (or non-human) versus human. Focusing on what humans do in relation to/with/in materials is still rooted in a Cartesian logic full of dualist or binary ways of seeing the world (e.g., body/mind, female/male, nature/culture; for further discussion on Cartesian logics, see St. Pierre, 2000).

Theories are not fixed nor does someone (neither the author nor reader) own or hold the "right" interpretation. Deleuze and Guattari's scholarship prompts us to consider that theoretical concepts are always on the move or are intellectually mobile. Concepts are always new, always becoming something more, and help us to think beyond what we already know. Theories are concepts and ideas about the world that are malleable and change as we think-with them (hence, theory-practice). Perhaps we could think of concepts as a verb: concepting. We must read, read, and read more (theory) *as we are also* be(com)ing/doing/knowing literacies (practice). As St. Pierre (2015) writes, nobody can read for you and those who read a lot can tell when others have not. In other words, don't rush to use a theoretical concept. Concepts don't float alone but rather are entangled in a web or meshwork of philosophical assumptions (and practices) that make them thinkable. We need to read theories, so as we think with them, we might understand better not only how the author conceptualized the concept *but also* how the theory is becoming anew as we plug it into our thinking/knowing/be(com)ing/doing. Deleuze (2004) writes, "A theory is exactly like a tool box . . . a theory has to be used, it has to work" (p. 208).

Wondering and Wandering With Posthumanism: Three Underlying Assumptions

For the remainder of this chapter, we will focus on three posthumanist concepts and revisit the videos of Billy composing (and watching peers play) a game board. Next I share three quotes about posthumanist theoretical concepts to help us think and I leave spaces in between for you to write, respond, question, and think-with the ideas. I encourage you to browse the reference list at the end of the chapter and find readings that you can dig into these concepts further.

Ethico-Onto-Epistemology

We come to know through being and doing; we cannot separate epistemology (knowing) from ontology (being) and axiology (doing).

> With this stance [posthumanism], ontology (theories of being) and epistemology (theories of knowledge and knowing) cannot be separated as they traditionally have been in research and teaching. In order to understand the relationship between learning, the child, and the material reality, we must lean into what Barad refers to an onto-epistemology, which is the study of knowing in being. 'It is impossible to isolate knowing from being since they are mutually implicated.
> (Lenz Taguchi, 2010, p. 40)" (Kuby & Gutshall Rucker, 2016, p. 15)

How does ethico-onto-epistemology connect to literacies?
What are you wondering and wandering with/about this concept?

> Take a moment to think, write, sketch, and respond to this concept; go ahead—get out a pencil or pen and write down your thoughts.

Relational Be(com)ing

Posthumanism is not (solely) a theory on materials or materiality. If as educators we focus on that, we've missed the point. Humans, non-humans, and more-than-humans are entangled in non-hierarchical and material-discursive relationships in their be(com)ing.

> Sociomaterialism [theories that focus on social, cultural, material relationships] is based on a relational ontology, where individual or discrete entities are not seen to pre-exist relationships—rather they are constituted through relationships, as is agency. Karen Barad (2007) refers to this as "entanglement" while Deleuze and Guattari (1980/1987) refer to it as "assemblages."
> (Leibowitz, Bozalek, & Kahn, 2017, p. 4)

How does relational be(com)ing connect to literacies?
What are you wondering and wandering with/about?

> Take a moment to think, write, sketch, and respond this concept; go ahead—get out a pencil or pen and write down your thoughts.

Working to Resist Binary Logics

The third assumption focuses on working against binary logics. Scholars such as Elizabeth St. Pierre, Alecia Youngblood Jackson, and Lisa Mazzei (2016) state that since at least the beginning of the 21st century, scholars from a range of disciplines and fields have been working in what are being called the "new empiricisms" and "new materialisms." Scholars in these areas have intensified their arguments against foundational assumptions of Western thought that enable binary oppositions such as mind/body, object/subject, female/male, human/non-human, and nature/culture.

> This is why we came to see theory as methodology as pedagogy with recursive arrows (theory ← → methodology ← → pedagogy). We believe all three aspects are mutually constitutive of each other.
> (Kuby & Gutshall Rucker, 2016, p. 47)

How does working to resist binary logics connect to literacies?
What are you wondering and wandering with/about?

> Take a moment to think, write, sketch, and respond this concept; go ahead—get out a pencil or pen and write down your thoughts.

As posthumanism works to resist binary logics such as subject/object, nature/culture, human/non-human, and mind/body (and so forth), we must also (re)think the binary of theory and practice. They are already, always entangled. In addition to rethinking these binaries, Tara and I also worked against (and simultaneously found ourselves within) binaries such as theory/methodology, literacy/not literacy, researcher/teacher,

Knowing/Be(com)ing/Doing Literacies   155

and writing/not writing. The binaries are many in literacy education and research practices! Let's pause and think back to the opening quotes on theorypractice by Olsson and Lenz Taguchi as well as the etymological roots and attempted merging of theory and practice. What are your thoughts and questions now?

> Take a moment to think, write, sketch, and respond; go ahead—get out a pencil or pen and write down your thoughts.

Theorypractice With Billy-Game Board-Peers

Let's return to the video clip of Billy-Game Board-Peers[10] coming to be. Before you view the clip again, choose one of the three theoretical concepts to *think-with* as you watch. What does thinking-with this concept *and* the video clip produce for you? How are you now thinking about literacies? Pedagogies? Re-watch it again and choose a different concept to think with. Re-watch it a third time with the final concept to think with.

> Take a moment to think, write, sketch, and respond; go ahead—get out a pencil or pen and write down your thoughts.

In the opening minute, Billy is sharing with me how the game will (hopefully) unfold, and in the moment of doing so, he picks up a pencil to revise the draft (i.e., game board design). He adds a rectangle on the draft to signal where people will pick up cards to tell them how many spaces to move on the game board/baseball field.

In the next scene, two friends are playing the game/personal narrative. Instead of making a game board with a lot of spaces, there are only four—the four bases of a baseball field. Billy wants players to "play" baseball, hit balls, and score points to see who "wins" the game. In doing so, as they draw cards, they will learn of his personal narrative—the stories he wants to tell about baseball experiences in his life.

In the process of playing the game/learning the personal narrative, the boys keep score in their heads and periodically share the updated score. Hands-paper baseball players-game cards engage in "un-sportsmen-like conduct." In the moment, they create a "dugout," which is needed in response to what is produced when a card is drawn. In doing so, they revise the game and add in a necessary component for where players need to go when they get out of the game. It seems the game is over when they run out of cards.

One of the players prompts Billy, who is the "cameraman," to ask, "How did the game go?" They comment on the game rules #6 and #7.

Billy responds to a question about bad sportsman-like conduct by revising the directions to the game as he talks to the players. Only in the moment of playing the game did relations come into being for the players (i.e., "losing a turn"). By playing the game, it became evident that a dugout is needed for players to be thrown out of the game for bad conduct. So, although Billy knew (epistemology) how to create a game and the components needed, it wasn't until the game came into being or reality (ontology) that the need for a dugout become realized. It was through relationships that (being and doing) revisions (knowing) came to be.

Personal narrative compositions (and processes of composing) such as this one cause me to wonder how we often draw lines around what is writing or not. Or what is literacy or not. These demarcations produce binaries (writing/not writing, literacy/not literacy) and thus produce certain relations in the world (Zapata, Kuby, & Thiel, 2018). Must there always be alphabetics for something to be counted and legitimatized as writing? Or literacies? How might we (re)think writing and literacies based on our theory-practice with children, theories, materials, discourses, languages, and . . . and . . . and . . .?

Teachers at Theorists-Pedagogists (or Pedagogists-Theorists)

Returning to the opening definitions and quotes, I believe teachers are some of the best theorists. If we believe theory and practice are mutually constitutive of each other, teachers are daily working-with and living-out theories and pedagogies with children, discourses, and other material bodies. Often people are good at categorizing, boxing off, closing up, and drawing lines and boundaries. However, this chapter (and this edited volume) is an attempt to mix, merge, play-with, disrupt, open-up, shock thought, and do differently when thinking about posthumanist theories and practices. While at times this is uncomfortable, the authors provide a generosity to go-with-it and lean into stuckness—not knowing where the uncertainty will go.

As I stated at the beginning and throughout, my focus with Tara is on what is being produced, in the moment, when students are invited to be writers with a range of artistic and digital materials. As we share in our book and other publications, we believe this intra-active pedagogy with humans, non-humans, and more-than-humans is an ethical stance—because all children should have spaces to think, learn, grow, compose with a variety of tools and supplies across many disciplines (without a pressure to produce an end product or state ahead of composing what the goal or purpose is). This connects to the idea that posthumanist theory is an orientation to how one views the world, a relational ontology, an ethico-onto-epistemological approach to pedagogy. Often schools focus on the future—on benchmarks, on ending objectives, on preparing for the next grade or even for after graduation, and so forth. However, we are concerned with the now, the in the moment—the realities produced in schools and the relationships when students are invited to be writers, composers, and learners with a range of artful (and discursive) materials.

Let's revisit the opening definitions and quote one more time and put them in conversation with the following statement:

> Consciously or not, we educators and educational researchers are used to looking at schools as places where humans dwell together to learn what it means to be human and to accumulate the kinds of skills and habits required to participate in human societies as adults. This occurs in spite of the fact that schools are connected with the nonhuman world in so many explicit and implicit ways . . . we are not the center of the universe. Indeed, we should not be the center of conversation.
> (Snaza et al., 2014, pp. 39 & 40)

As You Continue to Think with This Statement, Here Are Some Invitations to Ponder

- What is/are literacy(ies) in human/non-human/more-than-human entanglements (and what do they produce)?
- What are the ethics and justice of posthumanist literacies?
- How might educators notice ways humans/non-humans/more-than-humans are already producing literacies? Already doing theories?
- How do we support literacy desirings—unpredictable, fluid, relational ways of producing literacies?
- What new ways do you imagine working with children and other bodies (digital tools, texts, art supplies, school policies, and so forth) to foster spaces for pedagogical practices that honour posthumanist ways of knowing/be(com)ing/doing literacies?

Take a moment to think, write, sketch, and respond; go ahead—get out a pencil or pen and write down your thoughts.

Notes

1. I use the term "educator" as a more inclusive term rather than "researcher" and/or "teacher." "Educator" is used to signal a both/and (teachers and researchers—of which one person could identify as both).
2. Definitions retrieved from Google dictionary on March 15, 2018.
3. Candace authored this chapter, and therefore many statements are written with "I". However, "we" is also used in the chapter to signify and acknowledge the collaborative teaching/researching partnership with the teacher Tara Gutshall Rucker. Our research meetings and thinking together since 2010 heavily influenced this chapter.

158 Candace R. Kuby

4. I use "classrooms" as plural here to indicate that since 2010 when our partnership began, Tara has taught first, second, and fifth grades. However, the example in this chapter comes from a year she taught second grade (i.e., her room number was 203 as signaled later in the chapter).
5. I write "theory-practice" to show the mutually constitutive relationship of both. However, this puts theory first. "Practice-theory" is another way to write it; however, it privileges practice first. Ideally, writing them superimposed on each other would better "represent" the concept I am writing about.
6. All student names are pseudonyms.
7. The neologism *intra-action*, coined by Karen Barad (2007), focuses on the forces and productions among humans, nonhumans, and more-than-humans. Hillevi Lenz Taguchi (2010) writes about intra-active pedagogies in her book which inspires our thinking on literacy pedagogies.
8. You may also access the video with this link: https://drive.google.com/file/d/1UrAmAJMUrreHe0MRnpZFT9HVpHD06oiB/view?usp=sharing
9. I draw on Karen Barad's (2007) concept of entanglement, which comes from her work as a feminist-philosopher-physicist. Entanglement is about the phenomenon of particles—the wholeness produced when parts are together creating newness—a new whole (the physical proximity of parts isn't necessary for an entanglement to occur). The wholeness is not identifiable by the parts or individual components, but as a new whole.
10. I write these together with a hyphen to show the entanglement of Billy, game board, and peers.

References

Barad, K. (2007). *Meeting the universe halfway: Quantum physics and the entanglement of matter and meaning*. Durham, NC: Duke University Press.
Davies, B. (2014). *Listening to children: Being and becoming*. New York, NY: Routledge.
Deleuze, G. (2004). *Desert Islands*. Los Angeles, CA: Semiotext(e).
Deleuze, G., & Guattari, F. (1980/1987). *A thousand plateaus: Capitalism and schizophrenia*. (B. Massumi, Trans.). Minneapolis, MN: University of Minnesota Press.
Gutshall Rucker, T., & Kuby, C. R. (forthcoming). *Making and unmaking literacy desirings: Pedagogical matters of concern from Writers' Studio*.
Kuby, C. R., & Gutshall Rucker, T. (2016). *Go be a writer! Expanding the curricular boundaries of literacy learning with children*. New York, NY: Teachers College Press.
Leander, K. M., & Rowe, D. W. (2006). Mapping literacy spaces in motion: A rhizomatic analysis of a classroom literacy performance. *Reading Research Quarterly, 41*(4), 428–460.
Leibowitz, B., Bozalek, V., & Kahn, P. (Eds.). (2017). *Theorising learning to teach in higher education*. New York, NY: Routledge.
Lenz Taguchi, H. (2010). *Going beyond the theory/practice divide in early childhood education: Introducing an intra-active pedagogy*. London, UK: Routledge.
MacLure, M. (2013). Researching without representation? Language and materiality in postqualitative methodology. *International Journal of Qualitative Studies in Education, 26*(6), 658–667.
Murris, K. (2016). *The posthuman child: Educational transformation through philosophy with picture books*. London, UK: Routledge.

New London Group. (1996). A pedagogy of multiliteracies: Designing social futures. *Harvard Educational Review*, 66(1), 60–92.

Olsson, L. M. (2009). *Movement and experimentation in young children's learning: Deleuze and Guattari in early childhood education*. New York, NY: Routledge.

Pahl, K., & Rowsell, J. (2012). *Literacy and education: Understanding the new literacy studies in the classroom* (2nd ed.). Thousand Oaks, CA: Sage Publications.

Smith, D. W. (2012). *Essays on Deleuze*. Edinburgh, UK: Edinburgh University Press.

Smith, L. T. (2012). *Decolonizing methodologies: Research and Indigenous peoples* (2nd ed.). London, UK: Zed Books Ltd.

Snaza, N., Applebaum, P., Bayne. S., Carlson, D., Morris, M., Rotas, N., . . . Weaver, J. (2014). Toward a posthuman education. *Journal of Curriculum Theorizing*, 30(1), 39–55.

St. Pierre, E. A. (2000). Poststructural feminism in education: An overview. *Qualitative Studies in Education*, 13(5), 477–515.

St. Pierre, E. A. (2011). Post qualitative research: The critique and the coming after. In N. K. Denzin & Y. S. Lincoln (Eds.), *The Sage handbook of qualitative research* (pp. 611–625). Thousand Oaks, CA: Sage Publications.

St. Pierre, E. A. (2015). Practices for the "new" in the new empiricisms, the new materialisms, and post qualitative inquiry. In N. K. Denzin & M. D. Giardina (Eds.), *Qualitative inquiry and the politics of research* (pp. 75–96). Walnut Creek, CA: Left Coast Press.

St. Pierre, E. A., Jackson, A. Y., & Mazzei, L. A. (2016). New empiricisms and new materialisms: Conditions for new inquiry. *Cultural Studies ← → Critical Methodologies*, 16(2), 99–110.

Tuck, E., & Yang, K. W. (2014). R-words: Refusing research. In D. Paris & M. T. Winn (Eds.), *Humanizing research: Decolonizing qualitative inquiry with youth and communities* (pp. 223–247). Thousand Oaks, CA: Sage Publications.

Wall Kimmerer, R. (2014). *Braiding sweetgrass: Indigenous wisdom, scientific knowledge and the teaching of plants*. Minneapolis, MN: Milkweed Editions.

Wohlwend, K. (2011). *Playing their way into literacies: Reading, writing, and belonging in the early childhood classroom*. New York, NY: Teachers College Press.

Zapata, A., Kuby, C. R., & Thiel, J. J. (2018). Encounters with writing: Becoming-with posthumanist ethics. *Journal of Literacy Research*, 50(4), 478–501.

Plateau III

Relationships That Matter in Curriculum and Place

Mairi McDermott and Kim Lenters

In critical literacy, we are well aware of the importance, or shall we say, the materiality of questions in teaching and learning—questions posed by us and questions asked by the students. Asking the "just-right-question" can reorient the classroom's trajectory, assembling new lines of flight and possibilities for engaging the curricular material, one another, and the place in which learning is happening. The intra-active collectivity experienced by teachers, students, materials, and practices in the classroom thus highlights another important aspect of a posthuman understanding of classroom literacy learning: the notion of *throwntogetherness*. As a concept, throwntogetherness draws our attention to the somewhat random and always changing character of classroom assemblages. In each of the chapters in this plateau, readers are invited into throwntogetherness, facilitated through mundane questions as the authors map potential lines of flight set in motion from the questions: "What was your first encounter with Indigenous people?" (McKay & Whitty, this volume), "Do you want to go for a walk?" (Hirst & Burnett, this volume), "What will happen to us?" (Honeyford & Trussler, this volume), and "How are you doing?" (Perry & Seel, this volume).

As you can see from the questions, they may not always be situated as profound and critical questions. What is important is that each question punctuates a particular jolt in the authors' conjunctures. What is important is what the questions do when we take the time to engage our embodied and sensed responses. While deliberate choices are often made by teachers and administrators (think of lesson planning or organizing class rosters and reading lists) configuring the porous limitations of the assemblage, because people, things, practices, and events are always emerging or becoming something new, we cannot know how the various participants in a classroom assemblage will **intra-act** with each other. Thus, the chapters in this plateau, grounded in reorienting questions, take up the role of relationships in curriculum and place.

Often enough, curriculum becomes positioned as *material* to cover, and as many have noted before, in *covering* the curriculum, in trying to keep up with a linear trajectory of learning, we miss so much of the thisness, the haecities, contingencies, and indeterminancies of learning (Gannon & Davies, 2009). Posthuman understandings of literacy learning embrace the incommensurabilities of learning, providing new openings for exploring the potential and capacities of the various participants (human and more-than-human) in the classroom assemblage.

Classrooms, as assemblages, then, are particular places that are also always in-process of becoming *with* the bodies, materials, intentions and affects, curriculum, and culture (of the school, of the students, of the broader community). Posthumanism, and the chapters in this plateau, provide us with alternative understandings of *place*. In conventional Western epistemological regimes, our tendency may be to think of place as something rooted or fixed, static and immutable. Posthumanism, with its emphasis on *relations*, emergence, and fluidity, views place as configured through relationships among the things, people, events, and practices associated with a material place. As Comber (2016) states, "Schools, as material places located in particular geographic sites, with different social, cultural, and physical histories and characteristics, are dynamic and subject to change" (p. 7). In Hirst and Burnett's chapter (this volume), we are invited to think about how we move through place as embodied beings through their story of what unfolded after Burnett asks Hirst if she wants to go for a walk. Both authors, with different historical, material, and temporal relations with the place(s) in/on/with which they walk, animate the impossibility of place as static and immutable. Indeed, for the rest of their chapter they tell a "new" story of the students and the place of Hirst's school, one that differently positions the students as constituting the place—the physical and historical discourses of the neighborhood.

Whitty and McKay (this volume) also animate the importance of the stories we tell/teach (and that we are able to hear). The role of texts, of stories in opening possibilities for alternative relations with those who have been marginalized becomes the ethical commitment of their work as educators and their work in writing in this chapter. While places are constituted by an ever-shifting lamination of social, political, cultural, and physical trajectories, places also play a role in shaping the relations and entities associated with them. For example, a person's history with a place, such as the literacy classroom, will shape how they intra-act, as a student, with literacy instruction and texts, or how they, as a parent, take part in their child's schooled literacy learning. Whitty and McKay each invite us into their commitments to Canada's *Truth and Reconciliation* Report (2015) by sharing their vulnerabilities in the kinds of texts they encountered growing up, those which tell a particularly damaging narrative of the Indigenous Peoples of Turtle Island (colonially named Canada).

Relationships That Matter in Curriculum and Place 163

While Whitty and McKay focus on the role of story and texts in shaping the configurations of literacy learning materializing particular relations with *others*, Honeyford and Trussler (this volume) map the ways in which material objects may become sites for making connections and ethical relations with others across time and place. As noted earlier, Trussler's end-of-school-day routine was interrupted by a question from a recently resettled refugee high school student who was looking at the graduation photos from the previous year: "What's going to happen to us?" What futures are made available to these youth who come to Canada through refugee resettlement programs? How might we connect with them, and how might they connect with this place, here and now? In their chapter, Honeyford and Trussler take us through several pop-up installation projects they position as pedagogical in that they teach us to re-connect to place, objects, and others differently. The posthuman conceptualization of place gives us much to consider in relation to the way past relationships with place, positive or negative, may be implicated in a student's literacy learning. It also provides a space for considering how we, as educators, might change the trajectory of a place and what our students are able to be or do within it. Thinking with the concepts of affect, place, and throwntogetherness, as the chapters in this plateau do, can assist us, as educators, in setting students (and perhaps their families) on new literacy trajectories.

What might happen if we were able to help students who have had difficult relationships with the literacy classroom to begin to experience it as a place where they are effective, engaged, and energized? How might we do this? In the final chapter of this plateau, we are taken into the adult literacy classroom, a space where the students often had precarious relations with school and literacy for a variety of reasons. Perry and Seel (this volume) dig into the central importance of relationships, as beyond instrumental configurations conventionally practiced, in adult literacy. As they note, for adult literacy to become a space of altered relations (between self and perceived identity, between self and literacy, between materiality of literacy in 21st century and curriculum, between pedagogy and ethics) for re-imagining place and belonging, we must tend to the historical and mundane relationships that contour adult literacy as a pedagogical field.

Overarchingly, the chapters in this plateau animate the ways in which posthumanism draws our attention to relations in/through/with/against curriculum and place, inclusive of disrupting historical relations that accumulate through time limiting our imaginations of what could be through repetition and the taken-for-granted. The musings provoke us to shift our relations and relations to relations, situated as porous. Importantly, these shifts are compelled in these chapters through the importance of listening to and being with questions as part of critical literacy practices.

References

Comber, B. (2016). *Literacy, place, and pedagogies of possibility*. New York, NY: Routledge.

Gannon, S., & Davies, B. (Eds.). (2009). *Pedagogical encounters*. New York, NY: Peter Lang.

Truth and Reconciliation Commission. (2015). *Calls to action*. Retrieved from www.trc.ca/websites/trcinstitution/File/2015/Findings/Calls_to_Action_English2.pdf

10 Walking Together In and Through Stories

Pam Whitty and Heather McKay

When we think of literacies in contemporary times, we think about literacies as stories, as multiple and multimodal. We are immersed in stories that link to place, time, and matter. Stories transcend our physical place; they are fluid and transformative. We see the possibilities for stories and their intra-actions with each other, with ourselves, and with the more-than-human as "articulated moments in networks of social relationships and understandings . . . which includes a consciousness of its links with the wider world" (Massey, 1991, p. 28). These intra-actions bring to us a "simultaneity of stories-so-far" (Massey, 2005, p. 130) and hold promise for changing the past, present, and future.

In our place, Canada, Turtle Island, story and stories bring together the local and global—creating a literate landscape rich with cultures, peoples, languages, and histories. As two settler educators, Heather living in Treaty Seven territory in Calgary, Alberta, and Pam living on the homelands of the Wabanaki Peoples in Fredericton, New Brunswick, we are affected by the flows and intensities of all matter of stories. As educators, we use this space to intra-act and explore story and storytelling as one possible way to walk forward together, in a good way.

What Stories Do

Margaret Kovach (2009) whose family "stems from the traditional territories of the Plains Cree and Saulteaux peoples of the Great Plains" (p. 3), tells us that stories "remind us of who we are and of our belonging. . . . They are active agents within a relational world, pivotal in gaining insight into a phenomenon" (p. 95). Kovach's deep sense of stories, and their agential place in a relational world, intersects with the thinking of Karen Barad (2012). When Barad speaks to the agential nature of phenomenon—she theorizes that, "what we take to be 'past' and what we take to be the 'present' and the 'future' are entangled with each other" (p. 66). Various entanglements, then, materially and discursively constitute what becomes excluded and what comes to matter.

Decolonizing Literacy

Literacy, in Canadian schools, has historically been considered through a settler lens, thereby contributing "to the erasure of Aboriginal Peoples' ways of being and knowing" (Steeves, 2010, p. 18). This is a local reality for us as educators on Turtle Island. Indigenous Peoples, their languages and cultures, have been devalued, distorted, and excluded—othered from settler ways of knowing and being, creating dualistic systems. At the same time, colonization is a global reality for most educators—for colonization is not singular to Turtle Island. Our joint decolonizing intent is to make visible continuities of past, present, and future (Kovach, 2009, p. 95) and stories entangling with each other, our place, ourselves (Barad, 2012), so that we can and upturn inequities of colonizing stories to co-create socially just ways of knowing and being. As educators, we think together about the possibilities and the potentialities of classrooms as rich intergenerational collectives of stories—oral, written, ancestral, and contemporary—cutting across differences. We choose to think and act together with Canada's Truth and Reconciliation Commission (TRC) to offer multiplicities of stories and ways of living with/in story to reveal how colonizing practices affected, and affect, bodies, lives, and lands, thus, actively creating the deeply ingrained separation of peoples from each other over time, space, and matter.

Act Now

- Consider the definitions of literacies in your current space—what are your beliefs, and how are they enacted?
- What are ways literacies, including localized and globalized stories and the intra-actions between them, act to upturn inequities in your context?
- How do storying and Indigenous ways of knowing live in your own literate lives?

Encountering the Truth and Reconciliation Commission: Voicing Past Silences

> Residential schools disrupted families and communities. They prevented elders from teaching children long-valued cultural and spiritual traditions and practices. They helped kill languages. These were not side effects of a well-intentioned system: the purpose of the residential school system was to separate children from the influences of their parents and their community, so as to destroy their culture. The impact was devastating.
> (Eigenbrod, 2012, p. 1)

They Came for the Children: Canada, Aboriginal Peoples, and Residential Schools, a publication of the TRC (2012), intends to educate the Canadian public about residential schools and their traumatic intergenerational legacy. Commissioners Justice Murray Sinclair, Chief Wilton Littlebear, and Marie Wilson write: "For the child taken, and for the parent left behind, we encourage Canadians to read this history, to understand the legacy of the schools, and to participate in the work of reconciliation" (p. vii). *They Came for the Children* is a multi-layered series of stories: stories of loss, pain and shame; stories of humility, colonialism, and destruction; stories of the failures of schools, and the resistance of Indigenous peoples; a multi-layered, Turtle Island story still being told, written, rewritten, and retold.

Encountering Residential School Stories: Affect Is Agentic—A Story from Pam

As a child, I was *not* taken from my family and community, while at the same time, I was taught a singular damning Indigenous story, perhaps familiar to many of you. My deeply learned understanding of Turtle Island's First Peoples resonates with that of Margaret McKay's (2011). In *The Embedded and Embodied Literacies of a Young Reader*. Mackey enumerates the racist and pervasively negative constructions of First Nation peoples and cultures she encountered in school textbooks, library books, and popular culture from her childhood in the 1950s and 1960s. These material-discursive productions were rationalized by Christian and economic practices, through colonial exploration and exploitation, and eventually national policies of assimilation, including the Indian Act and Indian Residential School policies. As is explicated in the TRC (2015a): "The 'civilizing mission' rested on a belief of racial and cultural superiority." (p. 50).

Over my (Pam) past 27 years as an educator-researcher at the University of New Brunswick, on the traditional lands of the Wabanaki Peoples, I have read residential school stories with the people, mostly settlers, in the courses I teach. For example, in our Cultural Constructions of Childhood class, initial readings include Isabelle Knockwood's *Out of the Depths* and *Poems of Rita Joe*, both Mi'kmaq women who attended the Schubenacadie Residential School as children in Nova Scotia. In her article, "For the child taken, for the parent left behind": Residential school narratives as acts of "Survivance," Renate Eigenbrod (2012) theorizes Knockwood's explanation to Rita Joe for writing her book as an act of survivance. "The reason I wrote the book was to heal the people who were in there. There is a lot of healing that has to be done" (in Eigenbrod, pp. 279–280, quoted from "Song of Rita Joe," p. 48).

Eigenbrod (2012) contends that literature about residential school childhoods is not about victimization; rather, this accumulating body of work evokes "survival, resistance, and continuance of cultures against colonial policies aimed at the annihilation of Indigenous presence most aggressively in the residential schools" (p. 280).

Currently, in our Children's Literature and Literary Theory class, we are reading Nicola Campbell's *Shi' shi'etko* (2005) and *Shin-Shin's Canoe* (2008), Jordan-Fenton and Pokiak's *Fatty Legs* (2010), and Richard Wagemese *Indian Horse* (2012)—all stories of survivance. Surprising to me, there are a few people who have indicated no previous knowledge of Indigenous residential schools. Yet for most people, these residential school stories reveal the disturbing, deliberate, systematic nature of Canadian government policies which, over time, worked to assimilate Indigenous children into the dominant settler culture while eradicating familial connections and the cultures and languages of Canada/Turtle Island's First Peoples—cultural, cognitive, and linguistic imperialism (Battiste, 2013; Eigenbrod, 2010) hand in hand with destruction of families.

Our individual and collective responses to these stories are emotional, transformative, and intimate. Parents in the class speak to how these stories evoke terrifying images of their own children being taken from them—something they cannot imagine. Almost everyone expresses a range of emotions from shame to anger to rage. These stories are as affective and effective as are the Calls to Action, articulated within *The Truth and Reconciliation Commission Canada: Calls to Action* (TRC, 2015b). Almost every class participant—typically teacher candidates and longstanding teachers—has expressed their desire to make a difference with the children and families in their classrooms; they want to take action and believe that working from within story is one way. Actions they have taken include sharing *Shi-shi etko* (2005) and *Shin-Shin's Canoe* 2008) with first and second grade children and their families, *Fatty Legs* (Jordan-Fenton & Pokiak-Fenton, 2010) with older children, and incorporating *Indian Horse* (2012) into secondary school curricula. Some teachers, inspired by the upsurge in Indigenous graphic novels, have brought these into their classrooms. Most have taken a close look at the bookshelves in their classrooms and school libraries, removed books, and worked with their school librarians to update Indigenous collections. Many have registered for Indigenous courses so that they might continue with their personal and professional (re)education. There is a felt urgency to their actions.

Act Now

How might you provision your learning space with diverse texts to open new conversations and build dialogue about and between a variety of worldviews?

Example Collections and Lenses

- http://empoweringthespirit.ca
- https://diversebooks.org/
- https://americanindiansinchildrensliterature.blogspot.com/p/best-books.html
- www.cbcdiversity.com/about

Encountering April Raintree: Unconscious to Conscious—A Story From Heather

I was raised learning the "Western tradition of creating and telling stories about other peoples' histories, societies and cultural practices . . . which has enabled Western Europeans to impose their stories as universal truths, while mis-representing non-Western narratives" (Hampton & DeMartini, 2017, p. 250). I have lived in Canada for 43 years but only recently have I consciously encountered Indigenous histories and peoples outside of popular culture. My consciousness came unexpectedly, calling into question to what I thought I knew about myself and my home. A single request, posed by Indigenous educator Dr. Phyllis Steeves, to tell the story of my first experience with Indigenous peoples opened my eyes and my heart. This single question revealed histories and worldviews through story that I did not know existed. I first felt ashamed. I thought I had no story to tell.

Tereasa Strong-Wilson (2007) teaches us as educators that we "can revisit our literacy memoirs "(p. 124) and bring to that experience counter-stories to confront our storied pasts. When I recalled reading *April Raintree* (1984) in grade 11, this remembrance invited me to look into my own storied past with new eyes. My first experience with Beatrice Culleton Monsionier's book *April Raintree* (1984) is different from the stories Pam encountered in her youth and different from the stories my own children encounter today. By the 1980s, printed narratives were beginning to tell Indigenous truths previously unwritten. Over time and place, I understand *April Raintree*, my unconsciousness, and my affect differently each time I intra-act with this story. For me, *April Raintree* (1984) now presents "the racialized, gendered, and sexual nature of [Indigenous women's] colonization . . . [and] in doing so, they transformed the debilitating force of an old social control, shame, into a social change agent in their generation" (Million, 2009, p. 54).

Through stories, shameful secrets of Indigenous childhoods and their complicated relationships with Canadian policies leap out of the of the private realm and into the public, standing alongside and disrupting dominant stories. When we "focus on the importance of people telling their own stories (reading the world) in a place where people may be both affirmed and challenged [we can] see how individual stories are connected [to] larger patterns of domination and resistance in a multicultural, global society" (Gruenewald, 2003, p. 312). The invitation to tell my story led to my awakening. I want to learn about and live in all the stories bound to the place I call home. Story became my beginning into Truth and Reconciliation for Education on Turtle Island.

As a Canadian educator and mother, I wonder how a more thoughtful encounter with story might have awakened me sooner. What if our single stories can connect and become something better and more to learn from? How can we as educators construct storying intra-actions that lead to knowing ourselves and our place in authentic and expansive ways? Jo-ann Archibald (2008) teaches us that stories "vary from the sacred to the historical, from cultural traditions to personal life experiences and testimonials. Some stories are "just for fun, while others have powerful teachings" (p 83). Approaching stories with a purpose, the purpose of Truth and Reconciliation, becomes a tangible act each of us as educators can embrace.

Act Now

- Call forward your own storied past. What was your first conscious, eyes wide-open experience with Indigenous histories and peoples?
- What stories have you adopted as truth? How might revisiting the stories you were taught, in this time and place, offer new perspectives about the stories and yourself?
- How might you intentionally offer and connect story and stories for the learners you work with?

Encountering Story on the Land

As educators, we act as central storytellers or cultural workers for our students (Strong-Wilson, 2007). Leroy Little Bear suggests we seek places on the land that can act as "pathways that facilitate communication" (Hill, 2008) and to discover the stories the land holds for us. Land is different from the colonial texts many of us grew up revering. When we open ourselves up to land-as-text and land-as-teacher this supports "anti-colonial praxis (thinking and acting against coloniality), without reducing Indigeneity and decolonization to depoliticized metaphors (Hampton & DeMartini, 2017, p. 248). When we embrace story, we embrace land and from the land, language is born.

Stories Discovered in the Coulee—Treaty 7 Land

Embracing Critical Land Literacy (Gruenewald, 2003) is one way to disrupt and enact literacies for Truth and Reconciliation. Stories from and intra-actions with the land offer critical opportunities towards decolonization and reinhabitation. Through decolonization we learn "to recognize disruption and injury" (Gruenewald, p. 9) followed by reinhabitation where we learn "to live well socially and ecologically in places that have been disrupted and injured" (Gruenewald, 2003, p. 9). To call forward some of the stories that dwell in Treaty 7 territory, and in particular at Twelve Mile Coulee, two local teachers and their students started their relationship with story on the land. A 2000-year-old teepee ring and a Buffalo statue marked this particular place as a space to discover land-as-teacher (Monica Huebner, personal communication, October 24, 2017). They walked and sat together on the land, listening with open hearts for the stories the coulee would whisper to them. Inspired from their time on the land, two of the young people took it upon themselves to learn and share the formal written Acknowledgement of the Land, gifted to the Calgary Board of Education from Elders. This honouring of the land became a repeated intra-action between an oral acknowledgment and multi-layered print text, teaching and becoming something more through each sharing.

Inspired by Barbara Comber's description of place-based Alphabet books in *Literacy, Place and Pedagogies of Possibility* (2016), the group gathered in their coulee and used the Latin alphabet as an invitation to become aware of the stories that came to them. By dwelling together in this sacred space, the land spoke to them through the language of verbs. They documented and questioned their learnings through different materials—photographs, words, videoconferencing, and various art supplies—to help them understand what the stories meant to them. The result was a collection of stories—a printed and localized *A-B-Coulee* book—inspired by their local place and connected to the global through their intra-actions with others who had similarly taken up story as a way of learning. This one example, from a moment in time in one Canadian classroom, illustrates what can be possible when teachers invite/guide students to engage with place and story as one way to take up Truth and Reconciliation for Education.

Act Now

- What are local places you might approach to explore land-as-text and land-as-teacher?
- What do you know about the land and language where you currently reside and work? How could you learn more?
- Who are the local storytellers that you might walk with to help you, and your students, see the Land through new eyes?

Encountering Story in the Classroom

A group of teachers meet to discuss Fatty Legs, *a book they had all agreed to read over the holiday break. Each teacher speaks to an experience*

> with the story that resonated with them personally. Together they wonder
> how they might introduce this particular story about one girl's experience
> in the Canadian Residential School System to their grade four students.
> Recognizing themselves as settler teachers, they want to find ethical and
> heartfelt ways of bringing Indigenous stories such as Fatty Legs to their
> learners. How to begin? The teachers begin with the text itself but soon
> move into a discussion about story as a way of learning, story as a way
> to participate in Truth and Reconciliation for Education, and their own
> encounters with story which brought them to this moment in time. They
> collectively feel the power of this one story and begin to consider how
> story could help build wider worldviews for themselves and their students. They are excited to walk this unfamiliar road with each other and
> with their students.

Classrooms are places where identities are constructed and enacted, individually and collectively. Classrooms are places of knowing, becoming, and feeling. When we consider how to "build student capacity for intercultural understanding, empathy and mutual respect" (TRC, 2015b, p. 7), one possibility becomes the classroom storying practices themselves. We can learn to be storytellers so that we can embrace and tell stories in our classrooms. By inviting Elders and community members into our classrooms to share their stories, students can experience the power of story-as-teacher firsthand. The elements of story that bring it alive, "the tone, volume, and pacing of voice . . . the gestures that make the story come alive, and the input of the audience" (Reese, 2007, p. 247) can only be experienced through oral storytelling. Providing opportunities for students to participate in yarning circles, a storytelling structure that places students in a circular gathering formation, invites students to learn and use story as a community. Yarning circles are "a speaking and listening practice that can be used for reflecting on new experiences or for rehearsing ideas in preparation for writing or drama activities" (Mills, Sunderland, & Davis-Warra, 2013, p. 286). Story structures such as yarning circles are equitable places where stories and truth assemble and intra-act. During circle, "the child also brings memories of people, places and events" (McKeough et al., 2008, p. 151), bringing together the local and the global and strengthening the constellation that binds us together in this time and place.

The materials, the books on our physical and/or digital classroom shelves, also call teachers and students towards new intra-actions with story. What possibilities might the familiar classroom bookshelf offer? What intra-actions are made possible with the thoughtful construction of the classroom bookshelf and the practices enacted in relationship with students and texts? Rudine Bishop (1990) asks us to consider how texts can act as mirrors, windows, and sliding glass doors. When students enter the classroom as a place, what parts of themselves are mirrored back to them, and what windows are opened for them? When teachers and students construct the classroom bookshelf, who and what are positioned as important to know about? Who and what are missing—how do we know, and what can we do about it? How can we can critically choose stories for our wide-ranging classrooms while being responsive to the local?

The schooled practice of privileging print means that printed stories claim a dominant/dominating space in most Canadian classrooms. From the first days of school, stories are read aloud and shared with students. Teachers use books to entertain, teach, and invite children to become curious about their world around them. Classroom texts become a living part of the political landscape through which literacies are constructed. Teachers have an ethical opportunity to use story as a tool for Truth and Reconciliation. The choice of which books are shared ensures the untold stories become known and through these intra-actions, the reader and the text itself are changed through each transaction.

Sometimes a particular story presents itself as a door to enter into Truth and Reconciliation for Education. *Fatty Legs* (2010) by Christy Jordan-Fenton has become a popular text in classrooms at this time and place on Turtle Island. Teachers select this text to learn about residential schools and to begin to understand histories differently from those they embodied in their schooling. The constructed "truths" many of us encountered and embodied in our education as children and young people dominated past curriculum and carried forward as unchallenged truths into our adulthoods and as settler-teachers in our classrooms. These embodied truths demand (re)education, including encounters with multiple stories to disrupt, displace, and dislodge what has become stuck in our bodies, minds, and hearts. Heather's encounter with *April Raintree*, for example, and the affect and shame this powerful telling evoked for her represent the beginning of a significant shift in understanding. When we seek a new horizon—"one that looks beyond what is close at hand—not in order to look away from it but to see it better" (Gadamer, 1975/1998, p. 305, as cited by Strong-Wilson, 2007, p. 118), the possibilities of the texts living and coming into our classrooms can become something new and good. Thankfully, some wise individuals and collectives have already offered starting points around building inclusive practices and diverse bookshelves.

Act Now

- Chimamanda Ngozi Adichie and Grace Lin challenge us to go beyond the "single story" and examine how we listen to and come to "know" from story. How can you disrupt the single stories brought into your classroom?
- Broadening our definitions of text itself invites a reconsideration of the many ways story and knowledge lives in our world.
- Teachers can use social issues texts to enter into critical literacy, disrupting, interrogating, and taking a stance through story itself (Lewison, Flint, & Van Sluys, 2002).

- Building text sets around essential questions, themes, and topics leverages the assembling of multiple stories and multiliteracies (Cunningham, 2015) to help teachers and students better understand historical events and Truth and Reconciliation for Education.

Opening our eyes to whose stories are being privileged and the ways in which arbitrary references have and continue to dehumanize and distance readers are ways we can challenge the texts themselves (Reese, 2007). Through relational curriculum and community, embodied in partnerships with texts, we find tangible ways to use story as both a resource and an action towards Truth and Reconciliation for Education. We are made of and live inside stories. Together we invite story into our lives as we journey towards Truth and Reconciliation for Education. And, as Thomas King reminds us, "the truth about stories is that is all we are" (2003, p. 2), and through stories, we can co-create better truths and different stories together.

Act Now

- How will you take up story and stories—in their multiple forms—in this time and place?
- How will you intra-act with story and stories to find your own Truth and Reconciliation?
- How will you bring story-as-teacher alive in your literacy practice?

References

Archibald, J. (2008). *Indigenous storywork: Educating the heart, mind, body and spirit.* Vancouver, BC: UBC Press.

Barad, K. (2012). Interview with Karen Barad: Matter feels, converses, suffers, desires, yearns and remembers. In R. Dolphijn & I. van der Tuin (Eds.), *New materialisms and cartographies* (pp. 48–70). Ann Arbor, MI: Open Humanities Press.

Battiste, M. (2013). *Decolonizing education: Nourishing the learning spirit.* Vancouver, BC: UBC Press.

Bishop, R. S. (1990). *Presenting Walter Dean Myers.* Boston, MA: Twayne Publishers.

Campbell, N. (2005). *Shi Shi-etko.* Toronto, ON: Groundwood Books.

Campbell, N. (2008). *Shin Shin's canoe.* Toronto, ON: Groundwood Books.

Comber, B. (2016). *Literacy, place and pedagogies of possibility.* New York, NY: Routledge.

Cunningham, K. E. (2015). *Story: Still the heart of literacy learning.* Portland, MA: Stenhouse.

Eigenbrod, R. (2010). A necessary inclusion: Native literature on Native studies. *Studies in American Indian Literature, 22*(1), 1–19.

Eigenbrod, R. (2012). "For the child taken, for the parent left behind": Residential school narratives as acts of "survivance." *English Studies in Canada*, *38*(3–4), 277–297.

Gruenewald, D. (2003). The best of both worlds: A critical pedagogy of place. *Educational Researcher*, *32*(4), 3–12.

Hampton, R., & DeMartini, A. (2017). We cannot call back colonial stories: Storytelling and critical land literacy. *Canadian Journal of Education*, *40*(3), 246–271.

Hill, D. (2008). Listening to stories: Learning in Leroy Little Bear's laboratory: Dialogue in the world outside. *Alberta Views*. Retrieved from http://www.appropriate-entertainment.com/files/Download/ListeningToStones.pdf.

Jordan-Fenton, C., & Pokiak-Fenton, M. (2010). *Fatty legs*. Toronto, ON: Annick.

King, T. (2003). *The truth about stories: A native narrative*. Toronto, ON: House of Anansi Press.

Kovach, M. (2009). *Indigenous methodologies: Characteristics, conversations, and contexts*. Toronto, ON: University of Toronto Press.

Lewison, M., Flint, A. S., & Van Sluys, K. (2002). Taking on critical literacy: The journey of newcomers and novices. *Language Arts*, *79*(5), 382–392.

Massey, D. (1991). A global sense of place. *Marxism Today*, *35*(6), 24–29.

Massey, D. (2005). *For space*. London: Sage Publications.

McKay, M. (2011). The embedded and embodied literacies of a young reader. *Children's Literature in Education*, *42*, 289–307. doi:10.1007/s10583-011-9141-4

McKeough, A., Bird, S., Tourigny, E., Romaine, A., Graham, S., Ottman, J., & Jeary, J. (2008). Storytelling as a foundation to literacy development for Aboriginal children: Culturally and developmentally appropriate practices. *Canadian Psychology*, *49*(2), 148–154.

Million, D. (2009). Felt theory: An Indigenous feminist approach to affect and history. *Wicazo Sa Review*, *24*(2), 53–76.

Mills, K. A., Sunderland, & N., Davis-Warra, J. (2013). Yarning circles in the literacy classroom. *The Reading Teacher*, *67*(4), 285–289.

Monsionier Culleton, B. (1984). *April raintree*. Winnipeg, MB: Pemmican.

Reese, D. (2007). Proceed with caution: Using Native American folktales in the classroom. *Language Arts*, *84*(3), 245–256.

Steeves, P. G. (2010). *Literacy: Genocide's silken instrument*. Unpublished doctoral dissertation. University of Alberta Edmonton, AB, Canada.

Strong-Wilson, T. (2007). Moving horizons: Exploring the role of stories in decolonizing the literacy education of white teachers. *International Education*, *37*(1), 114–131.

Truth and Reconciliation Commission (TRC). (2015a). *Honouring the truth, reconciling for the future: Summary of the final report on the Truth and Reconciliation Commission of Canada*. Retrieved from www.myrobust.com/websites/trcinstitution /File/Reports/Executive_ Summary_English_Web.pdf

Truth and Reconciliation Commission (TRC). (2015b). *Calls to action*. Retrieved from www.trc.ca/websites/trcinstitution/File/2015/Findings/Calls_to_Action_English2.pdf

Truth and Reconciliation Commission of Canada. (2012). *They came for the children: Canada, aboriginal peoples and residential schools*. Winnipeg, MB: Public Works and Government Services.

Wagemese, R. (2012). *Indian horse*. Vancouver, BC: Douglas & McIntyre.

11 Wibbly-Wobbly-Timey-Wimey
Place-Based Pedagogy Across Time and Space

Megan Hirst and Cathy Burnett

We were both apprehensive about writing a chapter with someone we didn't know. All too quickly we found ourselves in a room together with time and the expectation that we should produce something. It was on the eighth floor and filled with light, reminiscent of other clean, smart, multi-purpose meeting rooms in newly built university buildings. Clean bare walls, a central table surrounded by chairs, a window looking over the edges of suburbia to Nose Hill. We settled either side of the table and started telling each other how we got here, getting to know each other through our stories. As we talked, things started to feel more comfortable. But it did still feel a bit odd, being thrown together in a strange room in what, for Cathy at least, was a strange city. Through the window the clear blue sky and glistening light hung over Calgary, a promise of something else. So, after lunch Cathy tentatively offered, "Do you feel like a walk?," "Yes!" said Megan, and off we went. Up the road for a mile, walking fast, away from the campus, to the children's hospital and a small wetland with a jetty and benches. It was enchanting. And so, of course, this became our writing place. Megan cross-legged on a bench. Cathy with a laptop in the shade. The walking there and back the backbeat for our conversations, working out which ideas flew for both of us, what held sway, accepting and building usually, sometimes letting things slide. Doing theory perhaps as we learned a little of each other's lives. So, the room, the sky, the unfamiliarity, our histories as teachers, as people, our families all played a part in how this chapter fell into shape. A spontaneous suggestion—to walk!—re-placed our time together, allowed us to pause, to think, and start to write.

We begin with these personal reflections because we want to disrupt the idea that this chapter—like any writing—provides a neutral or objective account. Writing is always done somewhere. It is always placed, and places themselves are not static or singular but constructed through relations. That shifting sense of emplacement filters into the process of writing and into what gets written. And at the same time, our sense of place maybe shifts through the process of writing. Rather than thinking of ourselves as *in place*, then, we might think of ourselves as *of* or *part of* place (Somerville, Davies, Power, Gannon, & de Carteret, 2011).

We both had very different senses of Calgary. Megan has lived there most of her life and can read events of her life into the map of the city (her family home, her school, her flat, the site of her marriage proposal). Cathy was there for the first time, jetlagged and displaced and searching for ways to anchor herself. But as we worked together—through working together—we made a temporary shared space, and the places we went opened out spaces for our writing. All this was short-lived. After 3 days, we headed off in different directions. But our ongoing, evolving, and reciprocal relationships with place helped form this chapter.

These themes—of emplacement, of identifications with place, of place as a resource, of place as constantly shifting—are central to what we want to explore in this chapter. Just as place played into and out of our own writing, in this chapter, we consider how place can play into and out of classroom literacy practice. We draw on stories from Megan's classroom in exploring how a focus on relationships with place can support a place-focused, strengths-based approach to literacy provision and consider some principles and approaches for working in this way.

In a chapter that takes place as its theme, it seems appropriate to begin with a walk through the neighbourhood and school where these stories are set, with Megan as guide.

What would you see if you were to walk the streets of the neighbourhood I teach in? You would see lots of faces. Faces of people waiting at bus stops, chatting outside the 7-11, leaning against the low wall outside the high school. Familiar faces, new faces, faces that look as if they have been in the neighbourhood for generations, and faces of those who have just arrived.

In the warmer months, you would see kids on scooters, bikes, skateboards, kids shooting hoops, kids walking beside a parent, one hand on a sibling's stroller. In the long, summer evenings, you'd hear the whoops and laughter of kids on our school playground well after the bell has gone, current students bringing along their younger and older siblings, some of whom were members of the year group that designed that very playground.

If you kept walking around the school, you would encounter colourful fence art that was brainstormed, designed, and painted by students I currently teach, and as you approached the main door, you might notice a garden to your left, filled with flowers, vegetables, and herbs. It was designed and is cared for by the kids, a responsibility shared by students from all grades and passed on through a rolling mentorship.

Entering the front doors of the school, you couldn't fail to see a large hanging mural of the Circle of Courage, an Indigenous "model of positive youth development" created by Dr. Martin Brokenleg, Dr. Larry Brendtro, and Steve Van Bockern (1990; 2001). Surrounding it are colourful identity art pieces created by students—a visual explanation of what it means to be them. Hang a right to walk through the learning commons (it's not "the library" anymore!), one of the biggest community gathering places in the school that was redesigned and campaigned for by students as a "21st Century Learning Commons." You could peruse the shelves stocked in part by a neighbourhood fundraiser or examine the fabulous art by students and our librarian. On many days, you would see students re-centring themselves in the mindfulness room next door. Then, walking through the halls, you could pause at each bulletin board and examine the stories which very intentionally document the students' learning processes. It will be abundantly clear that in this school, there is a focus on the learning journey and not the end product.

But most important of all, you feel a sense of community that lives both within and beyond these walls and this moment; you feel the presence of former students, teachers, and administrators, their collective visions and actions through the legacies they left for those who come after them. You will also feel the excitement our current students have to leave a legacy of their own. And in that, you also feel their hope for the kids who will come after them.

If you googled the name of the area in which this school is located, you would come across other accounts, reports summarizing employment statistics, numbers in households, and so on. Such accounts circulate widely in the media, with certain areas of our cities indexed through measurements of low income, low attainment, low aspirations, and high crime levels. These narrowly framed representations omit not only the diversity and humanity of those that live there but also political, economic and historical realities, the chains of decisions and actions made elsewhere that inflect what is available and what is possible (Husband, Alam, Huttermann, & Fomina, 2016; Jones, 2014). Pervasive as they may be, such accounts bound an area, disconnecting it from what happens elsewhere. This is problematic for, as Somerville et al. (2011) write, "Storylines shape our modes of thinking about ourselves and others, and our place in the world" (p. 5). Moreover, literacy is often very much part of such deficit accounts: "poor literacy levels" have long been associated with *the poor* (Hayes et al., 2017; Jones, 2014) despite the many studies suggesting that low levels of attainment reflect not so much the ability of students but the ability of educational institutions to generate literacy provision that values and builds on the diverse literacies students bring to the classroom (e.g., Comber & Kamler, 2005; Heath, 1983).

Megan's walk-through provides a messier, more multi-layered story about place. It tells of how locations are repurposed and practiced in different ways: the playground is sometimes a meeting place for families to congregate, sometimes a place to play long after school's out. Students' histories too are written into the environment. Some will remember designing the playground, garden, and fence-art and see them get re-made and re-used by younger students. Of course, the people, locations, and events featured in Megan's story might be described very differently by those depicted. If you listened to the stories circulating the area, you might see it differently again, perhaps through the eyes of the First Nations and Métis people on whose traditional territories the school is found or inflected by urban legends that have sedimented over time. Scattered through this chapter are cartoons (drawn by Megan) which provide alternate takes on some of the places, events, and approaches we describe, bringing them to life, we hope, but also perhaps unsettling them a little. Places, like the stories we tell, are slippery, as multiple past events and future possibilities fold into them.

In reflecting on how place might be important for literacy pedagogy, we drew on different sources and analogies. For Megan, it was words spoken by The Doctor, a hero of the longstanding UK television series *Doctor Who*, which documents the adventures of a travelling time-lord with the power to regenerate (a handy plot device that has kept tales of the Doctor alive over 10 series spanning six decades). The idea that any location has past and possible futures folded into it chimes with The Doctor's explanation of the fluidity of time and space as "wibbly-wobbly-timey-wimey" (Moffat, 2007).

For Cathy, it was the work of the geographer Doreen Massey. Massey (1991) critiqued the idea that "places have single, essential, identities" (p. 26), arguing that they are fluid and complex and are generated through multiple relations that cross sites and work on different timescales. The contours of place (both physical and felt) are shaped, among other things, by geological shifts and intersecting ecologies; economic and political decisions about neighbourhood facilities, housing, transport links, and so on; and the layered histories of those who have lived (and live) there and their personal, economic, social, and cultural lives. We can think of any site, as Massey suggests, "as a meeting place" crossed by multiple trajectories running across time and space that merge and diverge in multiple ways,

> People's routes through the place, their favourite haunts within it, the connections they make (physically, or by phone or post, or in memory and imagination) between here and the rest of the world vary enormously. If it is now recognized that people have multiple identities then the same point can be made in relation to places.
> (Massey, 1994, p. 153)

An important implication here is that any location is inevitably connected to others and that what happens in that location happens because of, and leads to, activities elsewhere. Rather than focusing on boundaries around places, Massey argued that we need to think of place in terms of relatedness and permeability. Our sense of place needs to accommodate both a connectedness between sites and the movement of ideas and activity across sites. Often—and this is important for a chapter on literacy—this connectedness and relatedness is mediated by text, for example, through multivariate forms of personal communication, through literature, or through the trails of official documentation that work to sustain commercial, institutional, and/or government policy and practice (Kell, 2011). As Comber writes,

> literate practices are always relational, both in terms of the microvisible activities of the present, but also historically and translocally, in that they are formed out of various traditions borne of particular times and places.
>
> (Comber, 2016, p. 152)

So how might these ideas be useful when thinking about school literacy provision? Comber (2016) argues that "Massey's approach nudges us to think further about schools and classrooms as meeting-places; places where people are forced to negotiate ways of being, relationships, ways of acting and indeed ways of knowing" (p. 8). School is not singular but is traversed by multiple experiences, histories, and possibilities. Expanding on how attention to multiplicities and relationality might play into practice, we offer three stories, all from Megan's work with her class of 10- and 11-year-olds, which tap into different ways of working with relationships among literacy, pedagogy, and place.

School as a (Multiple) Meeting Place

Google Maps

Inspired by Comber's (2016) neighbourhood walk project (pp. 43–45), I asked my students what spaces in our neighbourhood are most important to them. Many chose their home, but some chose quite unexpected spots—a fort against a fence they built with their sibling, a tiny nearby playground, the neighbourhood swimming pool, or a secret place in the trees across the railway tracks. Then on Google Maps, the students found their important places and walked the class through our neighbourhood, making me realize how intimately many of them know their space.

Later, I realized how potentially unique that was. Students at other schools were usually driven everywhere, and their internal maps of their neighbourhoods were made of little islands joined by unnamed roads. School here, library here, but how on earth do you get from one to another?

I began to think of my students' more nuanced maps of their neighbourhood as a massive source of strength. To know your space so well, to love it and to have effected change on it (creating forts, hideouts, shortcuts, and so on) had given my students a real sense of ownership. They felt responsible for and engaged with their neighbourhood in a way that students at other schools had rarely experienced.

Playground Changemakers

Children are natural observers. They are fascinated by people and their surroundings. They notice the smallest changes. So, when one of our basketball hoops broke, the backboard sadly hanging by one bolt, believe me, they noticed. It was left for months, right through the summer holidays, and my students arrived back in August to find it still lamentably broken.

They started asking questions: Why isn't it fixed? Whose job is it to repair it? Can we call them and convince them to fix it? But before we could tackle the basketball hoop, it was fixed overnight, the students returning to a shiny new hoop. There was no longer a problem to be solved, but the kids' questions made me realize how aware they were of our shared space, their responsibility to that space and of their intrinsic sense of ability to effect change on their space.

So, we embarked on a new mission, to see what other spaces in our school could be changed. The goals that were outlined by the students themselves were to make our school a more mindful and welcoming place to be. We examined possibilities through the lenses of "changemakers" and "legacy," exploring the idea that students change the school and that the school in turn changes students, in particular, future students, who will look at the legacy left by our class and feel empowered to make changes just as my students feel empowered by those student changemakers who came before them.

Figure 12 A sudden change of plan

182 *Megan Hirst and Cathy Burnett*

Figure 13 No limit to their imagination

Food Waste

Our focus on food waste began with a viral video posted by the French supermarket Intermarché (Intermarché—"Inglorious Fruits and Vegetables," 2014). When I showed it to my class, many had already seen the video or heard of "ugly food." as the concept was starting to spread to Canadian grocery stores at that time. Our class decided to dive into this project head first (at times, literally!), and we began researching food waste and hunger in our world.

We examined photos from Europe, Canada, and the United States that documented the extent to which food was being wasted in the developed world. We watched documentaries, found statistics, and interviewed a retired CEO of a grocery store chain. Finally, we wrote persuasive letters to grocery stores asking them to consider adopting "ugly food," as a concept that the students had embraced with passion and vigour. When the grocery stores we had intended to target began selling "ugly food" of their own accord, our conversation shifted and became "What can we do as a class? As a school? How do we ensure we are taking responsibility for the part we play in the problem?" Once they had asked these questions, the next logical question was, "What is our role in the issue of food waste?"

As a teacher team, we got in touch with master's student Tamara Cottle and asked her in to help us assess our impact. Together we landed on a study of the garbage produced in our school. First, we surveyed students' opinions and assumptions regarding food waste; then we examined one morning's and one lunch's worth of garbage.

After digging, sorting, counting, weighing, and documenting the garbage, the kids were astounded by the quantity of perfectly viable food being wasted. They put together presentations using the survey data and the garbage study data and then shared their findings with every class in the school. Finally, they asked for feedback and ideas on how we as a school could reduce our food waste. They came up with concrete and adoptable suggestions, such as: "Tell your parents if they're packing you

Wibbly-Wobbly-Timey-Wimey 183

Figure 14 Best school day ever!

food that you never eat," "Offer your extra food to a friend," "Compost what you can," "Pack your lunch with your parents," and "Bring home the food you don't eat."

This study prepared the students and staff to effectively implement a city-wide change in waste management requiring all garbage to be sorted into compostables, recyclables and waste. The switch was readily embraced as the students were already familiar with the concept of food waste and its implications.

Wibbly-Wobbly-Timey-Wimey: Working With the Fluidity of Time and Space

The three stories trace different ways in which the relatedness and permeability of place can play through educational practice. Of course, we cannot know what these activities felt like to the students or how they were significant to them. They do, however, tell of different *kinds* of relationships with place: with the local area, with the school grounds, and between life in the locality and global movements of money, food, and ideas. Holding in the mind the idea of school as a meeting place and The Doctor's "wibbly-wobbly-timey-wiminess," they illustrate three different ways of working across time and space.

1. **Sharing local knowledge.** In Google Maps, the students' personal experience of the locality meshes with a globally distributed mapping product. Given the opportunity, the children demonstrated their intimate knowledge of the local area: their personal mappings and the

stories, practices, and meanings they make with place. Their felt connection to the area was allowed into the classroom and shared with peers and with Megan, shifting her perspective on their engagement with the world around them. Of course, this activity prized open just a tiny chink through which to see the breadth and depth of their experience, and there is much we can't know: how these engagements shifted day to day, for example, or how memory or sensation played into what they felt or did (just as memory and sensation of place played into our own experience of working on this chapter). It did, however, foreground students' lived knowledge of their area and highlight how the pasts, presents, and futures embedded within place were resources for their lives.

2. **Building a legacy of change.** *Playground Changemakers* has its roots in critical pedagogies that work to empower learners to take charge of their world and unsettle the power structures that hold certain realities in place (Freire, 1970). Specifically, it draws on place-based pedagogies that connect students' interests, passions, and experiences with the spaces and places where they live (Comber, 2016). Invited to shape these spaces and places—to fix things and take charge—the students were positioned as active participants in the world around them. We are interested in how the cumulative effects of this pedagogical work—the legacy of previous students and staff—is materialised in the school buildings, on the walls, and in the playgrounds and, as such, in how it may help to construct what it means to be an educator or a student at this school. Future students may more likely imagine making changes themselves if they've lived with the changes made by their predecessors, and staff, too, may be inspired to facilitate such work. As place shifts, new possibilities are generated for what might come next. Students' legacy of changes becomes part of the messiness of place and lives on for subsequent cohorts of students.

3. **Connecting the local, regional, national, and global.** In *Food Waste*, the students acted across multiple sites to fix the problem of wasted "ugly food," circling between the local and the distant. As students carried out their investigation, their focus of interest moved: from classroom; to a French supermarket; to local grocery stores; to food wastage in Europe, Canada, and the United States; to a national chain of stores; to a citywide scheme; and back again to their homes and school lunchboxes. In tapping into local, regional, national, and global developments, *Food Waste* foregrounds the nesting of near and far, the relationships between what happens here and elsewhere. It also hints at how practices are always local even when activities travel across sites, traversing the globe.

In each of these activities, the students negotiate their relationships with place, and as they do so, activities across different timescales intersect.

Rather than framing literacy provision in discrete lessons or blocks, these activities make use of longer trajectories of students' lives within day-to-day literacy practice. They acknowledge that:

- time is folded into students' relationships with place in different ways;
- place plays into students' relationships over time; and
- what students do changes places over time.

In these examples, place is something complex and fluid into which multiple possibilities are folded. The activities encouraged children to work *with* this relatedness and in doing so position them as empowered and informed individuals who are able to leave their mark on their school, local, and sometimes even trans-global community.

Approaching Literacy as Relational Work

Literacies are threaded through all three stories, from the readings of Street View images to the analysis and interpretation of data for the food waste study and writing the letters to CEOs. They tell how the students explored diverse ways to communicate in managing and mediating relations with others across space and time. Rather than seeing literacy education in terms of discrete outcomes, this approach helps position students—and literacy—in relation to the other people and things that are implicated in and help construct their lives.

There are many other ways in which these students might have worked with the relatedness of place. Tracing other connections or pathways through this "meeting place" would have generated other kinds of enquiries. They might, for example, have tracked the movements of those at the school or in the area (e.g., through migration stories) or investigated the origins of Google Maps to understand the values and imperatives that shape how such apparently neutral websites map the world. They might have explored oral histories or continued to investigate the inter-relatedness of their lives with other than human populations—with the animals, plants, soil, and rock, both locally and elsewhere.

Tracks: Some Principles for Practice

We recognize, of course, that there are many barriers to such work, that things do not always turn out so well, and that students will have experienced these activities—and, indeed, place—in different ways. Moreover, the power to change is uneven; not everyone's ideas or activities move freely, and children cannot always make the changes they want. However, as Massey (2005) writes, "This is a space of loose ends and missing links. *For* the future to be open, space must be open too" (p. 12). Working with permeability and relatedness, however, can help to generate this openness, we suggest.

For Megan and her colleagues, this kind of work relies on a *strengths-based approach*, which builds on what students know, recognising the diversity of their social and cultural resources (e.g., see González, Moll, & Amanti, 2005). We emphasize, however, that thinking with place, as we present it in this chapter, does not just foreground individual strengths but encourages us to notice what students do *in relation with* other things, places, and people. We refer to this way of working as a *place-focused, strengths-based approach*. Such an approach emphasizes what Somerville describes as

> a responsive and emergent learning that draws on and extends the rich variety of experiences of which learners are capable. It recognizes the particularities of people in relation to place, and extends their responsiveness and responsibility in relation to place.
> (Somerville et al., 2011, p. 63)

It might involve, for example, learning more about and working with students' histories of engagement with a particular site (as in *StreetView*), their concerns about the locality (as in *Changemakers*), or the wider world (as in *Food Waste*).

Teaching in this responsive way with limited resources and external pressures can feel like riding the bronco, and this isn't something one teacher is likely to be able to do alone. In Megan's school, many people are involved in making it possible to notice and build on the opportunities generated through what students do, suggest, and produce. These people include the students, former students and their families, the principal, teachers, mentors, local residents, artists, school supporters and community leaders, the university, occupational therapists, counsellors, and the parent council. A place-focused, strengths-based approach, depends on building a sense of teamwork that recognizes literacy education "as a joint enterprise" (Comber, 2016, p. 124) in which working and being together are seen as a source of strength and a resource for doing, making, appreciating, and helping; for critical friendship; and for shared noticing of a togetherness in and with place.

Considerations for Place-Based Pedagogies

- Any site can be conceived as a meeting place, crossed by multiple trajectories running across time and space that merge and diverge in multiple ways.
- Literacies are always emplaced, but at the same time, places are fluid and multiple.

- The pasts, presents, and futures entangled with places are resources for students' learning and their lives.
- A place-focused, strengths-based approach emphasizes what students do *in relation with* other things, places and people (both in the immediate locality and more widely); rather than seeing literacy education in terms of discrete outcomes, it focuses on literacies as ways of mediating students' relationships with people and places.

Final Thoughts

We opened this chapter with reflections on writing and place: on identifications with space, on place as a resource, on place as constantly shifting, on being *of* as well as *in* place. In what followed, we have tried to capture a little of Megan's work with/in her class. We hope that the stories and cartoons have given you a sense of what it might be like to be there. Of course, this sense will differ for each reader as our descriptions meet up with your life experience, your ways of knowing, and the (meeting) places you know and of which you are part.

We have tried to think of place as fluid and messy, and we acknowledge that place can at once confound potentiality while at the same time opening up new possibilities for action. We have presented place as felt, fluid, constantly re-worked and multi-layered. This perspective seems to offer much more to us as literacy educators than the bounded take we get from statistics and media representations. Dwelling on and with place brings relationality to the fore and this in turn disrupts individualist, time-bound constructions of literacy. Rather than thinking in terms of linear cause and effect, it helps us think of literacy provision as located in a web of complex relations and to approach our role as literacy educators in relation to what children know and do in relation to one another and the places they know.

In arguing for a pedagogy that works with, from and in place, we've used stories to paint a picture of possibility. The students that pass through the school change it, leaving a legacy in its very bones, and as they do so—as they work to shape and mould—the hope is that this process may nurture a sense of empowerment and possibility. Literacy, we have argued, is the means through which students can work with complexity, permeability, and relatedness to open up new possibilities.

References

Comber, B. (2016). *Literacy, place and pedagogies of possibility*. New York, NY: Routledge.

Comber, B., & Kamler, B. (2005). *Turn-around pedagogies: Literacy interventions for at-risk students*. Newtown, UK: Primary English Teaching Association.

Freire, P. (1970). *Pedagogy of the oppressed.* New York, NY: Continuum International Publishing Group.
González, N., Moll, L. C., & Amanti, C. (Eds.). (2005). *Funds of knowledge: Theorizing practices in households, communities, and classrooms.* Mahwah, NJ: Lawrence Erlbaum.
Hayes, D., Hattam, R., Comber, B., Kerkham, L., Lupton, R., & Thomson, P. (2017). *Literacy, leading and learning: Beyond pedagogies of Poverty.* New York, NY: Routledge.
Heath, S. B. (1983). *Ways with words: Language, life, and work in communities and classrooms.* New York, NY: Cambridge University Press.
Husband, C., Alam, Y., Huttermann, J., & Fomina, J. (2016). *Lived diversities: Space, place and identities in the multi-ethnic city.* Bristol, UK: Polity Press.
Jones, S. (2014). "How people read and write and they don't even notice": Everyday lives and literacies on a Midlands council estate. *Literacy, 48*(2), 59–65.
Kell, C. (2011). Inequalities and crossings: Literacy and the spaces in-between. *International Journal of Educational Development, 31*(6), 606–613.
Massey, D. (1991). A global sense of place. *Marxism Today, 38,* 24–29.
Massey, D. (1994). *Space, place and gender.* Minneapolis, MN: University of Minnesota Press.
Massey, D. (2005). *For space.* London: Sage Publications.
Moffat, S. (producer). (2007). *Blink,* Doctor Who. BBC. Season 3 Episode 10.
Somerville, M., Davies, B., Power, K., Gannon, S., & de Carteret, P. (2011). *Place, pedagogy, change.* Rotterdam, The Netherlands: Sense Publishers.

12 Red Dresses and Sequined Bras
Encountering Materiality, Place, and Affect in Pop-Up Installation Pedagogy

Michelle A. Honeyford and Patti Trussler

A Story of Saed: Encounters, Belonging, and Environments

> At the end of the day, the hallways of a high school are witness to different aspects of our students' lives. The bustle and chatter have walked out the doors, and what remains are pockets of private interactions. Teachers are not usually privy to these, but one afternoon, I (Patti) observed two of our refugee students contemplating the most recent graduate composite on the wall. What looked initially like an animated chat appeared to be more of a somber discussion. The one boy shook his head and pointed to the two of them. I realized then what had transpired. As they approached me, I experienced a pang of sadness mixed with shame. How was I going to answer their inevitable question? "Miss, what is going to happen to us?" Saed asked. After fumbling my way through a vague and unsatisfactory response, I redirected my route and made my way to the principal's office, where I recounted what had just happened. Two days later, the principal found me in my office to ask for suggestions on how we could include students like these boys in all future graduation ceremonies.

Our recollections of this encounter remind us that school spaces, as well as curriculum and practices convey a great deal about who and what are valued in education. Saed [pseudonym] came to Canada as a refugee, and despite having the resilience and courage to begin a new life, learn a new language, and participate in an academic community, he shared his alienation and regret: Saed would not have enough credits to graduate, to participate in this important rite with his peers, and to have his photo included in the composite on the wall. Despite his diligent efforts, his accomplishments would not be acknowledged; there would be no trace that he was ever there.

While education portends to be about promise and future possibilities, for many adolescents like Saed, their experiences of high school are those of isolation and disengagement. Schools are contested spaces where social, material, physical, and emotional forces shape how well students belong and flourish. Despite efforts to redesign school buildings and curriculum, Saed and others continue to feel the tyrannical effects of time and scheduling; the linguistic and cultural biases of assessment; the discrimination of standardized curriculum and accountability measures; the denial of culturally responsive and sustaining pedagogy; and the dearth of teachers who know, understand, and reflect their racial, gender, and cultural identities.

Purpose

These issues concern us. In my role as teacher/counsellor, I (Patti) have been supporting refugee youth who find themselves in worlds in which they must establish a sense of belonging while navigating a new identity. My doctoral research interest is in capturing the stories of these youth and the role *place* and *belonging* have had in their journeys. For me (Michelle), my work as a literacy researcher and teacher educator has been situated in partnerships focused on opening up spaces for learning where the cultural identities and ways of knowing of students, teachers, and communities can flourish.

Our shared interests have led us to explore how to activate and create a stronger sense of belonging and purpose for all students. In this conceptual piece, we begin with the understanding that education is political and of immense social, economic, and cultural consequence to people and that inequity and disparity continue to be a tremendous issue (Perez, Breault, & White, 2014). We believe young people can realize change in their communities and world not by preparing for a distant tomorrow but by engaging critically and creatively in the complex geopolitical, environmental, and social issues in which we are entangled today. Our schools need to value listening, celebrate difference, and model ethical and caring relationships with the world and one another.

Overview of Chapter

In this chapter, we explore three concepts—*encounter*, *belonging*, and *environment*. Drawing from curriculum studies, critical space-place and material pedagogies, literacy studies, and art/design, these concepts raise important questions related to space, bodies, literacy practices, and pedagogies. We explore these concepts through narratives and examples, with a vision for pedagogical change. Finally, we offer possible themes and considerations for actualizing installation pop-ups in schools.

> **We explore *encounter, belonging,* and *environment* *in theory and practice* to consider how:**
> - Changing our thinking of place (schools) into space (possibilities) shifts our relationships with our students and communities.

- Practicing an "installation pedagogy" embodies more diverse ways of knowing, transforms school environments, and provides students with opportunities to contribute to social change.
- Embracing interdisciplinary inquiry around issues that matter to our local communities produces intentional spaces for meaningful dialogue.
- Cultivating a strong sense of identity, purpose, and belonging happens when we engage our students' voices and perspectives.

Thinking with Concepts as Pedagogy

Our approach is to think with "concept as pedagogy," inspired by Hillevi Lenz Taguchi and Elizabeth Adams St. Pierre (2017), whose "concept as method" offers a post-qualitative approach to educational research. Concepts—rather than traditional research methods—"act as practices that reorient thinking, undo the theory/practice binary, and open inquiry to new possibilities" (Lenz Taguchi & St. Pierre, 2017, p. 643). These concepts provoke for us pedagogical practices that resituate curriculum in the "complicated conversation . . . with oneself . . . and with others threaded through academic knowledge, an ongoing project of self-understanding in which one becomes mobilized for engagement in the world" (Pinar, 2012, p. 47). These concepts suggest possibilities for curriculum and classrooms to become both a "civic square and a room of one's own" (Pinar, 2012, p. 47), where learning academics is animated with learning about self, always with a focus on the larger sociocultural and sociopolitical context—what Megan Boler (1999) describes as "collective witnessing" (p. 178), learning that is "always understood in relation to others and in relation to personal and cultural histories and material conditions" (as cited in Pinar, 2012, p. 47).

- *Encounter* provokes us to wonder: to what extent do our schools and curriculum reflect the varied voices and perspectives of our students and communities? Where and when do students encounter experiences that stimulate their minds and emotions?
- *Environment* suggests that we consider: what relationships do our students have to our schools, the spaces and places where they live and learn, and to one another? What connections do we foster between our students' local environments and their learning?
- *Belonging* moves us to ask: how can we honour our students' identities so that their diverse realities are recognized? How can our work with students to inspire a sense of belonging and purpose?

Curriculum Encounter: The REDress Project

The concept of *curriculum encounter* as pedagogy reorients the nature of our relationship with curriculum. *Encountering* curriculum motivates us to imagine a much different relationship than *covering* or *mastering* curriculum. Curriculum encounters evoke embodied and affective experiences; they require us as teachers and students to be "aesthetically present . . . to subject matter rather than assuming [we] possess it and can manipulate it in decontextualized projects" (Slattery, 2003, as cited in Pinar, 2012, p. 189). Encounters can put us off-balance, create disequilibrium or discomfort, or can catch us by surprise.

> *I (Michelle) was walking across campus to meet a graduate student for coffee, watching my step to avoid a large puddle, when a flutter of red caught my eye. I looked up, surprised to see a beautiful red silk dress hanging from a tree. It blew in the breeze, dancing in the wind. I wondered if someone had found the dress, hanging it on the tree, to wait for its owner to return. I noted its elegant cut and design, imagining the person who might wear it and the occasion for which it might be worn. I encountered the next red dress in the foyer and then caught sight of three more hanging in an alcove often used for art installations. I waved to my student and then quickly detoured to the alcove, curious about the significance and intent of the display.*

Curriculum encounters occur in the realm of our everyday lives, inclusive of human and non-human intra-action. They are multidimensional and material, and as part of a materialist pedagogy, they call for a reconceptualization of curriculum around "matters of concern" (Latour, 2005, p. 231) that open "diverse ways of analyzing, thinking, and imagining that cannot be restricted within customary disciplinary boundaries" (Snaza, Sonu, Truman, & Zaliwska, 2016, p. xxi). I learned that a local artist, Jaime Black (2014), initiated The REDress Project as "an aesthetic response" to the more than 1000 missing and murdered Indigenous women and girls in Canada (Artist statement, para. 2). The installation of 600 community-donated dresses in public spaces (Figure 15) was intended to serve as "a visual reminder" of the gendered and racialized nature of violent crimes against Indigenous women and girls, the dresses evoking "a presence through the marking of absence" (Black, 2014, Artist statement, para. 2). According to Black, red is a sacred color for Indigenous peoples and believed to be the only colour spirits can see. Thus, the red dresses are "calling back the spirits of these women and allowing them a chance to be among us and have their voices heard" (Black, as quoted in Suen, 2015).

The concept of curriculum encounter suggests change: that an encounter will a/effect us in some way but that we may not know immediately *how* or *why*. Encounters suggest individual variance and differentiation: as Snaza et al. (2016) suggest, "a host of relations are at work in every encounter and produce different ongoing affects as a result of both a legacy of events and through each new affective moment. Those

Red Dresses and Sequined Bras 193

Figure 15 Jaime Black's The REDress Project, University of Manitoba
Source: (EcoHealth Learning Circle, n.d.)

affects-effects matter to the individuals involved, but they may matter in different ways" (p. xxiii).

Months later, I discovered The REDress Project in the Canadian Journeys gallery at the Canadian Museum for Human Rights and then again that winter, installed along the river skating trail. The red dresses hung in stark contrast to the white snow, their delicate fabric an anti-thesis to our heavy winter coats. There—along the river that has been dredged for the bodies of local Indigenous women and girls—I thought of families and friends gathered on the riverbank seeking the missing or mourning their loss. As we continued our walk with a scholar visiting from the United States, the dresses sparked a lengthy conversation about residential schools in Canada, the Truth and Reconciliation Commission, and Calls to Action for education. The red dresses had produced the a/effects Black had intended, "creat[ing] a dialogue around social and political events and issues, through provocation or creating space for reflection" (Black, 2014, Artist bio, para. 2).

Thinking with curriculum encounters as pedagogy requires "a new politics of attention" in education attuned "to the world" (Snaza et al., 2016, p. xxii). As a curriculum encounter, The REDress Project utilizes art to provoke aesthetic and relational awareness across disciplines and through authentic issues, in this case, of "feminism and Aboriginal social justice, and the possibilities for articulating linkages between and around these movements" (Black, 2014, Artist bio, para. 2). In her artist statement, Black (2014) articulates a vision that we believe should also inspire literacy pedagogy: to be informed by and emerging from "the places where the social, cultural, political and personal intersect"; that utilizes material and tools "for exploring, connecting and questioning our current and historical socio-political framework and the ways in which we behave within that framework"; with the intent to "provoke and incite dialogue . . . making work that provides viewers with the opportunity to approach [issues] from a different perspective" (Artist statement, para. 1). In thinking with encounter as pedagogy, we would ask, *isn't that what curriculum should do?*

Belonging as Pedagogy

Belonging as pedagogy moves us to cultivate in students a strong sense of connection, purpose, inclusion, and respect in the spaces/places of our classrooms and schools. We have witnessed a growing sense of disconnection in our students' lives; migration and movement as a result of political instability or economic in/opportunity and social media have contributed to this phenomenon. Belonging as pedagogy moves us to foreground powerful questions about who we are, how we should live, and why it matters.

The REDress Project was designed to inspire other artists and communities to "take on and start doing public installations" to raise awareness and understanding (Black, as cited in Suen, 2015, October 3). While attending a conference, I (Michelle) visited an exhibition by students from Soaring Eagle Indigenous Secondary School. There, I found a photo essay inspired by The REDress Project. Set in a lush green forest, several photos featured a young woman in a red dress wearing a red silk blindfold.

In some, a long red silk ribbon also hung from the trees around her. The collection spoke to how "materialist pedagogy is open ended, processual, and attentive to the aleatory nature of encounter" (Snaza et al., 2016, p. xxii). With a symbolic blindfold, the artist was calling for change to a justice system that has ignored the violence—an injustice that the trees and land, traditionally cared for by Indigenous women, were protesting as well. By choosing to wear the red dress, the artist was calling attention to the body—its youth, strength, and beauty—active in a movement to redress the racist victimization of Indigenous women.

The belonging and flourishing of children and youth is critical to the health of a community. Justice Murray Sinclair, chair of the Truth and Reconciliation Commission of Canada, has argued that for "any society to function properly, it must raise and educate its children so that they can answers what philosophers such as Socrates, and Plato, and Aboriginal Elders, call 'the great questions of life' . . .: Where do I come from? Where am I going? Why am I here? Who am I?" (2014, p. 7). We believe these questions provide an important (and often missing) sense of relational purpose and curricular relevance for students. High school classrooms are spaces of "throwntogetherness" (Massey, 2005), meeting places where learners are expected to negotiate multiple ways of relating to each other and knowing their worlds (Comber, 2016). When posed collectively in the classroom, these questions provoke encounters with the social and material world that can become the focus of the curriculum: where do we come from? Where are we going? Why are we here? and Who are we? Such questions can inspire students, like Saed and those at Soaring Eagle, to inquire into the issues of belonging that matter to them, creating a pedagogy of openings for encounters that produce environments for students and communities to learn, engage, and act.

Environments as Pedagogy: Installation Art

Thus, we are also thinking with *environments* as pedagogy. The importance of educational environments has long been established: "For more than a century, educational theorists have written about space, place, and bodied encounters in educational environments" (Snaza et al., 2016, p. xxiii). When we think with environments, we become more aware of the potential of teaching and learning from and with the materials and ecologies around us. We are inspired to think more about literacy as connected to and embedded in the relationships we have with our environments. We also become more aware of the limited ways in which environments inform education and thus of the many literacy practices and epistemologies of our students that we ignore and negate. In thinking with environments as pedagogy, we also become more critical about how our school environments may be limiting our students' access to rich and meaningful curriculum encounters.

More specifically, we are thinking with environments as installation art: "An alternative term for installation art; environments are mixed-media constructions or assemblages usually designed for a specific place and for a temporary period of time" (Tate, n.d., "Art Terms"). Thinking with environments as pedagogy pushes us into productive, multimodal spaces, where students are engaged in inquiry and learning through creating installations, pieces that aim "to inform the public through strong visuals and striking subject matter, and often invite viewers to reach their own conclusions through contemplation" (My Modern Met, 2018, p. 3). We are particularly drawn to site-specific installations: works of art "designed specifically for a particular location and that [have] an interrelationship with the location" (Chodzko, 1999, "Site specific," para. 1).

We are inspired by artists around the world who are drawing attention to social, cultural, environmental, and geopolitical issues, with and through their art and through a pedagogy of relational aesthetics (Bourriaud, 1998). These artistic practices are aimed to explore human relations and their contexts. A recent installation by French street artist JR (2017), for example, features a 70-foot tall image of the face and hands of Kikito, a 1-year-old boy from Tecate, Mexico, peering playfully over the fence of the U.S.-Mexico border (see JR, 2017). The last day of the installation was celebrated with a picnic on both sides of the fence, as Kikito, his family, and hundreds of people from Mexico and the United States shared a meal at a table (featuring JR's photo "The Eyes of a Dreamer") extending across both sides of the border. As a concept to think with pedagogically, environments suggest that educators, too, are designers who need to understand our locations, learn from our students and communities about the issues that concern them, and build on the knowledge and vision they have as resources for an aesthetic education.

For us, these examples illustrate the possibilities for thinking with the concepts of curriculum encounter, environments, and belonging as pedagogy. They provide a point of reference for enacting literacy practices "that are both familiar and strange, converging spaces, places, time periods, semiotic modes, and cultural traditions" in order "to see ourselves, others, and the worlds around us in new ways" (Honeyford et al., 2017, p. 121). But what might this look like in practice?

Encounters, Belonging, and Environments in Practice

Bras for Cancer

> *Imagine asking high school students attending an exhibit of bras, each bra having been re-designed to express a personal story of someone's experience with cancer. In glass cabinets, all possibilities and combinations of colors of beautifully sequined, artfully decorated bras were each poignantly annotated and displayed alone. Curious teenagers awkwardly*

paused to view, read, and react to how fellow students in a "Fashions" class had articulated how the harrowing disease had impacted their worlds. The relationships, the journeys, the emotions were expressed in a concrete form. These objects of intimacy evoked complex responses.

Breast Cancer Awareness Month has been adopted internationally to leverage the emotional connections and experiences of those touched by cancer to empower survivors and raise awareness within society. By participating in campaigns such as the pink ribbon/pink hijab or an effort such as "Bras for Cancer," conversations are started, stories shared, and personal connections made. Furthermore, when we wear something or create something using our hands, it becomes an embodied experience that can both evoke or awaken a lasting memory. This "site-specific" installation allowed its creators to explore and then share their own narratives regarding cancer; this encounter inspired further dialogue. It provoked questions and emotions that each student had to negotiate. What is this? What does it mean? Why am I responding this way (discomfort, embarrassment, shame, sadness)? It revolved around a personal story but became public.

Figure 16 Bras for Cancer

Source: (Photo printed with permission by Theresa Birkholz)

If a teacher were to take this encounter to facilitate further student inquiry, it could foster curriculum possibilities in topics such as advocacy, personal loss, cultural practices related to health care, medicine, death, fashion, or artistic voice. Such inquiry could generate opportunities to share stories and perspectives, engage in research, and create multi-modal provocations. Students could create "pop-up" installations to invite the broader student body and community to encounter these issues in new and powerful ways. This speaks to the "new materialist discourse [which] extends these longstanding notions of the importance of affect and space in pedagogical encounters by conceptualizing space and place not as predefined containers but 'the product of interrelations' and 'always under construction'" (Massey, 2005, p. 9, as cited in Snaza et al., 2016, p. xxiii).

Installations such as The REDress Project, the Breast Cancer Awareness project, and JR's "Eyes of a Dreamer" rally around a common purpose. Each illustrates an evolving effort—moving across sites, through collaborations with other artists, and in public events—to make critical issues visible and to invite participation from a greater audience in physical or digital spaces. The participatory nature of these projects energizes their message. *How can we mobilize this potential in our schools?*

Catalysts and Possibilities

Our relational contexts and the issues that impact our communities suggest productive possibilities. In creating a theoretical list (Figure 17), we considered a number of cross-curricular concepts with the purpose of opening engaging, interconnected learning environments. These possibilities are intended to provoke our imaginations to re-envision curriculum, teaching and learning—perhaps by starting a conversation with a colleague, launching a wonder wall with students, rethinking a tired unit, or seizing an opportunity to utilize a new resource.

We see opportunities for rich learning experiences in these themes. For example, an inquiry into power, responsibility, or community may build on or lead to an inquiry into privilege or silence. We see many connections to the knowledge, skills, and dispositions included in the official curriculum in multiple content areas (e.g., social studies, English language arts, science, technology, business). But the concepts of curriculum encounter, environment, and belonging open up the curriculum—and how we teach and learn—in more responsive, aesthetic, and holistic ways. This is an open-ended approach to curriculum; it is what Roth (2014) describes as "curriculum*-in-the-making" (p. 4), in which the asterisk is a reminder that curriculum is always living, unfinished, and ungraspable. This is inquiry—a rich and iterative process of research, question-posing, and documentation—that incorporates "making" as part of the process. As learners, designers, and makers, students would keep working portfolios

Theme Concept	Questions for Inquiry/Possible Openings
Perspective Voice	What does voice mean? Whose voices are heard? What role does voice play? Where is your voice welcomed (and not)? Where do we see voice in our school?
Land Environment	What relationship do you have with the land? What role does the environment play in your life? How is the idea of the land expressed?
Power or Oppression	What is power? How does it feel to be powerful? To not have power? Can power be negotiated or distributed? What systems of power have you experienced?
Community Relationships	How do we express relationships? Who defines relationships? What relationships are sanctioned or official and why?
Belonging Home	Where do you feel like you belong? How do you define home? Where is home?
Beauty	What is beauty? How do we express or display beauty? What role does beauty play in society? Who defines beauty? Where is beauty?
Responsibility	What does responsibility look like? Who defines responsibility? Who or what are we responsible for?
Health	How do you define health? What do we need to be in good health? Who is responsible for the health of a society?

Where: Classroom, Hallway, Cafeteria, Front foyer, Bulletin board, Display case, Outside

When: Before/after school, Lunch hour, During school or community event, For a day, week, or month

What: Interactive or experiential, Conversation wall, response cards to post or leave in box, audiovisual booths, Twitter, blog, discussion threads, websites, Multiple perspectives

How: Visual, Written, Audio, Digitally mediated, Multi-modal

Encounter

Figure 17 Possibilities

of documents, research notes, drawings, images, and other resources that would contribute to designing an installation.

Considerations

As Figure 17 suggests, students (and teachers) would need to consider the environment and modalities they want to use: where they would like others to encounter their "pop up" (i.e., how the installation might change/transform/disrupt a space to draw attention to its message?); when it would be available; what materials might be used; and how it would be designed to invite students, teachers, administrators, parents, or the public into the interactive encounter.

These encounters should evoke embodied experiences with material artifacts that can be touched, worn, and smelled. In one of my (Michelle's) graduate classes, for example, a student created an encounter with high-heel shoes to examine issues of gender (see Honeyford et al., 2017). High heels in a variety of styles, colours, patterns, and textures hung from the ceiling at eye height, encouraging visitors to touch, smell, and hold them as they read the texts hanging beside them that explored research from historical, economic, art/design, and physiological perspectives. Shoes in a range of sizes and heights were available to walk around in. Similarly, art installations can include sound (e.g., spoken language, song, community events, or nature) to elicit strong connections to the place of the encounter.

Thus, this is not a traditional individual or group project that is "handed in, graded and done" but intended to create meaningful inquiry and dialogue beyond the space of the classroom. Students would build into their design a method to elicit responses to discover what the installation produced for those who "visit": what did the installation make visible or bring to their consciousness? Methods might include inviting participants to write on a conversation wall; add to a mediated discussion thread, website, or blog; share their own story in a recording booth; participate in a brief interview; or create something to add to the installation. These responses then become "data" to analyze and prompt further questions, a pivot to new curricular directions.

Conclusion

It was the composite graduation photo that sparked Saed's visceral response to being excluded from his high school's most significant rite of passage: graduation. Like a red dress hanging from a tree or a glass trophy case transformed by a collection of embellished bras, an installation has the potential to disrupt the routine spaces of schools and invite students to imagine their everyday environments differently. By creating and experiencing these encounters, students' own stories will become interwoven with those of others and embodied in the physical spaces of their school.

To return to our initial questions and the plight of the Saeds in our schools, we believe there is a need to address the disconnection and alienation many students experience in our buildings. We see a possibility for pedagogy that disrupts oppressive school structures, practices, curriculum, and spaces through the unexpected by having students claim and transform schools as places of belonging. Students like Saed would see themselves in these spaces: they would be designers, artists, and collaborators in their learning. They would challenge the barriers that exclude them and contribute to redesigning curriculum and learning spaces in ways that we—educators, administrators, researchers—might never imagine. We see a possibility for schools to become rich meeting places where students' lives and the curriculum become entangled (Massey, 2005, as cited in Comber, 2016, p. 39) through spaces of story and study, where we learn to better understand ourselves and nurture relationships with others. We see opportunities to unlearn heartlessness and learn how to care so that "*what matters* and *how I know*" become "essential, concomitant, epistemological studies" (Fowler, 2012, p. 26, italics in the original). We see environments where all students have the opportunity to pursue the answers to questions such as: "Where do I come from?," "Who am I?," "Why am I here?," and "Where am I going?" (Sinclair, 2014, p. 7). We see—and we feel—possibilities for change. We hope you do, too.

References

Black, J. (2014). *The REDress project*. Retrieved from www.theredressproject.org

Boler, M. (1999). *Feeling power: Emotions and education*. New York, NY: Routledge.

Bourriaud, N. (1998). *Relational aesthetics*. Dijon, France: Les Presses Du Réel.

Chodzko, A. (1999). "Site specific." Retrieved from www.tate.org.uk/art/art-terms/s/site-specific

Comber, B. (2016). *Literacy, place, and pedagogies of possibility*. New York, NY: Routledge.

EcoHealth Learning Circle. (n.d.). *REDress show at UofM: The REDress project*. Retrieved from http://blogs.cc.umanitoba.ca/nri-ecohealth/redress-project-show-at-uofm/

Fowler, L. (2012). Unlearning heartlessness, restorative education. In C. Chambers, E. Hasebe-Ludt, C. Leggo, & A. Sinner (Eds.), *A heart of wisdom: Life writing as empathetic inquiry* (pp. 24–34). New York, NY: Peter Lang.

Honeyford, M., Amy Penner, J., Beyak, T., Beyer, D., Borton, A., Fewer, K., . . . Purdy, D. (2017). Artifacts as catalysts for reimagining transcultural literacy pedagogies. In R. Zaidi & J. Rowsell (Eds.), *Literacy lives in transcultural times* (pp. 117–135). New York, NY: Routledge.

JR. (2017). *Photo of the day: JR in Tecate*. Retrieved from www.jr-art.net/news/gigantic-picnic-at-the-us-mexico-border-fence

Latour, B. (2005). *Reassembling the social: An introduction to Actor-Network-Theory*. New York, NY: Oxford University Press.

Lenz Taguchi, H., & St. Pierre, E. A. (2017). Using concept as method in educational and social science inquiry. *Qualitative Inquiry, 23*(9), 643–648.

Massey, D. (2005). *For space*. London, UK: Sage Publications.

My Modern Met. (2018, April 15). *Best of 2018: Top 10 amazing art installations that defined the past year*. Retrieved from https://mymodernmet.com/what-is-installation-art-history-artists/

Perez, D. M. C., Breault, D. A., & White, W. L. (2014). *Curriculum as spaces: Aesthetics, community, and the politics of place*. New York, NY: Peter Lang.

Pinar, W. (2012). *What is curriculum theory?* (2nd ed.). New York, NY: Routledge.

Roth, W.-M. (2014). *Curriculum*-in-the-making: A postconstructivist perspective*. New York, NY: Peter Lang.

Sinclair, J. M. (2014). Education: Cause & solution. *The Manitoba Teacher, 93*(3), 6–10.

Snaza, N., Sonu, D., Truman, S. E., & Zaliwska, Z. (2016). *Pedagogical matters: New materialisms and curriculum studies*. New York, NY: Peter Lang.

Suen, F. Y. (2015, October 3). Red dresses seek to draw attention to missing, murdered aboriginal women. *CTV News*. Retrieved from www.ctvnews.ca/canada/red-dresses-seek-to-draw-attention-to-missing-murdered-aboriginal-women-1.2593772

Tate. (n.d.). *Art terms*. Retrieved from www.tate.org.uk/art/art-terms

13 Relationship Matters in Adult Education
The Practice of Literacies In-Between

Mia Perry and Keith Seel

Introduction

Neither teaching nor learning happens in a vacuum or as a neutral exchange. Literacy education is no exception. Educational scholarship has provided us with broad and rich discourses, concepts, and practices to address the myriad intermingling aspects of the literacy encounter, from the role of socio-cultural contexts of literacy practices (e.g., Barton, Hamilton, & Ivanic, 2000; Brandt & Clinton, 2002; Heath, 1983; Street, 1995), to the role of place (e.g., Comber, 2015; Somerville, 2013), politics (e.g., Friere, 1994; Luke, 2018), and technology (e.g., Coiro, Knobel, Lankshear, & Leu, 2014), and the list goes on. This chapter acknowledges the complexity of the individual, and the individual conditions, of teaching, but rather than focusing attention on any one component of the literacy learning experience, we look at the relationship between them.

Literacy education in the context of adult learning is heavily weighted with the practices of reading and writing, second or additional language acquisition, and skills training. In this work, we take up literacies in the much broader context of meaning making and emergence in the world through multiple modalities and sense making practices. These literacies are embodied, situated, and interrelational. This approach to literacy positions the decoding and interpretation of print text as a form of literacy but not the only goal. Furthermore, this allows for non–text-based communication and methods of meaning-making and representation to have relevance, recognition, and role in the literacy classroom. Regardless of how we take up literacy as a practice, we postulate that literacy beckons us to *relate*. The practice of relating is a physical and technical one but, of course, also a personal and situated one. It is the practice of relating in literacy education that we grapple with herein. We wonder what emerges when we pause in that space of relation, what happens when we take it up as a possibility, differenciation (Davies & Gannon, 2009; Perry, 2018), and a space of agency.

Posthumanist theory allows us to consider the classroom as an assemblage of the intermingling, always evolving, forces or "ingredients": our students, their influences, our materials, their vibrancy (see for e.g., Barad, 2007; Bennett, 2010; Braidotti, 2013; Deleuze & Guattari, 1987). Indeed, it gives us the starting point of entanglement, from which we select ways, reasons, and methods to disentangle and organize our understandings of the classroom space and practice. We disentangle the students from the teacher, the furniture from the curriculum, the inside from the outside. But, of course, this practice is partial and yet pragmatic. Our interest in this chapter is in the nature of the entanglements, or relationships *in-between* things. These in-between spaces can be understood as the grease, the glue, and the tensions of the assemblage. Our assumption is that all things carry the force of influence on the educational encounter when considered in terms of their relationality. We can think, for example, of the relationship between the student and their materials, between the teacher and their past, between the student and the teacher, and so on. It is in the relationship in-between things and "intra-action" that produces change, that generates agency and energy (Barad, 2007).

With this in mind, our commitment within this chapter is for ethical literacy education practices that are responsive and relevant to the learners and place that they aim to support. Calling to mind specific instances of relationship in a classroom setting orients one to the numerous things at play—roles, materials, histories, and expectations. In the following narrative, Mia re-stories examples from her classrooms to illustrate potential practices of relationship that can become substantive in the pedagogies that emerge. We see from the experiences in this chapter examples of engagement with students that lead to emergent spaces and create time for personal and interpersonal reflection infused with a kind of vulnerability necessary in relationships. In the example that follows, new relations shift both teacher and student and new threads of relationship are built.

A Moment in Class

I walked into the classroom (or *a* classroom—this is a constructed narrative reflecting my practice developed over time). I wasn't the first one there, so I made small talk with a few students, adjusted some of the furniture, set up the projector, and prepared for the start of the class. When we started the class, I had exchanged at least a few comments, eye contact, and smiles with every individual student (about 20 of them). My slides and notes were ready, and the students were ready, sitting with notepads out and pens poised, settled. I began by giving the students an overview of what I had planned to cover during the 3 hours of our class. No surprises; some notes jotted down. Then I asked the whole class again at once, how they were: simply: "How are you doing?" Some nods, smiles, "good, thanks." I added an invitation for the group to close their eyes or look down for just about 30 seconds. A few people giggled; one student, an older man, often the class clown or spokesperson, made a sarcastic comment. I continued to extend the invitation, which by now most students had taken up. The older man seemed to be unable to stop breaking into giggles. I didn't admonish but simply tried to support the rest of the class by adding occasional small instructions: "Think about how you are feeling, how you are doing today; think about how you're sitting . . . try putting both feet on the ground . . . are you breathing? . . . just 15 more seconds to go." Crucially, I added: "try to find a couple of words, or statements if you like, but two words is all that's necessary, to represent a glimpse of how you are doing—something that you're happy to share." "When you are ready, open your eyes."

One outcome involves a student, a young man who, unbeknownst to me, had just found out that his mother had been diagnosed with cancer. He stood up quickly and left the room, clearly upset. I asked another student, who I knew to be his friend, if he would go out to check if he was OK. Shortly afterwards, I went to him, we had a short conversation, between the three of us, and we agreed that the two students would go for a walk (we were near a park) and re-join us in class after the break.

Back in the classroom, students share their words and statements, and after a sudden and quite visible exposure of one student's feelings, as if a light had been turned on, the sharing of these words emerged as if a veil was slowly being lifted from the room. In this process, we *realized* the space, the collective, the people that we were to be in engagement with for the rest of the class. It was a collective of many tired, even exhausted, people and many anxious and stressed people. Amongst us, there were some who were excited and some who were calm, some who were simply happy and grateful, and some who were hungover and hungry.

So, now I know. I've asked the question ("How are you?"). What do I do with the knowledge of the answers as I move into the planned content of the class?

Chapter Road Map

The authors of this chapter bring different positions, pasts, and perspectives to our work in adult and literacy education. Mia's work brings arts practice to literacy research and education in intercultural and interdisciplinary spaces, and Keith's path has moved from teaching young offenders to a dean responsible for providing adult upgrading. Our diverse positions brought related but different perspectives to this chapter. The ideas and experiences shared in this chapter emerged out of a series of conceptual encounters, meetings and confrontations, exchanges and misunderstandings, agreements and disagreements. This chapter, then, results from a short and intense project that builds on some long standing and ongoing practices and inquiries that cross geographical, cultural, and disciplinary contexts.

We begin by first looking at how the idea of relationship has already been thought about in educational research. We explore the history and experience of relationship that touches on how each one of us "feels" or "experiences" relationships. Discourses of affect and interrelationality are put into relation with etymologies and ethics. We argue throughout that this concept and related attention to practice has substantial ethical and pedagogical implications to adult education and indeed educational practice and theory across all contexts.

Looking for Relationship in Education

The predominant view in educational research acknowledges that "relationship" in education is instrumental, meaning that there is a specific purpose for having the relationship—namely, the accomplishment of educational goals. For example, Bernstein-Yamashiro and Noam (2013) look specifically at teacher-learner relationships and conclude that they "are instrumental to teaching" and that "relationships enable academic success" (pp. 48–50). They extend this conclusion to note that "academic attention" and "good behaviour" depend on having a good relationship in place. Furthermore, teacher-learner relationships help bring curricula to life and help to "redefine the terrain on which learning and growing take place" (p. 55). Along this line, the student-teacher relationship can also be understood as "process of 'co-learning'" (Howitt, 2000; Gibbs, Angelides, & Michaelides, 2004; Le Heron, Baker, & McEwen, 2006). There are variations within this line of thinking and a body of work that is gradually expanding. Zandvliet, den Brok, Mainhard, and van Tartwijk (2014) have edited a representative array of expansive studies in this area, whilst acknowledging the relative dearth of research overall. Other disciplines—for example, theology—reveal engagement with the topic from an ethical and philosophical perspective (e.g., Wessels, 2015).

Within the largely instrumental view of teacher-student relationships, the opportunities, risks, and vulnerabilities called for in human relationships often becomes operationalized into checklists and tips. For example, Steele Royston (2017) suggests the following "tips" (p. 35): know yourself, know your students, be aware of perceptions, keep your emotions in check, understand proximity, and care. Lists like these oversimplify the complexity of relationships and highlight the instrumental nature of what is happening in the classroom. Other research (e.g., Hobson & Morrison-Saunders, 2013) suggest that the teaching relationships that are most academically productive are teacher-subject-learner relationships. Here, the "entanglement of both teacher and student in relationships with the subject" rather than each other, is the preferred sense of relationship (p. 774). The sense from this perspective, is that "the classroom should be neither teacher-centred nor student-centred but subject-centred" (Palmer,

1998, p. 116). Perspectives like this, while still instrumental, suggest that the one to one relationship ought to be mitigated through the subject being examined in the classroom.

Whether such a thing is possible or not, some believe that learning in the classroom is "based on the personal relationship between the teacher and the learner" (Rogers, 2002, p. 27). It is in this betweenness of the relationship, or the nature of the relationality, where we can begin a different exploration into the possibilities of relationship in an educational context. The sense of relationship as other than the entities between which, through which, and around which it flows is open to transformation—to being opened up to its own future. Using etymology as a prompt to further inquiry, a paradox can be attributed to relationship: the relational (from the Latin *relatio* meaning a bringing back, a restoring) moment of the relationship, as it starts something new, also grows backwards into the history, to tradition, and opens again, to something received from the past. The sense of other can be seen as central to the notion of relationship. Other, as the-other-than-self, calls, summons and motivates that which forms into what we could think of as a relationship. This call—an evocation and a provocation—affirms the relationship as that which comes forward in a generative impulse while at the same time opens back towards the histories, places, and cultures of whatever is engaging in what we label a relationship. In practice, relationships materialize with or without awareness or "an openness towards the other" (Kearney, 1984, p. 124) but rather as an ontological state.

From its Latin roots, the relationship carries the sense of telling, of restoring and of bringing back. It opens a space of possibility, of generativity, of sharing and rediscovery. It could be thought that through relationship, learners and teachers create a narrative that renews the bond between them and brings them back to what each is individually and collectively in the space of a classroom. When the classroom is an adult classroom, the bonding through a shared and evolving narrative is critical. If adults do not feel a sense of belonging, relevance, or commitment, they can (and do) simply walk away from the classroom.

Language has histories, but it also has materiality. New materialist and posthumanist theories prompt us to recognise, sense, and account for the force of affect that comes with words and the relationship between the matter of the word and the meaning of it. When we loosen our attachment to what relationship means, or has meant, we allow ourselves to attune to what relationship *does* (Deleuze & Guattari, 1987; St. Pierre, 1997). This requires a non-representational onto-epistemology that both feeds from but also repositions etymology, as a material resource in comparison with others such as visual marking, tone or volume of voice, and so on. It is not the purpose of this chapter to explore the relationship between the history, meaning, and affect of the signifier "relationship," but it is worth recognising that it carries a force, and we play out a response, depending on our individual personal material-discursive repertoire, history, and literacy.

These multiple perspectives and approaches have direct implications on practice. Practicing from a poststructural or posthuman position involves engaging with students as learners always in relation to the contexts and materialities around them. This impacts broadly on the way we think about students and the learning experience (Taylor & Hughes, 2016). In addition, poststructuralism lends a focus on the constitutive and practical force of discourse in relation to self, subjectivity, and performance (Davies, 2005). In other words, *how* and *what we use* to talk, communicate, and relate can determine our understanding of reality and experience and therefore our agency and action in it. Ultimately, this colours the representations of learning that structure the school experience, that is, the exam, the presentation, the project, the "answer." These constructs can no longer be seen as independent or complete. The binary logic that distinguishes student from classroom; self from other; and indeed, success from failure, is challenged with these theoretical frames. Knowledge, truth, and the human subject are constituted by discourses, materials, and affect, making all three contingent, in relation, and always emerging. In poststructural and posthuman notions of education, knowledge is unstable, and subjectivity is fluid. In this way, we consider students as individual learning selves always in motion and in relation (Davies, 2000; Ellsworth, 2005).

Practicing in Relation

Whether we take up a heuristic, an etymological, or an affective approach to relationship in education, we can productively consider the meanings and affects of relationship as interconnected. In working in literacy spaces, especially where the learners are adults, the contrasting approaches to relationship might open up possibilities for educators in the following kinds of ways:

Relationship as

An invitation to engaging with the immaterial and imaginary:

- A space in which learners and educators share aspects of themselves that contextualise and inform the curriculum (e.g., memories, stories, desires, fears)

A connection to literacies of globality:

- A practice of inquiring, storying, imagining, and mapping the invisible connections among materials, for example, the paper on the desk and the forest; the coffee and the country in which it grew

> A creative emergence of new unexpected assemblages:
>
> - Putting oneself in different relations to an "other" through playing a "role" or repositioning oneself in new ways in play or/and movement; exploring the liminal spaces at the intersection of one context or thing and another
>
> A critical practice of understanding the materiality of language:
>
> - Ask, sense, map what words *do* to the nature of your relationship to learning, to certain content, to outcomes

The concept of relationship assumes the implication and responsibility of all parties involved. For many, therefore, this suggests a level of risk in the endeavour and implies the vulnerability that comes with interrelationality. With instrumental purpose, as described earlier, relationship is a more controlled and predictable practice but also limited in its advantage. When we engage more expansively in relationship, we allow other layers of curriculum, other literacies, and other possibilities to enter into our teaching and learning. Part of that expansive treatment of relationship involves de-centring the self from our perception and understanding of the world, moving beyond a humanist stance whereby relationships are between or defined by human. Beyond this, we can see relationality as ubiquitous, the practice of relating as an ontological constant.

The Spaces in Between

Relationship carries an acknowledgement of the other, or *more than one*, more than subject. Acknowledgement is in itself an ethical act, and much harm has been done in the opposite process of subjugating and denying the value of certain peoples, the existence of certain knowledge (Singh, 2018). The act of acknowledgement of the other reveals a space for the relationship (and ethics) to emerge and be possible. With relationship, the other cannot be transformed into an object of transformation (Derrida, 1978, p. 138) because the other is outside of the metaphysics of subject and object.

Letting the other be other opens up a mode of being that is being in-between. Davey (2006) proposes that being in-between is not concerned with what, from an empirical perspective, would be called the "subjects" that are encountering one another, be they human or non-human. Rather, the being in-between is a process of an encounter that exposes the differences of other-ness and the "transformative possibilities for further understanding" (p. 15). According to Davey, the encounter necessitates engagement which is "more than an acknowledgement of the proximity of perspectives and horizons other than my own" (2006, p. 15). The encounter with the other is therefore generative in that the in-between uncovers and reveals the contrast of one perspective and that of the other and discloses "the reality of alternative possibilities not presently my own but which might yet become *my* own" (Davey, 2006, p. 15, italics in original). Furthermore, the encountering of the other has the potential to reveal in the in-between the "unquestioned past self-understandings and future potentialities" (Davey, 2006, p. 16). Past self-understandings such as personal history, culture, and association with place and time arrive with one and with the other at the moment of the encounter. So too, arrive all the possibilities that could grow out of the encounter. To be in a relationship then is to have remained in the face of an encounter—rather than leaving—to step into the in-between, to be whole in the sense of affirming one's presence in the moment as having past, present, and future connections out into the world.

In the day-to-day reality of a teacher at work, these conceptual dynamics permeate our classrooms and teaching contexts whether or not we attend to them. The experience of being in-relation, the nature of the encounter with people and perspectives, and the engagement with others underpins, if not, determines how and what we hear, think, see, and feel. How attuned to that inter-relation we are depends on the individual and on the context. In other words, we might be with a group of very receptive but nervous students or a group of sleepy and bored students and may or may not notice it depending on where our attentions are focused. If our focus is on the lecture we planned to deliver, or the activity we planned to facilitate, we may focus on our relationship with that task rather than our relationship with the recipients or participants of that task.

Taking relationship seriously, to the extents of its possibility, can be an ethical, a methodical, a personal, a vulnerable, and a generative activity. In the narrative recounted at the beginning of this chapter, the facilitation of "How are you?" was an invitation into a new type of relationality and into a space that was unplanned and unknown. Within that 2-minute period, the classroom became a space of explicit relation. A genuine question was asked, along with a practice to support the answering. An active practice of listening was carried out in response. Students asked themselves a question and shared to the extent that they were able or willing, and they listened, to the extent that they were able or willing. Once that had occurred, the space, previously made up of and navigated according to these people, their actions, and our spatial and role arrangements, now included the myriad forces, influences, imagined pasts and futures, that make up context: the party the night before, the family living through trauma, the other two assignments due tomorrow for another two courses, the infrastructure of the city that requires some students to leave their homes 3 hours before the start of class, and on and on. The pedagogical practice (at least partially pre-planned), always located in space, is now positioned in a different space, transformed only by a commitment to a certain type of relationship.

The literacy classroom is an assemblage of things: individuals, collectives, materials, subjects, and social and historical and imaginary contexts. Curriculum and instruction can delineate, prioritise, and authorise literacies and experiences in this space. It can do this as a blunt tool, with the relative certainty of time management and content "covered." Alternatively, curriculum and instruction can enter into the relation assemblage of the classroom, with the students, spaces, and teachers of literacy. The relative certainties in this scenario look very different: in relation, we can achieve relevance to learners and responsiveness to needs.

References

Barad, K. (2007). *Meeting the universe halfway: Quantum physics and the entanglement of matter and meaning*. Durham, NC: Duke University Press.

Barton, D., Hamilton, M., & Ivanic, R. (2000). *Situated literacies: Reading and writing in context*. New York, NY: Routledge.

Bennett, J. (2010). *Vibrant matter: A political ecology of things*. Durham, NC: Duke University Press.

Bernstein-Yamashiro, B., & Noam, G. G. (2013). Learning together: Teaching, relationships, and teachers' work. *New Directions for Youth Development*, 137, 45–56.

Braidotti, R. (2013). *The posthuman*. Cambridge, UK: Polity Press.

Brandt, D., & Clinton, K. (2002). Limits of the local: Expanding perspectives on literacy as a social practice. *Journal of Literacy Research*, 34(3), 337–356.

Coiro, J., Knobel, M., Lankshear, C., & Leu, D. J. (Eds.). (2014). *Handbook of research on new literacies*. New York, NY: Routledge.

Comber, B. (2015). *Literacy, place, and pedagogies of possibility*. New York, NY: Routledge.

Davey, N. (2006). *Unquiet understanding: Gadamer's philosophical hermeneutics*. New York, NY: State University of New York Press.

Davies, B. (2005). *A body of writing: 1990–1999*. Walnut Creek, CA: AltaMira Press.

Davies, B. (2000). *(In)scribing body/landscape relations*. Walnut Creek, CA: AltaMira Press.

Davies, B., & Gannon, S. (Eds.). (2009). *Pedagogical encounters*. New York, NY: Peter Lang.

Deleuze, G., & Guattari, F. (1987). *A thousand plateaus: Capitalism and schizophrenia* (B. Massumi, Trans.). Minneapolis, MN: University of Minnesota Press.

Derrida, J. (1978). *Writing and difference* (A. Bass, Trans.). Chicago, IL: University of Chicago Press.

Ellsworth, E. (2005). *Places of learning: Media architecture pedagogy*. New York, NY: Routledge.

Friere, P. (1994). *Pedagogy of the oppressed* (M. Bergman Ramos, Trans.). New York, NY: Continuum.

Gibbs, P., Angelides, P., & Michaelides, P. (2004). Preliminary thoughts on a praxis of higher education teaching. *Teaching in Higher Education, 9*, 183–194.

Heath, S. B. (1983). *Ways with words: Language, life, and work in communities and classrooms.* Cambridge, UK: Cambridge University Press.

Hobson, J., & Morrison-Saunders, A. (2013). Reframing teaching relationships: From student-centred to subject-centred learning. *Teaching in Higher Education, 18*(7), 773–783.

Howitt, R. (2000). Editorial: For whom do we teach? The paradox of "excellence." *Journal of Geography in Higher Education, 24*(3), 317–323.

Kearney, R. (Ed.). (1984). *Deconstruction and the other: Dialogues with contemporary continental thinkers.* Manchester: Manchester University Press.

Le Heron, R., Baker, R., & McEwen, L. (2006). Co-learning: Re-linking research and teaching in geography. *Journal of Geography in Higher Education, 30*(1), 77–87.

Luke, A. (2018). *Critical literacy, schooling, and social justice.* New York, NY: Routledge.

Palmer, P. (1998). *The courage to teach.* San Francisco, CA: Jossey-Bass.

Perry, M. (2018). Unpacking the imaginary in literacies of globality. *Discourse: Studies in the Cultural Politics of Education.* doi:10.1080/01596306.2018.1515064

Rogers, C. (2002). The interpersonal relationship in the facilitation of learning. In R. Harrison, F. Reeve, A. Hanson, & J. Clarke (Eds.), *Supporting lifelong learning: Volume 1 perspectives on learning* (pp. 25–39). London: Routledge.

Singh, J. (2018). *Unthinking mastery: Dehumanism and decolonial entanglements.* Durham, NC: Duke University Press.

Somerville, M. (2013). *Water in a dry land: Place-learning through art and story.* New York, NY: Routledge.

Steele Royston, N. (2017). Improving music teaching through interpersonal relationships. *Music Educators Journal, 103*(4), 34–39.

St. Pierre, E. A. (1997). Methodology in the fold and the irruption of transgressive data. *International Journal of Qualitative Studies in Education, 10*(2), 175–189.

Street, B. (1995). *Social literacies: Critical approaches to literacy in development, ethnography, and education.* London: Longman.

Taylor, C., & Hughes, C. (2016). *Posthuman research practices in education.* London: Palgrave Macmillan.

Wessels, F. (2015). The critical role of relationship in education. *Theological Studies, 71*(3), 1–8.

Zandvliet, D., den Brok, P., Mainhard, T., & van Tartwijk, J. (Eds.). (2014). *Interpersonal relationships in education: From theory to practice.* Rotterdam, The Netherlands: Sense Publishers.

Plateau IV
In(Conclusions)

Mairi McDermott and Kim Lenters

As we noted in the introduction, this section of the book invites us to hear from two Travellers (Miriam Ramzy and Gina Ko) who were introduced to the ideas, theories, and possibilities of posthumanism in literacy through their participation in the workshop. As the project unfolded and we began to think about the questions, struggles, and even resistances to what posthumanism might offer to teaching and learning literacy in contemporary times, we asked Ramzy and Ko if they would share some of the ways their learnings have come to (re)shape moments in their teaching practices, research, and personal lives. What is particularly notable in their reviews is the importance of zooming in on one moment-in-time to propel us to think/be/do differently. In other words, we are not so naive as to imagine that everyone who moves through this book will identify as becoming posthumanism literacy educators. Remember, that is the importance of the in-process language, for example, becoming. Our identities are not static, unified, and complete for all time, but rather our hope is that, much like Ramzy and Ko share, you may find yourself beginning to notice things/relations/literacy differently, even for one moment.

In her Traveller Review, Ramzy (this volume) tells us how posthumanism alerted her to the ways in which space matters in literacy learning. She shares her recollection of encounters with a young child she thought was struggling to make connections to learnings she seemingly expressed with ease the previous day in a different space. As she returns to these moments with young Lea in multiple spaces, Ramzy provides an important reminder of the highly contingent nature of literacy assemblages. Ko, then, maps an ongoing and unfolding story of youth activism and critical environmentalism in which she, her daughter, and her daughter's friend are immersed. With the posthuman language and orientation, she is able to locate a nodal point that propelled a line of flight, which seems to be ever expanding in its reach. Sparked by a question asked by her daughter about where disposable cups from coffee shops go, Ko identifies significant shifts in her pedagogical and consumption practices.

This work can be uncomfortably inconclusive, and that is yet another aspect of it that we are drawn to. So, we leave you here to wander through Ramzy's and Ko's wonderings as they thought with posthumanism as a place to invite your (in)conclusions.

Traveller Review I: Space Matters
How a Change in Space Can Influence Learning

Miriam Ramzy

"Leah, you knew this yesterday. How do you not know this today?" I was working with a student in grade 2 on math. We had been practicing quickly identifying teen numbers—13, 14, 15—and representing them using various manipulatives for just under 3 weeks. The day prior to asking Leah these questions, we had been working in our regular space: a small room with a low table, bright windows, and empty shelves. Today, we were in a new space, as our regular room was occupied: the tables were higher, the shelves around us were colourful and filled with teacher stuff, and there were no windows. Leah was still working with the same materials and the same number chart, but she was confusing her teen numbers again! Three mornings a week, we practiced them in various ways, to develop number sense. Today was day 9, and it seemed she was regressing. I could not understand how this could be, and I left school that day questioning my teaching abilities and competencies.

In my own teaching practice, I have asked myself something similar to "Why do you not know this today?" many times: "Brandon, how do you not remember this letter? Last time you knew it.," "Fran, you knew this sight word yesterday. What is happening today?" I have asked myself these questions, and immediately after, I felt guilty for two reasons: first, because the child could see and feel my frustration and consequently felt bad for forgetting, and second, because I felt like an incompetent teacher. I wanted my students to feel successful at school, yet they were forgetting what I thought they had already learned.

That is how I used to interpret these situations. As I prepared for the 3-day workshop, engaging with readings and in conversations with my peers, I developed an understanding of all of the layers than mediate student learning. The environment, learning spaces, and materials students use and engage with influence their learning. In Kuby and Rucker's (2016) book, they delve deeply into the importance of the materials we provide for students in our classrooms and how humans and non-humans are entangled together in learning. Just as our bodies and brains work together to learn, our bodies and the non-human materials around us also influence our learning, including the space we occupy.

For Leah, the space we occupied during our sessions played a crucial role in her learning and ability to recall. For this particular session, we moved to a new space. Posthumanism would explain that there are multiple external factors that influence our learning at any given moment. Biological, physical, environmental, cultural, institutional, and even our materials are some of the dimensions that influence student learning constantly; "all of these work together in a contingent interplay to produce any literacy event" (Nichols & Campano, 2017, p. 246). The day I worked with Leah in the new room, the physical space changed drastically, as did the environment; rather than walk across the hall to our regular room, we descended two flights of stairs and worked in a space that was unfamiliar to Leah. The environment changed, from a bright, open space, to a small, fluorescent-lit, *busy* room, filled with teacher boxes and photocopying materials. For Leah, someone who was already a positioned as a struggling learner, a change in these dimensions confused her.

Spaces matter. As teachers, it is our responsibility to consider how changes in space, and changes in any non-human element, can influence learning. Students negotiate their learning in light of these factors and in response to them. In my own teaching practice, this has deeply shifted my responses to students and analysis of the situations when they do not seem to get it or forget what they learned. I step back and consider what has changed in the child's surroundings and possible previous inter- and intra-actions; I ask about recess or their morning at home before school and then move forward. Rather than fixate on what they cannot do, I focus on the space, the environment, and the materials they have access to or that I can provide for them. Now, as I work with Leah, rather than push my frustration on her, we might skip our meeting until our regular space is available, or we will play games and build numbers in a non-evaluative environment. For myself, it is no longer, "Why don't you remember this?," and instead, "What is this child feeling and negotiating, and what can I do to support them?" and "What has changed?"

In our classrooms, and as teachers, there are so many factors we need to be constantly monitoring, facilitating, changing, and attending to, so it can be easy to get lost in it all. For myself, it comes down to the little humans we are responsible for. I have observed the influence spaces play in our learning. For Leah, a new space challenged her learning.

I would like to conclude by letting you know that I am not a posthumanist scholar. These theories and concepts are still new and, at times, difficult for me to understand and "see" in practice. What I have found most effective is reading examples of how these theories can live in a classroom and with students, sometimes in the simplest ways. I hope that through my presentation of this experience, the theories have become further apparent to you as well. One of my most profound learnings while participating in this project is that "one of post-humanism's strengths is that it does not require us to abandon our existing practices altogether, but rather provides new dimensions that help better account for the complexities of the classroom" (Nichols & Campano, 2017, p. 249). I encourage you to reflect on your current practices and use the theories discussed in this book as resources to think and plan with (Nichols & Campano, 2017).

References

Kuby, C., & Rucker, T. G. (2016). *Go be a writer! Expanding the curricular boundaries of literacy learning with children*. New York, NY: Teachers College Press.

Nichols, T. P., & Campano, G. (2017). Post-humanism and literacy studies. *Language Arts*, *94*(4), 245–251.

Traveller Review II: Used Once and Disposed
Collaborating With Youth Environmental Activists in Posthuman Times

Gina Ko

> *Kevin Johnson, here is our petition in a USB stick. Please consider making a better cup, one that is tree-free and can be recycled everywhere. We love our earth.*
>
> Mya Chau

My daughter Mya and her friend Eve started a petition on Change.org to ask Starbucks to make a better cup. This idea began several years ago when Mya (9 years old) and I talked about how bad disposable cups are for the environment. We thought we would informally ask people at the mall to ask how many cups they use and throw away per year. We surveyed family and friends; as well, I asked my colleagues at the university, at my counselling agency, and my Bachelor of Education students. We were astonished by how many cups per person are thrown in the trash. We initially sensed that disposable cups were a problem; however, after engaging with others on the matter, we came into a different sense of urgency! After conducting research and learning about how disastrous single-use cups are for the environment (they get incinerated in the landfills, and many end up in our precious oceans), Mya and Eve (11 years old) were propelled into action. They (with my assistance) started a petition using Change.org titled "Starbucks, we know you can make a #Bettercup" and garnered more than 346,000 signatures. We had the support of family, friends, faculty members, colleagues, and students who signed and shared the petition. The campaigner, Julie, at Change.org supported us in revising the petition and reached out to media outlets. We flew to Seattle and were invited to the Starbucks headquarters to meet with the global social impact team and CEO of Starbucks. Mya handed the petition to him (the opening quote above captures the moment she handed it off), and the Starbucks representatives promised they would do better by investing $10 million over 3 years to make a cup that can be recycled everywhere.

Thinking with Nichols and Campano (2017), posthumanism can "draw us into deeper reflection about the urgent and profound ways that our lives, technologies, and activities exert tremendous pressures on our planet, cities, schools, and students—and can help us envision how these might be better reconfigured for mutual flourishing" (p. 248). Through intra-action between human (Mya, Eve, the Change.org campaigner, and myself) and non-human entities (the disposable cups, the environment, the petition, and public discourse) as part of an assemblage, I began to notice the ways in which we were affected (set into motion to *do* something) and had the capacity to affect (securing a promise from the CEO to change their practices with the hope that we could better engage with our environments in more sustainable and ethical ways). Dwelling in this reconfiguration, we engaged in new acts, focusing on the mutual flourishing of humans and non-humans in sustainable assemblages. My experiences in the 3-day workshop—learning about posthumanism, assemblages as generative concepts—have strengthened my sense that supporting youth activism can cultivate critical literacies that are beyond the conventional human-centred foci. This moment-in-time journey has propelled Mya and Eve continue to question, act, and move toward ongoing commitment for environmental justice.

The Unfolding of a Journey Propelled by a Moment-in-Time

Together, we contemplated environmental concerns and wanted to speak out to do something about it. Mya and Eve were invited to speak with the media in newspaper, radio, and television interviews. And the assemblage grew. Throughout this unfolding, the embodied experiences (Ehret & Hollett, 2014) of concern (rapid heartbeats), excitement (screaming for joy), hope (big smiles), and determination (heads held high) contributed to the assemblage. The embodiment of learning was powerful and has propelled us to continue to push for social and environmental change. One example of such change is our increased consciousness of plastic waste and its affects on animal life in the oceans. Now, we use re-usable shopping bags, stainless steel straws, beeswax, bar soap, shampoo, and conditioner (non-human) to reduce the plastic accumulated in our household and eventually the landfills and oceans.

In addition to the changes in our everyday practices at home, Mya and Eve went on to receive a WE Day (WE Charity, 2019) bright Future Award and attended the Take Action Camp in Tuscan, Arizona. There they learned about global social issues such as environmental justice, gender inequality, poverty, socioeconomic disparity, water conservation, and more. Upon returning to Calgary, they partnered up with another young environmentalist, who was successful in asking Starbucks to phase out plastic straws by 2020. Now together, they have started a new petition to ask a Canadian coffee and donut shop franchise to make a #Bettercup, and the petition has garnered over 171,000 signatures to date.

Nichols and Campano (2017) noted "humans are not independent, rational agents whose actions are unfettered and transparent, but rather, are always interdependent with other humans and non-humans around them" (p. 247). The simultaneous unfolding of Mya and Eve's activism with my learning of these posthuman orientations has led me to notice the importance of recognizing our human and more-than-human interdependencies. I notice my spouse, Tom, moved by Mya's activism, bringing his own re-usable coffee cup and water bottle to work. My son, Koen, now joins in conversations about the environment, and we regularly seek out and listen to podcasts together and talk about ideas to care for our planet. In returning to these unfoldings through posthumanism, I have gained a deeper understanding of how to think/be/do with this theory; my life and relationships (with human and more-than-human entities) have shifted to become more congruent with thinking, being, and doing posthumanism. Walking the talk has been crucial in animating the generative possibilities of posthuman theory to inform my everyday practices. The journey continues as I devote my academic, personal, and professional lives to social justice issues using this posthuman lens.

References

Ehret, C., & Hollett, T. (2014). Embodied composition in real virtualities: Adolescents' literacy practices and felt experiences moving with digital mobile devices in school. *Research in Teaching of English*, 48(4), 428–452.

Nichols, T. P., & Campano, G. (2017). Post-humanism and literacy studies. *Language Arts*, 94(4), 245–251.

WE Charity. (2019). *WE day*. Retrieved from www.we.org/we-day/

Orienting Map IV

Why Theory? Thinking, Being, Doing Literacy With Posthumanism

Kim Lenters and Mairi McDermott

Familiarizing ourselves with posthuman concepts of affect, becoming, assemblage, relationality, emergence, embodiment, and the importance of place can move us to focus anew on our pedagogical practices. In this final chapter, we take up the relationship between theory and practice and what shifts we believe posthumanism invites us to think-be-do with in literacy.

We began this project with a sense that posthumanism might expand literacy practices; simultaneously, we are aware that theory/Theory/theories can tend to distract us or take precedence over practice. Throughout this project, from the conceptualization to the collaborative workshop and onward to the writing up of this volume, our desire has been to animate the importance of theory while honouring the role of practice. This desire leads us to share how theory is placed within our work, as well as within posthumanism at large. Rather than positioning theory as prior to practice, or at least as a distinct entity from practice, we situate theory and practice as entangled aspects of the same thing.

Indeed, often enough, even while theory is positioned *a priori* to practice, it is our practices and experiences that also generate theory. Harwood, Hickey-Moody, McMahon, and O'Shea (2017) show the foregrounding of practice in a practice-theory relationship in this way: "*Doing something different allows us to think about it in new ways*. Practical acts can be the beginning of new systems of thought and meaning" (p. 41, emphasis original). Contemporary practices of literacy offer us an example of the ways practical acts shift systems of thought, while simultaneously, the emergence of particular theories (in this case, posthumanism) provide us a language to notice and work with the shifts in practices. Shifts in how we engage with texts (e.g., Instagram, Twitter, Snapchat), in fact, even the question of what counts as a text, propel us to re-think how we imagine (theorize) literacy. Posthumanism has oriented us to capture these shifts.

The multitude of ways in which we now represent thought and ideas through platforms that undo the linearity of words on a page can move our thinking-being-doing literacy in literacy teaching and learning spaces. In many ways, we are trying to put theory to work to catch up to the changing literacy landscape in this volume. Remember, back in the introduction, we named several theoretical turns in literacy teaching and research—sociocultural, sociolinguistic, multimodal, and critical—each of which continues to substantively shape our understandings of what literacy is and how it is approached pedagogically in schools. What we hope this volume contributes to these conversations is that no single approach can do it all. We believe that attuning ourselves to posthumanism further contributes to the ways in which we move with and through literacy practices.

Furthermore, with posthumanism, theory takes a different position, one wherein theory is agentic rather than positioned as static (e.g., capital "T" theory). By suggesting that theories emerge in dynamic relation to practices and experiences, we want to note that theories can also help us in noticing differently. Through intentional engagement with posthumanism, we believe that we can intervene further in literacy understandings. Whatmore (2006) locates theory as a "technology of practice and an intervention in the world" (p. 601). In doing so, she disrupts the one-way relation between theory and practice, instead alerting us to a posthuman understanding of theory and practice as mutually entangled. One does not come *before* the other; rather, theory is practice and practice is theory. In the context of this volume, this relation between theory and practice, or theory-practice and practice-theory, returns us to our guiding principle: that practitioners theorize, and theorists practice. In many ways, as we discuss in our preface, while we have distinguished literacy educators from literacy researchers, our hope in this volume is to flatten the hierarchical emphases on research as distinct from practice. In flattening the value of what educators theorize and what researchers practice, our goal is to honour the ways in which we are differently oriented to this work, and that is the power of conversing and composing across our worlds!

Navigating Problems of Practice in Literacy Education With Posthumanism

To amplify our position on theory and why theory matters, the figure we offer two things: 1. a brief outline of some of the shifts a posthuman approach to literacy offers and 2. a more detailed discussion of some literacy problems of practice through a posthuman orientation.

Engaging these shifts, we turn to a discussion of some present-day problems of practice that putting posthumanism into conversation with literacy instruction can illuminate.

- Theory and practice as divided → Theory-as-practice and Practice-as-theory
- The Individual → A relational collective
- Difference as located external to us → Difference as constant for all entities, where each entity is becoming different all the time
- Human-centred → Human + more-than-human
- Agency as residing in the individual → Agency as distributed among humans + more-than-humans
- Ethics informed by an exterior code or set of rules → Ethics that flow from relationalilty
- Cognitive ways of knowing (epistemology) → Embodied ways of knowing and being (onto-epistemology)
- Contingencies as barriers → Contingencies as opportunities, openings
- Critical literacy as being in the world → Critical literacy as being-with-the-world (Spector, 2015)
- Task + individual → Task + the biological + the environmental + the physical + the cultural + the institutional (i.e., non-human participants) + the individual (Nichols & Campano, 2017)

We have drawn on the works of Karen Barad, Suzanne Gannon, Phil Nichols & Gerald Campano, Karen Spector, and Carol Taylor to inform these articulations of posthuman theoretical shifts that have grown out of the work of Gilles Deleuze and Felix Guattari. All of these scholars are cited in our reference section.

Figure 18 Theoretical shifts in posthuman thought

Rigid Parsing of Learning

Literacy educators and curriculum writers make decisions about how to "divide" learning so as to highlight certain skills or certain types of texts. For example, years ago, elementary school teachers worked with the adage "Children learn to read in the primary years and read to learn in the intermediate years" (see Chall, 1983). More recently, this has been disrupted with the recognition that young children can use literacy to learn. In part, this disruption is guided by the realization that children enjoy expository texts from a young age and are more than capable of taking meaning from them. It is also driven by the recognition that children, from a very young age, think deeply about the hows and whys of the world and this should be reflected in the ways literacy instruction is carried out.

This example highlights the artificial boundaries we sometimes place on learning. Another example is developmental continua. Originally conceptualized to provide educators and parents with a sense of what a child might be expected to do at a particular stage of literacy development, these continua were developed with a Western conception of child development, what constitutes literacy, and the acceptable times by which a child in a Western school system should be achieving those developmental benchmarks. As helpful as developmental continua may be for understanding what a student could be doing at a particular age, we never want the continua to serve as the arbiters of what students are capable of doing. Even more important, we don't want them to become the final judge making pronouncements regarding what students cannot do. When outcomes or developmental continua become that which tell a child s/he is a reader or not-a-reader, a writer or not-a-writer, they actually stand in the way of that student's progress. Rather than viewing outcomes as barriers, posthumanism guides us to use literacy learning outcomes in ways that open up possibilities for students. Posthumanism leads us to ask what students are capable of doing and use this inquiry to guide pedagogy.

Accountability Measures

Over the past two decades, many school systems have been required to engage assessment practices that demonstrate student literacy learning in very particular ways (this relates to the discussion of developmental continua above). A focus on students meeting certain benchmarks at particular times in their educational careers was initially intended to ensure that children would not be disadvantaged by certain forms of early years instruction. However, through state policies in many jurisdictions worldwide, these measures have led to the problematic focus on what students cannot do to the exclusion of what they can do.

While it is not necessarily our intention to advocate for curtailing developmental outcomes and accountability measures, posthumanism leads us to question the way they have come to dominate the classroom assemblage and what we can do about this problem. How might we disrupt the tendency for rigid accountability measures to force out valuable practices and materials and place undue emphasis on the products of literacy instruction (e.g., comprehension tests, essays, stories)? How might we challenge the way a focus on product discounts the importance of the processes of becoming literate? When assessment is necessary, how might we think of assessment practices that consider the collectivity of literate becomings?

Learning by Design

As indicated in the previous to discussions of problems of practice, posthumanism in literacy encourages us to remain open to the not-yet-known, the unforeseeable. It draws us into what we cannot know in advance, what might emerge in the ever-shifting networks of relations in our classrooms, for example, the particular composition of students present that day, the materials brought in for the lesson, the spatial arrangement of the room, whatever happened *before* students entered into the shared space. Learning by design, popularized in the procedural model of backwards planning (Wiggins & McTighe, 2005), can become an exercise of calculation, control, and instrumentality that overdetermines learning processes. By beginning with the end product of the unit or lesson, you then design learning activities that are meant to ensure "Students will be able to . . ." by the completion of the unit. With a conclusion pre-determined, not only about a final destination for a teacher and 20 to 50 students, we are left with little room for the not-yet-known. What, then, happens to emergence, to the moments of pause and lines of flight driven by curiosity and interest? Literacy approaches through posthumanism urge us to ask: how can we predict what the learning possibilities might be(come) in advance of the learning?

Conclusion

Certainly, we are in support of having particular literacy goals for and with our students; however, we are cognizant of the ways in which rigid adherence to developmental continua or outcomes, particularly for assessment and curricular design purposes, contradicts the indeterminacy present in all classrooms. We encourage those who have read through the various elements of this volume to consider what shifts have been prompted in your own literacy teaching and research. How have you come to think-be-do literacy differently (even if only momentarily) thinking with posthumanism? How does posthumanism support you in capturing some of the complexities in literacy practices?

References

Chall, J. (1983). *Stages of reading development*. New York, NY: McGraw Hill.
Harwood, V., Hickey-Moody, A., McMahon, S., & O'Shea, S. (2017). *The politics of widening participation and university access for young people: Making educational futures*. New York, NY: Routledge.
Whatmore, S. (2006). Materialist returns: Practicing cultural geography in and for a more-than-human world. *Cultural Geographies, 13*, 600–609.
Wiggins, G. P., & McTighe, J. (2005). *Understanding by design* (Expanded 2nd ed.). Alexandria, VA: ASCD.

Index

Note: Page numbers in italic indicate a figure and page numbers in bold indicate a table on the corresponding page.

accountability 22, 59, 190, 224
activism 9, 15, 213, 218–220
actualizations 55–58, 60
adolescent education 135–144, 189
adult education 1, 4–5, 13–14, 29, 163; experimentations in affective reading for 51–60; and relationship 203–211
affect 2, 6–7, 10–11, 20–23, 29–30; and adult education 52, 54–55, 59, 206–208; as agentic 167–169; and community engagement 35–36, 40; in pop-up installation pedagogy 189–191, 198–201; and what the body can do 30–32, *30*; *see also* affective texture; reading, affective
affective texture 117–119
agency 3, 9, 19–21, 23–24, 30–31; and adult education 203–204, 208; and community engagement 35, 41–42; and ethics and difference 86; and the personal narrative game board 154; and posthumanism 223; and youth environmental activists 218
allatonceness ix
aliveness ix, 62–64, 70
and-and 9, 12; and-and literacy pedagogy 10–11
Anzaldúa, Gloria 95
apparatus 94–95
April Raintree 169–170, 173
Arrival, The 30, 52–60
artifacts 111–112, 131–132, 142, 151
assemblage viii–ix, 9–11, 20–26, 29–38, 42; and adult language classrooms 53–54, 56–58; assemblage theory 19, 36; and ethics and difference 85–88; sensorial 31, 33–42; and throwntogetherness 139–140; *see also* classroom as assemblage

Baker, Jeannie 76
Barad, Karen 7, 22–24, 93, 95; and the personal narrative game board 152–154, 158n7, 158n9; and stories 165–166; *see also* entanglement; intra-action
becoming 21–25, 54–55, 58–60, 87–88, 91–92, 115–116; and the personal narrative game board 148, 151–154, 157; and posthumanism 223–224; and relationships 161–162; and stories 171–172; *see also* making-knowing-becoming
belonging 103–105, 108–109, *112*, 122–123, 189–191, 201, 207; as pedagogy 194–195; in practice 196–198
Bennett, Jane 26, 31, 41–42; *see also* thing power
binary logics 154–155, 208
Black, Jaime *see* REDress Project
bodymind 6, 8, 10, 21, 29
body-storming 67–70
boundaries ix, 3, 35, 67, 86–87, 92–100; and classroom cosmopolitics 130; making-knowing-becoming with 100–101; and the personal narrative game board 151, 156; and place-based pedagogy 179; and posthumanism 223; and throwntogetherness 136

Braiding Sweetgrass 127–130
Bras for Cancer 196–198, *197*
Brendtro, Dr. Larry *see* Circle of Courage
Brokenleg, Dr. Martin *see* Circle of Courage
Burnett, Cathy 162

Calls to Action xi, xv, 168, 194
Campano, Gerald 55, 60n1, 132, 219–220
Campbell, Nicola *see Shin-Shin's Canoe*; *Shi' shi'etko*
catalysts 30, 198–200
change 44–46, 48–50, 73–75, 82–83, 180–181, 183–185; and pop-up installation pedagogy 190–192, 200–201; and space 215–217
changemakers 181, *182*, 184
Chaudhuri, Anita 29–30
Circle of Courage 177–178
classroom as assemblage 4, 11, 25, 30–31, 40–41, **41**; and adult language classrooms 54; and ethics and difference 88; and relationships 161–162; and throwntogetherness 140, 142
Cliff Hodges, Gabrielle 142–143
collaboration 54–55, 80–82, 110–111, 218–220
collectivity 21–22, 29–30, 161, 224
Comber, Barbara 1–2, 11, 14–15, 33, 139, 171; and place-based pedagogy 180; and relationships 162
commonplaces 7, 109–110
community engagement 33–42
concepts 21–26, 29–30, 63–64, 151–153, 155, 191–192
contact zone 115, 117–124
cosmograms 126–132
cosmopolitanism viii–ix
cosmopolitics 126–133
curriculum xiv–xv, 11–12, 45–46, 77–78, 85–86, 173–174; and adult education 208–209, 211; and pop-up installation pedagogy 189–192, 194–196, 198, 200–201; and relationships 161–163; *see also* curriculum encounter
curriculum encounter 191–196, 198

decolonization 166, 170–171
De Freitas, Elizabeth 99
Deleuze, Gilles 22, 36, 153; and Pierre-Félix Guattari 13–14, 21, 23–25, 54, 63–64, 87, 149–150, 152, 154
Dewey, John x–xi
dialogue 104–105, 110–111
difference 45–46, 49–50, 63–64, 84–88, 223
differenciation 22, 86, 203
diffractive mapping 101
dolls 135–137, *137*

early childhood 80, 150
ecosystems 95–96
Eigenbrod, Renate 166–168
elaboration 106
elementary education 31, 34, 76, 105, 148, 223
embodiment viii–ix, 1–2, 5–6, 21–22, 29–30; and boundaries 97–100; and community engagement 35–36, 40–41; and gift-economy approaches 65–66; and pop-up installation pedagogy 200–201; and posthumanism 223; and relationships 161–162; and stories 173–174
emergence ix–x, 9–10, 12–13, 55–56, 203–204, 209; *see also* emergent learning
emergent learning 73–83, 186
entanglement 20–21, 23–24, 154, 157, 158n9, 204
environment 77, 122–123, 128–129, 131, 189–191, 198–201; built 78; as pedagogy 195–196; and space 215–216
environmental sustainability 34–35
epistemologies 22–24, 140, 152, 156, 162, 223; and pop-up installation pedagogy 195, 201; *see also* ethico-onto-epistemology; onto-epistemology
ethico-onto-epistemology 22–23, 153
ethics 6–8, 24, 58, 74, 85–87, 223; and adult education 206, 209–210; and boundaries 95, 100–101; and classroom cosmopolitics 126, 130; and the personal narrative game board 152, 157; and pop-up installation pedagogy 190; posthuman 23, 85–86, 88; and relationships 162–163; and stories 172–173; and worldmakers 85–88; and youth environmental activists 219; *see also* ethico-onto-epistemology

Index

evaluation 79, 106, 132
experimentation 51–60, 64

Fatty Legs 168, 171–173
feminism 150–153, 158n9, 194
fluidity 6, 70, 136, 140, 162, 179, 183–185
food waste 182–186, *183*
formulas 112

games 31, 37, 81–82, 97, 216; *see also* personal narrative game board
gestures 172; minor 30, 43–50
gift-economy approaches 62–71
Google Maps 76, 180–181, 183, 185
Guattari, Pierre-Félix *see under* Deleuze, Gilles

habitat 76, 94–98
Haraway, Donna 152
Hayes, Deb 78–79
Hirst, Megan 162
Honeyford, Michelle A. 163
Huddleston, Amanda 86

identity 10, 31, 44, 57–58, 64, 213; adolescent 137–138; and classroom cosmopolitics 129–130; and diversity 116, 120, 122–123; and ethics and difference 86–88; and making texts 121–122; and multiplicity and interrelatedness 103–104; and place-based pedagogy 177, 179; and pop-up installation pedagogy 190–191; and relationships 163; and stories 172; and throwntogetherness 136, 138–144
imagination 101, 126–128, 135–136, 138–139, 200–201, 210–211; imagining dynamic potential 75–80, 82; *see also* research imaginations
improvisation 31, 64–65, 70, 78, 110; systematic 132
Indian Horse 168
Indigenous peoples 76, 94, 150–151, 161–162, 177; and pop-up installation pedagogy 192, 194–195; and stories 166–170, 172
installation art 36, 163, 189–191, 198–201, *199*; Bras for Cancer 196–198, *197*; The REDress Project 191–196, *193*
interrelatedness 103–112

intra-action 7, 9, 20–21, 23–24, 29–31, 158n7; and adult education 204; and pop-up installation pedagogy 192; and relationships 161–162; and stories 165, 169, 171–172, 174; and youth environmental activists 219

Jordan-Fenton, Christy *see Fatty Legs*
junk 31, 33–36, 40–42

keystone species 95–96, 99, 101
Kimmerer, Robin Wall *see Braiding Sweetgrass*
knowing *see* local knowledge; making-knowing-becoming
Kuby, Candace R. 11, 15, 151, 215

land 75, 77, 94, 96, 112, 138, 195; land-as-text 170–171; *see also* Nose Hill
leadership 78–80
Leander, Kevin M. 31, 149
learning by design 224–225
Lenters, Kim 1–2, 11, 14, 92
lines of flight 9, 23, 25, 31, 213, 225; and community engagement 34; and relationships 161
listening 67–70, 103–112, 171–172
literacy desiring 151
Littlebear, Chief Wilton 167
Little Bear, Leroy 170
local knowledge 183–184

MacLure, Maggie 150–151
making-knowing-becoming 95–96, 100–101
Massey, Doreen 24–25, 123–124, 138–139, 142, 179–180, 185–186
Massumi, Brian 20–21, 23
materialism 7, 51–55; materialist pedagogy 192, 195; materialist teaching practice 55–59; new materialisms 7, 34, 95, 150–154, 198, 207
materiality 25, 33, 36, 152–153; of language 207, 209; of literacy 163; of questions 161; *see also* installation art
McDermott, Mairi 1–2, 11, 14
minor, the 44–45; *see also under* gestures
Monsionier, Beatrice Culleton *see April Raintree*

more-than-human 4, 9, 21, 23–24, 26; and boundaries 94, 96; and diversity 115; and gift-economy approaches 68–70; and moving with sensation and affect 29, 31; and the personal narrative game board 150–151, 157; and posthumanism 223; and relationships 162; and stories 165; and youth environmental activists 220
multiplicities 103–112, 140–142
mutual flourishing 87, 126–133, 219

Nichols, T. Philip 55, 60n1, 87, 219–220
non-human 3, 7, 19, 23–24, 29, 31; and adult education 209; and adult language classrooms 52, 54, 58, 60; and boundaries 100; and classroom cosmopolitics 126, 133; and community engagement 35, 41; and diversity 123; and ethics and difference 87–88; and the personal narrative game board 148–150, 152–154, 156–157; and pop-up installation pedagogy 192; and posthumanism 223; and space 215–216; and youth environmental activists 219–220; *see also* more-than-human
Nose Hill 91–92, 92–93, 94–96, 176; and diffractive light 92–94; and making boundaries 98–100; and making-knowing-becoming 100–101; and schools as habitats 96–98

onto-epistemology 8, 207, 223; *see also* ethico-onto-epistemology
ontologies 8, 22–23, 152–153, 156; materialist 52; relational 24, 152, 154; *see also* ethico-onto-epistemology; onto-epistemology

parsing 35, 223–224
pedagogies: place-based 78, 176–187, 181–183; of possibility 1, 13, 75–78; of poverty 78–80
pedagogues-theorists *see* theorists-pedagogues
personal narrative game board 147–157; place 5–6, 33–34, 76–78, 123–124, 136–144; multiplicities of 67–70; place-based learning 40–42, **41**; and pop-up installation pedagogy 190; relationships that matter in 161–163; and space 10, 24–25, 74–75, 198; and stories 165–166, 169–174; *see also under* pedagogies
planning 62–70, 76–77
plateaus 13–14, 23–24, 26
playgrounds 36–39, 177–178, 180–181, 184
Pokiak-Fenton, Margaret *see* Fatty Legs
positionings xv, 60, 75, 143, 221
post-critical literacy 6–9
post-critical literacy pedagogy 8–9
posthuman concepts 6, 19–26, 63–64, 71, 221
posthumanism viii–ix, xiii–xv, 3–13, 29–31, 213, 221–225; and adult education 207–208; and community engagement 35–36; and the personal narrative game board 148–154, 156–157; posthuman literacy resources 17; and relationships 161–163; and youth environmental activists 218–220; *see also* posthuman concepts; *see also under* ethics
post-pedagogy 9
potential 75–80, 99, 116, 144; and adult language classrooms 51–52, 54–58; and minor gestures 44–46, 48–50
practice-theory xv, 149, 158n5, 221–222
process and product 9–10
Project Engage 33–42, **41**
purpose 190–191

reader response theory (RRT) xi, 86, 140
reading, affective 51–60
REDress Project 191–196, *193*, 198
relational ontology *see under* ontologies
relational transformations 43–50
relationships 7–10, 22–25, 39–40, 47–49, 54–56, 162–163; in adult education 203–211; and classroom cosmopolitics 128; in curriculum and place 161–163; and diversity 120–121, 123; and gift-economy approaches 68–69; and the personal narrative game board 152–154, 156–157; and place-based pedagogy 184–185; and pop-up installation

pedagogy 190–191, 195–197; student-teacher 9, 103, 116–117, 206
relations of power 117–118, 123
research imaginations 80–82
response-ability xv, 24
response 65–66, 142–143; *see also* reader response theory (RRT)
Rorty, Richard ix, xi
Rosenblatt, Louise x–xi, 86; *see also* reader response theory (RRT)
Russell, Elaine 76

sensation 14, 29, 57, 66, 107, 184
sensemaking xv, 3, 9, 15, 26, 86, 106–110
Shin-Shin's Canoe 168
Shi' shi'etko 168
silence 67–68, 166–167, 198
Sinclair, Justice Murray 167, 195
Sinclair, N. 99
socio-material, the xiv, 51–52, 56–60, 80, 151
space 43–44, 68–69, 76–77, 81–82, 91–101, 109–111; and adult education 203–205, 207–211; change in 215–217; and classroom cosmopolitics 126–129, 132–133; and place 10, 24–25, 74–75, 198; and place-based pedagogy 176–187; poetics of 131; and pop-up installation pedagogy 194–195; smooth and striated 25–26, 31; spaces in between 153, 209–211; and stories 165–166; and throwntogetherness 138–141, 143–144
sticky note thinking 54–56
stories 37, 41, 59, 94–95, 165–174; and classroom cosmopolitics 129; and diversity 117, 121–122; and multiplicity and interrelatedness 104–106, 108–110, 112; and place-based pedagogy 176–180, 183–185; and pop-up installation pedagogy 197–198; and relationships 162; and throwntogetherness 135–136, 138–144
Strong-Wilson, Tereasa 169–170

TAHQ time 110–111
Tan, Shaun *see Arrival, The*
Taylor, Carol 19
teaching dilemmas 103–108
text x–xi, 8–9, 79–82, 85–88, 105–106, 109–111; and diversity 119–120; land-as-text 170–171; and stories 172–174; text-body 51–60; and throwntogetherness 140–144
theorists-pedagogues 156–157
theory-practice xv, 15, 51–60, 147–157, 158n5, 222; *see also* practice-theory
thing power 21, 26, 31, 41, 86; *see also* vibrant matter
thinking *see* sticky note thinking; thinking-with-theory
thinking-with-theory 2, 15
throwntogetherness ix, xi, 12, 25–26, 92, 97; and diversity 123; and pop-up installation pedagogy 195; and relationships 161, 163
transformations *see* relational transformations
Trussler, Patti 163
Truth and Reconciliation Commission (TRC) 166–168, 172, 194–195

Van Bockern, Steve *see* Circle of Courage
vibrant matter 21, 26, 31
visualizing 63, 142–143
voice xiv–xv, 191–192, 198–199, *199*
voicing 166–167

Wagemese, Richard *see Indian Horse*
Walker, Kara 36, 40–41
Waterhouse, Monica 29–30
Wells, Marg 75–78, 82
Wilson, Marie 167
worldbuilding 126–127, 130–133
worldmaking 2, 8, 23, 85–88